Praise For
CRISIS ON THE KOREAN PENINSULA

"Drawing on their detailed knowledge of Asia and of military realities on the Korean peninsula, Mike Mochizuki and Mike O'Hanlon provide in this volume an extremely thoughtful and timely contribution to the important debate on what to do about one of our most urgent foreign policy challenges—North Korea's renewed drive for nuclear weapons."
—Mike Armacost, former U.S. ambassador to the Philippines and Japan, former president of the Brookings Institution

"By far the best book yet written on the challenge posed by North Korea's nuclear weapons program, *Crisis on the Korean Peninsula* lays out a comprehensive and convincing diplomatic and military strategy for persuading and pressuring Pyongyang into relinquishing its atomic arsenal. Calling for a combination of steaks and sledgehammers, rather than the more traditional carrots and sticks, O'Hanlon and Mochizuki have come up with a proposal that Kim Jong Il may not be able to refuse and that George Bush may be willing to embrace. Let's hope so because the alternatives are almost too terrible to contemplate."
—Stephen J. Solarz, former Congressmen from New York, former Chairman of the House Foreign Affairs Subcommittee on Asian and Pacific Affairs

"Michael O'Hanlon and Mike Mochizuki make a major contribution to our efforts to find effective ways of coping with the vexing problems of North Korea's nuclear weapons programs. They are right to stress that North Korea's neighbors, including especially China, have as much of a stake as does the U.S. in a definitive termination of these programs and in North Korea's shifting its priorities from obsessive militarization to economic and political reform. The authors deserve credit for their thorough analysis of these controversial issues."
—Helmut Sonnenfeldt, Guest Scholar, The Brookings Institution, former State Department and National Security Council official

"A comprehensive proposal for addressing one of the most important issues of our day."
—George Mitchell, former Senate Majority Leader

"This thoughtful book pulls together some of the most interesting ideas about how to deal with the North Korea challenge. In proposing a grand strategic bargain to test North Korea's commitment to peace, O'Hanlon and Mochizuki offer a provocative prescription for the future."
—Senator Joseph R. Biden, Jr., ranking Democrat, Senate Foreign Relations Committee

"In describing their comprehensive proposal for negotiations with North Korea, O'Hanlon and Mochizuki exhibit the strategic creativity and analytical depth badly needed by United States policymakers dealing with this strange—and dangerous—place."
—Ash Carter, Professor, John F. Kennedy School at Harvard University, former Assistant Secretary of Defense

"*Crisis on the Korean Peninsula* deals with the most urgent security problem facing the United States today. The "grand bargain" it proposes is a thoughtful approach that should be given serious consideration by the administration."
—William J. Perry, 19th Secretary of Defense

CRISIS ON THE KOREAN PENINSULA
How to Deal with a Nuclear North Korea

MICHAEL O'HANLON
AND
MIKE MOCHIZUKI

A Brookings Institution Book

McGraw-Hill

New York Chicago San Francisco Lisbon London
Madrid Mexico City Milan New Delhi San Juan
Seoul Singapore Sydney Toronto

McGraw·Hill Companies

Copyright © 2003 by The Brookings Institution. All rights reserved. Printed in the United States of America. Except as permitted under the United States Copyright Act of 1976, no part of this publication may be reproduced or distributed in any form or by any means, or stored in a data base or retrieval system, without the prior written permission of the publisher.

1 2 3 4 5 6 7 8 9 0 DOC/DOC 0 9 8 7 6 5 4 3

ISBN 978-0-07-158979-6

Printed and bound by RR Donnelley.

McGraw-Hill books are available at special quantity discounts to use as premiums and sales promotions, or for use in corporate training programs. For more information, please write to the Director of Special Sales, Professional Publishing, McGraw-Hill, Two Penn Plaza, New York, NY 10121-2298. Or contact your local bookstore.

 This book is printed on recycled, acid-free paper containing a minimum of 50% recycled, de-inked fiber.

To our parents

CONTENTS

FOREWORD BY STROBE TALBOTT	vii
ACKNOWLEDGMENTS	ix
DEFUSING THE CRISIS	1
CHAPTER 1: THE HERMIT KINGDOM	23
CHAPTER 2: THE CRUX OF THE CONFRONTATION	57
CHAPTER 3: THE "GRAND BARGAIN"	83
CHAPTER 4: TURNING SWORDS INTO PLOWS	113
CHAPTER 5: FIXING A FAILED ECONOMY	127
CHAPTER 6: A NEW ALLIANCE	145
APPENDIX 1: MODELING AN ATTEMPTED NORTH KOREAN BREAKTHROUGH	167
APPENDIX 2: AGREED FRAMEWORK BETWEEN THE UNITED STATES OF AMERICA AND THE DEMOCRATIC PEOPLE'S REPUBLIC OF KOREA	177
APPENDIX 3: EXCERPTS FROM THE NATIONAL SECURITY STRATEGY OF THE UNITED STATES OF AMERICA, SEPTEMBER 2002	183
REFERENCES	195
INDEX	221

FOREWORD

Over the past year, various offices at the Brookings Institution have had the aspect of war rooms—almost literally so, since the subject on many of our scholars' minds has so often been war: the one the U.S. is waging against terrorism, the won that it fought and won in Iraq, and the one that could, *in extremis*, break out at any time on the Korean peninsula.

Our most thoughtful, knowledgeable, energetic and prolific scholar on military matters is Michael O'Hanlon, a Senior Fellow in our Foreign Policy Studies program. He is the author or coauthor of ten books, as well as dozens of journal articles and hundreds of newspaper essays, over the past nine years at Brookings. I think of him as the intellectual equivalent of a four-star general. In response to the ongoing crisis over North Korea's nuclear brinkmanship, he has teamed up with Mike Mochizuki, who is a specialist on Northeast Asia at George Washington University, to produce, in a burst of concentrated effort, this lucid and timely book, which Brookings is proud to co-publish with McGraw-Hill.

The two Mikes provide a short review of the historical, political, economic, and military context of the ongoing showdown between President George W. Bush and Kim Jong Il. In that respect, it's an excellent primer for understanding the headlines of today's newspapers—and, most likely, tomorrow's as well.

But their primary purpose is to lay out some suggestions for a new policy for dealing with North Korea's nuclear aspirations and propensity for blackmail. The authors believe that the approach of the Bush administration and its predecessors needs revision. For example, in their view the Clinton administration's focus on North Korea's nuclear and missile programs, while initially productive, inadvertently contributed to a North Korean tendency to use its dangerous weapons programs as bargaining chips. They also argue that the Clinton approach stood little chance of helping North Korea reform its economy (or its human rights practices), ensuring that even if one crisis was successfully addressed, others would likely follow.

They are critical of the Bush administration for going too far in the other direction, since, in their view, the American combination of stonewalling and coercion toward North Korea caused a breakdown in diplomatic progress, divided the United States from its regional allies (especially the all-important one, South Korea), and led to at least a temporary acceleration of North Korean nuclear activity.

As an alternative, the authors sketch out a "road map"—which the administration has recognized as a useful concept in diplomacy in other areas. It includes ideas for resolving the nuclear and missile issues, as well as human rights problems in North Korea. But the focus of the book is a concept for how a package of conventional arms reductions, economic assistance, and economic reform might steer North Korea in a more promising direction.

Altogether, this book is a model for what we try to do here at Brookings: bring independent analysis and expertise to bear on the most challenging issues of our times for the purpose of informing the citizenry and offering constructive ideas to policymakers.

Stobe Talbott

ACKNOWLEDGMENTS

The authors would like to thank Pedro Almeida, Richard Bush, Victor Cha, Julien Hartley, Kaori Lindeman, Aaron Moburg-Jones, Gary Samore, Scott Snyder, James Steinberg, and Strobe Talbott for their invaluable assistance. They also appreciate insights, in past conversations and also more recently, from Mike Armacost, Stephen Biddle, Bruce Blair, Kurt Campbell, Ash Carter, Kurt Chicowski, Robert Crumplar, Ivo Daalder, Tom Davis, Richard Dunn, Robert Einhorn, Joshua Epstein, William Gleysteen, Harry Harding, Scott Kennedy, Payne Kilbourne, Sung Han Kim, Richard Kugler, Nick Lardy, Ed Lincoln, Frances Lussier, Satoshi Morimoto, Marcus Noland, Eric Nyberg, Don Oberdorfer, Kongdan Oh, William Perry, Dingli Shen, Lee Sigal, Steve Solarz, Hal Sonnenfeldt, John Steinbruner, and Michael Swaine.

DEFUSING THE CRISIS

In this book, we propose a "grand bargain" that the United States and its regional security partners should pursue with the Democratic People's Republic of Korea (DPRK), more commonly known as North Korea. Although accords could be negotiated and implemented step by step, they would be guided by a clearly articulated and broad vision. That vision should help grab the attention of North Korean leaders, who would be presented with a clear alternative to their present dangerous and self-destructive path.

If this approach failed, the Bush administration would be much better prepared than it is now to argue to South Korea, Japan, and

China that more of a hard line policy was needed. Up to the present, these countries have not expressed a willingness to get notably tougher with North Korea should circumstances require unpalatable coercive options. The U.S.-South Korea alliance has suffered serious strains as a result. But there is very good reason, based on the history of negotiations with North Korea, to think an ambitious plan could succeed.

Some in the Bush administration oppose any plan that would prop up the reprehensible North Korean regime. That sentiment is understandable. But the means available to the United States for changing regimes, short of a war sure to be far more destructive than was the overthrow of Saddam Hussein, are not promising. Moreover, any policy that pursued regime change by strangling the North Korean economy would be likely to worsen the plight of the North Korean people, and increase the risks that North Korea would even sell nuclear materials to other dangerous states or terrorists, before it succeeded in its main objective. Before resorting to coercive regime change policies, therefore, the Bush administration should do its utmost to convince the current North Korean leadership to change its own ways fundamentally—just as China and Vietnam have done even as they retained their basic communist systems.

The agenda we propose would address the acute nuclear weapons crisis that has so dominated headlines in recent months, as well as the matter of the DPRK's ballistic missiles. But it would go much further. It would also emphasize human rights issues, such as the return of Japanese nationals kidnapped by North Korea decades ago, and even, over time, the internal practices of the North Korean regime toward its own people. The plan's centerpiece would be a combination of deep conventional arms reductions on the peninsula and economic assistance to North Korea. Only such a policy could reduce the enormous economic burden that North Korea's oversized military places on the country. Without such arms cuts, as well as economic reform, North Korea will probably continue to provoke future crises in order to extort resources from the international community simply because its leaders will see no other way to stay financially afloat.

The broad goal of our proposed road map would be to transform the overall nature of the outside world's relationship with North Korea—and ultimately that of North Korea itself. For this reason, the plan will remain relevant even in the unlikely event that the nuclear problem is quickly resolved. It will also remain relevant if the security situation deteriorates and the nuclear crisis worsens; even under such circumstances, U.S. objectives would still include the denuclearization and reform of North Korea.

This plan should also be immune to the charge, and the real worry, that it represents appeasement or blackmail. It would not provide cash aid for specific types of illicit weapons. Rather, it would provide development aid for a broader process of demilitarization, stabilization of the peninsula, and reform of North Korea. Aid would be disbursed over time, conditioned on continued compliance by North Korea with the overall plan's various terms and stipulations. This grand bargain proposal would aim to solve the problem posed by the DPRK based on an agenda determined in Seoul, Washington, Tokyo, and Beijing, not just to mitigate the latest acute symptoms of North Korea's hypermilitarization, belligerence toward the outside world, and self-destructive internal policies. It would not try to support and sustain the North Korean regime in its current unacceptable and horrendous form. It would insist that that regime change in key ways before receiving major help and benefiting from a fundamentally new relationship with the outside world.

The last decade of U.S. policy has, by contrast with this broad road map, been rather narrow and tactical. It has focused on the crisis du jour, mostly concerning North Korea's nuclear and ballistic missile programs. That approach has brought some successes, at least temporarily, notably in the 1994 Agreed Framework, which placed important caps on North Korea's nuclear weapons potential. But it also appears to have encouraged the DPRK to develop a worsening habit of extortionist behavior—whether out of malice or out of simple desperation, given North Korea's continued economic plight and inability to find legitimate sources of income. For that reason, it holds no appeal for President Bush.

At the same time, however, Mr. Bush's apparent policy preference—insisting that North Korea immediately stop its nuclear activities and severely limiting diplomatic engagement as well as any talk of possible incentives to Pyongyang until it does—may fail. North Korean leaders tend to become more intransigent when their backs are against the wall; in addition, they are clearly willing to see their own people starve before capitulating to coercion.

And if the hope is that North Korea would collapse as a result of a U.S. policy of strangulation, the odds of success seem remote. The DPRK has already survived more than a decade in a state of ongoing decline, surprising many. Pushing North Korea to the brink may also increase the odds that it will sell plutonium to the highest bidder to rescue its economy. That would be the worst of all possible policy outcomes for the United States. Given the fact that a bomb's worth of plutonium is about the size of a grapefruit, it is also an outcome that could not be reliably prevented even by a naval blockade.

We agree with the Bush administration's apparent view that North Korea needs to be presented with a broad range of demands in any future negotiations. But we also feel that, in contrast to Bush policy to date, North Korea needs to be offered concrete incentives to reform. In addition, the United States and its regional partners need to spell out their demands in detail and pursue them diplomatically with Pyongyang without particular concern about whether the next round of negotiations is bilateral or multilateral or a mix of the two.

The Bush administration may hope that the impressive U.S. military victory over Iraq in 2003 combined with diplomatic pressure from China and other regional parties will be enough to convince North Korean leaders to dismantle their nuclear programs. But this strategy may well not work. Under current circumstances, Kim Jong Il might now decide he needs his nuclear program more than ever to be sure he does not share Saddam Hussein's fate; indeed, his government has stated as much. Moreover, a hard-nosed strategy, as well as any U.S. talk of military preemption against North Korean nuclear facilities or the regime itself, has elicited little support in Seoul or Beijing to date.

Against this backdrop, we suggest a road map for a safer Korean peninsula. It is a diplomatic strategy that would demand a great deal of North Korea but offer that country much in return. The idea would be to present North Korea a clear choice and force it to choose one of two possible futures—engagement with the outside world and gradual economic recovery, similar in ways to what China and Vietnam have done in recent decades, or continued confrontation and further economic decline.

This proposal would be based on a broad vision like those that have guided Mideast and Balkan peace processes in recent years. Such road maps clearly do not guarantee success, but they can help parties accept the bitter medicine of measures they do not like in order to reap the benefits of other, more appealing measures. By establishing benchmarks for progress, they can also help parties that do not trust each other very much verify compliance by the other side and build up confidence over time.

Any such plan must start with a means of denuclearizing North Korea. This will remain the top U.S. priority in the region regardless of the specific circumstances that prevail in months ahead. Whether North Korea slows its moves toward a larger nuclear capability on the one hand or worsens the crisis—even taking a drastic step such as testing a nuclear device—on the other, the nuclear issue will remain paramount.

To address the nuclear crisis, we would begin with rapid restoration of fuel oil shipments to North Korea, provided that the North was willing to verifiably freeze its nuclear activities at the Yongbyon nuclear site while negotiations proceeded. The substance of the deal would then require accelerated implementation of the Agreed Framework's plan for getting plutonium out of North Korea; it would not be realistic to expect this step to occur instantaneously, but it should begin right away and be completed within a few years. Our proposal would modify the Agreed Framework by helping the North build conventional rather than nuclear power plants to replace the large, unfinished reactors at Yongbyon as well. It would also require rigorous inspections of known North Korean nuclear-related sites and eventually of the currently hidden uranium enrichment program, as well as "challenge" inspections at any places where intelligence agencies suspected that illicit nuclear programs were under way.

Although the nuclear issue is the most acute problem on the Korean peninsula today, the centerpiece of our proposal is the combination of conventional arms reductions and North Korean economic reform. We recommend an accord modeled after the NATO-Warsaw Pact Conventional Forces in Europe Treaty that was negotiated toward the end of the Cold War. A "Conventional Forces in Korea" accord would mandate cuts in tanks, other armored vehicles, artillery, helicopters, and combat jets on both sides of the demilitarized zone (DMZ).

North Korea, with the much larger military machine, would have to make the larger cuts, including proportionate reductions in forward forces near the DMZ. This approach would not eliminate the North Korean conventional threats to the capital city of Seoul and the rest of the Republic of Korea (ROK), or South Korea, but it would reduce them. Even more important, it would begin to demilitarize North Korean society and to lift the enormous economic burden that country's armed forces place on its economy.

Just as important, Japan, South Korea, China, and the United States would reward North Korea with a commitment to help it gradually restructure its economy. If Pyongyang agreed, it would benefit twice from this package deal. First, it would reduce the size and cost of its military which Pyongyang has itself recently recognized to be excessive (claiming it needs nuclear weapons to provide for its national security at lower cost). Second, it would gain greater technical and economic aid (as well as a lifting of trade sanctions) from Japan, South Korea, the United States, and China.

North Korea would have to continue to cut conventional forces and reform its economy to keep receiving aid each year; the assistance would not be provided in a single lump sum and would be conditional based on compliance with a series of benchmarks. This policy would reduce the core threat that has existed in Korea for half a century; it would also offer at least some hope that economic reform in the DPRK might begin to succeed.

This proposal moves beyond the current debate over whether the United States should engage in bilateral talks with North Korea (the main Clinton administration approach) or insist upon a multilateral venue as President Bush has done. The initial concept of a grand bargain could be proposed in either a bilateral U.S.-DPRK setting or in "minimally multilateralist" settings, such as China-U.S.-DPRK talks. Washington should be willing to engage diplomatically in that way to lay out its broad proposal (and the Bush administration is to be credited for deciding to accept such a forum for one round of discussions in April of 2003). But given the central roles that would have to be played by South Korea, Japan, and China in the broader aid and diplomatic policies we propose, these countries would have to be part of the meat of most negotiations and be involved in the implementation of any accords. Countries such as Russia, Australia, and Canada might play smaller roles as well.

Our proposal would also require North Korea to allow all Japanese kidnapping victims and their families to go to Japan permanently and to engage in a broader, longer-term human rights dialogue. Pyongyang would further pledge to continue its restraint in not supporting terrorism (and would be removed from the U.S. list of state sponsors of terrorism); it would also refrain from any further counterfeiting and drug trafficking. It would stop testing, producing, and deploying medium- and long-range ballistic missiles and stop exporting ballistic missiles of all kinds; ideally, it would also eliminate its existing stockpiles of these weapons, though there could be some flexibility on this point. Pyongyang would sign and accept the responsibilities of signatories to the chemical and biological weapons conventions.

For its part, the United States would offer a public nonaggression pact, contingent on full North Korean compliance with its denuclearization obligations and other stipulations of the grand bargain. Washington would also provide a no first use of weapons of mass destruction pledge, resumption of diplomatic relations, and lifting of economic sanctions. The two Koreas and the United States and China would also sign a peace treaty.

MILITARY ISSUES AND OPTIONS

North Korea probably has one or two nuclear bombs built with plutonium it extracted from its small "research reactor" at Yongbyon in 1989. By extracting additional plutonium from the spent fuel that was used in that reactor until 1994, North Korea could probably increase the size of its nuclear arsenal to six to eight bombs within months of a decision to do so. Unfortunately, there is some worry that it has already taken steps to move in that direction in 2003; it could have a dozen bombs by mid-decade.

U.S. military options do exist. U.S. and South Korean armed forces could in theory destroy the two larger nuclear reactors still under construction at Yongbyon before they could be finished, an option Secretary of Defense William J. Perry once raised publicly while serving in the Clinton administration. Doing so could prevent North Korea from ultimately developing several dozen more bombs a year. The United States and its allies might also conduct a military strike against the smaller nuclear reactor, the plutonium reprocessing facility, and/or the spent fuel rods at Yongbyon (though that latter option may be lost, since North Korea recently stated that it has already reprocessed a good deal of the spent fuel in question). Although some radioactivity would be released in such a strike, the amounts would probably not be great.

In response to any such preemptive attacks, however, North Korea might then strike back against South Korea and Japan. Given the pervasive influence and hard-line attitudes of the military and the Communist Party, this type of action would be likely even if Kim Jong Il were targeted along with his nuclear infrastructure and killed or cut off from his military as a result. Allied planners could hope for a different result but could not count on it. The result could easily be all-out war on the peninsula, with the likelihood of hundreds of thousands of deaths, including those of thousands of American soldiers.

Even if new U.S. technology and tactics enabled a swifter victory than expected, the carnage from any war would almost surely extend to tens of thousands of lost lives and tens of billions of dollars in property damage. Seoul would likely be subject to sustained artillery barrage for at least a period of days. This would almost surely be true even if U.S.-ROK forces began large-scale hostilities themselves with attempts to preempt North Korean artillery use; the North has just too much of such weaponry to think that most could be quickly destroyed. And history suggests that North Korean fighters are more motivated, tougher, and more loyal to their government than were most Iraqi soldiers under Saddam Hussein.

Moreover, in regard to the immediate threat, North Korea might soon move its spent fuel rods or reprocessed plutonium to a location that would be more difficult to hit. In addition, the United States and South Korea apparently do not know where the DPRK uranium enrichment program is located; if this is the case, they obviously could not strike it. Nor do we know where North Korea keeps any existing nuclear weapons. A military option may have to be eventually considered by Washington and Seoul in one form or another, but it is quite unappealing—and would possibly be of rather limited effectiveness, unless it turned into all-out war, with all the associated carnage. It is also wholly unacceptable to South Korea's government, making it politically and morally impractical for the United States to consider the option seriously at present.

North Korea would be unlikely to deliberately start a war even if it had many nuclear weapons. Nor are any of its nuclear weapons sure to be small enough to fit on its missiles. But should war somehow occur in the future, with an arsenal of eight or more bombs, at least one might well be successfully delivered by aircraft or boat or even a ground vehicle and detonated against allied forces or civilian populations. The existence of a North Korean nuclear arsenal would also risk sparking a nuclear arms race in Northeast Asia that could lead to the nuclearization of South Korea and perhaps even Japan or Taiwan. Worst of all, there is also the danger that North Korea would sell fissile material to other countries or terrorist groups to garner desperately needed cash—or that the country could collapse, with whatever group or faction that held the nuclear materials then selling them. Despite Secretary of State Colin Powell's claim in December 2002 to the contrary, the current situation in Korea is very much a crisis, and a major one at that.

The Bush administration needs to devote much more serious attention to the problem, not only by being open to talks with Pyongyang but also by developing, along with its allies, an agenda for such talks. The point should be to offer North Korea an alternative future to the path it has recently chosen. That alternative should include incentives but also stiff demands on the regime of Kim Jong Il—on issues ranging from the nuclear crisis to missile exports to Japanese kidnapping victims to conventional forces on the peninsula. This approach would emulate Ronald Reagan's tough negotiation strategy with the Soviet Union in the 1980s and his "trust but verify" concept as well.

The vision would be big and bold. That approach would present North Korean leaders with a clear alternative to their current plight. It could also reduce the excessive haggling over minutiae that has typified negotiations with North Korea in the past. The broad vision would not have to be captured in a single agreement. Although we think that a package approach would be the simplest and most promising, it could ultimately be discarded in favor of a series of smaller deals if they proved more negotiable. But the broader vision or road map should illuminate and guide any such step-by-step accords.

THE CLINTON LEGACY

When entering office, President Bush wanted to revise the Clinton administration's approach to North Korea. The latter had a number of important accomplishments over roughly a five-year stretch from 1994 to 1999, after a slow start during which the administration did not give the North Korean problem enough high-level attention or develop a workable strategy. But the Clinton team could not reach a deal on North Korean missiles before leaving office—and subsequent revelations that North Korea had started a secret nuclear program in the latter part of the 1990s tarnished its otherwise impressive accomplishments.

The Clinton administration produced the important 1994 Agreed Framework, under which North Korea froze its major nuclear programs and promised ultimately to undo whatever nuclear weapons progress it had earlier made at its small research reactor (the same one now at issue). At the time, the United States was accused of giving in to North Korean blackmail, but the deal the administration signed was a smart one: energy in exchange for energy and nonproliferation.

Washington and its allies did not provide $4 billion in cash for Pyongyang, as often claimed by critics, but instead promised the equivalent of $4 billion in power plants that would replace the Yongbyon nuclear facilities. If the deal had a flaw, it was that it left North Korea in possession of its spent fuel rods for too long, though it is not obvious that Pyongyang would have agreed to quickly surrender them. It also promised North Korea new types of nuclear reactors, purportedly "proliferation resistant" but not entirely free from the danger of having their spent fuel ultimately diverted to weapons purposes by the North Korean regime. But those reactors will almost certainly not be completed, so at worst, the 1994 accord bought time.

A few years of difficult relations marked by smaller crises and mutual recriminations followed the 1994 accord. But then a process of diplomacy and engagement began on the peninsula, especially after President Kim Dae Jung took office in South Korea in February 1998. It led to summit meetings between the leaders of the two Koreas, South Korean tourist visits to North Korea, limited South Korean economic investment in the North, and some reunions for families separated since the Korean War. Although North Korea did launch a long-range missile over Japanese territory in 1998, Pyongyang subsequently adopted a moratorium on future testing, which remains in place as of this writing.

This engagement process slowed by late 2000. After a North-South summit in June of that year, North Korea stalled on its promises to continue the series of summits and family exchanges. It provoked military clashes at sea. And meanwhile, though this was not known at the time to U.S. and allied intelligence, it had initiated a secret uranium enrichment program to add to its nuclear stockpile.

The Clinton administration continued to try to engage North Korea even as détente weakened. Secretary of State Madeleine K. Albright visited Pyongyang. President Bill Clinton considered a trip as well, if his administration had first been able to clinch a deal that would buy out North Korea's missile programs and end its missile exports in return for compensation worth perhaps several hundred million dollars a year. A similar idea had been contemplated by Israel in the early 1990s, until the United States discouraged it from pursuing the idea further. (That deal would have bought out possible DPRK missile sales to Iran.)

North Korean missile exports did not violate international law and constituted virtually the only remaining export (besides illegal drugs and a few mundane industrial goods) of the cash-starved regime. By compensating North Korea for ending the exports, the Clinton administration hoped to solve the main problem North Korea posed to the United States on the broader global stage.

But this approach risked encouraging North Korea to develop dangerous weapons programs as its primary means of gaining hard currency and diplomatic respect. By failing to address the broader security interests of all concerned, such as a peace treaty and reductions in conventional forces, it failed to change the basic way the three main parties thought about each other. For example, North Korea may have continued to think it needed a nuclear deterrent of some kind against American or South Korean attack, leading it to begin its underground uranium enrichment program a short time after the Agreed Framework was concluded. Moreover, a fix that did little to reform North Korea's economy was unlikely to solve the underlying problem facing that country's leaders, making it probable that Pyongyang would try similar tactics with other weapons given its desperate economic plight.

Whatever one thinks of the Clinton approach, it clearly needed to be revised once the United States uncovered evidence of North Korea's illegal and dangerous uranium enrichment program by the summer of 2002. Even though that program is quite modest in scale compared to the Yongbyon plutonium facilities, it is a clear violation of the Nuclear Non-Proliferation Treaty and thus of the Agreed Framework, and too dangerous to tolerate.

THE BUSH POLICY TOWARD NORTH KOREA

President Bush has taken a hard line toward North Korea since the start of his administration. The policy has varied a bit, from warmer to cooler, but has retained its essential character throughout.

Mr. Bush turned a cold shoulder to South Korean president Kim Dae Jung, known for his "sunshine policy" of engagement toward Pyongyang, when Kim visited Washington to request continued U.S. support for that policy in March of 2001. The Bush administration mused publicly that North Korea should reduce its threatening conventional military forces prior to receiving any additional U.S. help or diplomatic attention, but it never translated that sentiment into a concrete policy proposal. After the terrorist attacks of September 11, 2001, President Bush lumped North Korea into what he described as an "axis of evil" with Iran and Iraq, even though North Korea now has few if any real links to terrorists and even though recent history suggests it can be influenced through engagement. His subsequent emphasis on the potential need for preemptive action against extremist states armed with weapons of mass destruction led to considerable speculation about whether North Korea, like Saddam Hussein's Iraq, might be subject to attack. Mr. Bush also stated that he loathed Kim Jong Il, adding further fuel to the fires of speculation.

By the summer of 2002, U.S. intelligence had uncovered evidence of North Korea's illicit uranium enrichment program. The Bush administration promptly demanded that North Korea verifiably dismantle that program before diplomacy could begin. It also suspended the fuel oil shipments to North Korea pledged under the Agreed Framework. That step was justified in one sense, given North Korea's violations of its nonproliferation obligations under that accord. (As noted, the North Korean nuclear program also violates the 1968 Nuclear Non-proliferation Treaty, signed by Pyongyang in 1985. It further violates a 1991 accord it signed with Seoul—made possible by a withdrawal of U.S. nuclear weapons from South Korea—pledging that the entire peninsula would be nuclear weapons free.) But cutting off the fuel oil also reduced U.S. leverage.

Washington then found itself in an even worse dilemma. North Korea removed monitors and seals from its stock of waste fuel produced primarily in the early 1990s and expelled U.N. monitoring personnel. That put it in a position to add to its probable stock of one or two bombs by producing perhaps half a dozen more within months. It could quite likely do so before outside economic pressure could cause regime collapse or capitulation, even if Washington could somehow convince Beijing, Seoul, and Tokyo to join such a strategy of strangulation. (Indeed, North Korea may have already taken steps to expand its nuclear weapons inventory in this way in recent months.) Moreover, adopting such a policy would surely hurt North Korea's already beleaguered—and often starving—civilian population before it would affect the Kim Jong Il regime.

The Bush administration eventually relaxed its terms for talking to North Korea somewhat, agreeing to a session in Beijing in April of 2003 that involved Chinese but not South Korean or Japanese participation. It also agreed to talk before North Korea took any reassuring steps in regard to its nuclear program. But this session did not lead to very much except the possibility of future talks. Indeed, in some ways it was a step backward, since North Korea used the occasion to claim that it did indeed have a nuclear capability, as American intelligence had long suspected.

The situation is likely to evolve over coming months, but the basic nuclear standoff seems likely to remain. And even if it is somehow resolved, or at least temporarily defused, the broader problem remains. North Korea is a failing, hypermilitarized, and dangerous state, with few current prospects for reform or recovery and thus a high propensity to engage in further provocative behavior as a means of gaining economic assistance from the international community.

A NEW POLICY

The Bush administration is correct in its assertion that the United States must adopt a tough policy toward North Korea. But it is wrong in its apparent assumptions that a tough policy precludes offering Pyongyang concrete incentives to change. The right incentives are not bribes; they are catalysts to reform. If North Korea is prepared to change course, not only in its foreign policy and military posture but even in its domestic practices, the United States should be willing to help. Even if that approach fails, Washington will be in a better position to convince Seoul, Beijing, and Tokyo to join it in tightening the screws on North Korea and perhaps even in considering the use of military force.

North Korean leaders themselves are not likely to find the vision or courage to make big changes on their own. Nor are they likely to propose a grand bargain themselves, given their past patterns of negotiation together with their limited understanding of what steps would be needed to fix their economy and improve relations with the outside world. They also may doubt, and fear, the real intentions of the Bush administration given its "axis of evil" rhetoric as well as its emphasis on preemption and regime change. If there is to be progress, Washington will have to coax, persuade, and pressure DPRK hardliners to change their ways rather than expecting them to do so on their own.

In early 2001, the Bush administration stated that North Korea would need to reduce its threatening conventional force posture if it wished more aid and better diplomatic relations with the United States. The administration also advocated a multilateral approach to negotiating with North Korea rather than accepting bilateral U.S.-DPRK talks. But President Bush has given no concrete elaboration of the character of this proposed multilateral approach. And although he has suggested a comprehensive agenda for negotiations, going well beyond the nuclear and missile issues, just as we propose, he has yet to lay out any specifics or offer North Korea any concrete incentives to change its ways.

North Korea's nuclear and missile programs constitute the most immediate threat to the interests of the United States. But they are hardly the only issue. North Korea's conventional forces are unacceptably large and dangerous. They may pose the greatest threat to South Korea of any weapons in the DPRK inventory. They could produce tens of thousands of casualties in Seoul through artillery attack alone. Because keeping the North Korean conventional forces funded requires approximately 20 to 25 percent of the country's feeble gross domestic product, any policy leaving them intact will preclude hope for gradual economic reform in the North.

Seoul, Tokyo, and Washington should propose a grand diplomatic bargain—or at least a broad, long-term road map for future relations—to Pyongyang. It would make a number of demands on North Korea:

- Verifiably end all of its nuclear programs. This would require on-site inspections anywhere, and with little notice, of North Korea's plutonium and uranium enrichment facilities, as well as any suspicious sites. It would also restore continuous monitoring equipment at North Korea's plutonium facilities until they were all permanently dismantled.

- Reaffirm and accelerate its commitment to allow its spent fuel rods and extracted plutonium stocks to be taken out of the country, and again commit to eliminate whatever nuclear weapons it now has.

- Stop selling missiles abroad and ban all flight testing and further production of medium- and longer-range missiles (including the No Dong and Taepo Dong systems).

- Let all Japanese kidnapping victims and their families leave North Korea—not just the five victims allowed to visit Japan to date or the thirteen acknowledged as having been seized by Pyongyang. More broadly, begin a human rights dialogue with the outside world akin to what China has tolerated in recent years, without specific initial demands but with the clear expectation of gradual reforms in internal human rights practices over time.

- Make large (though not unilateral) cuts in conventional forces, as well as reductions in forward-deployed military capabilities near the DMZ. Reductions should involve around 50 percent of existing heavy weapons, if not even more.

- Verifiably eliminate chemical weapons and allow inspections to confirm the absence of biological agents as well.

As negotiations began, South Korea, Japan, and the United States, as well as other interested parties, such as China, would keep food aid flowing and resume fuel oil shipments. North Korea would freeze all nuclear activities immediately as well and allow monitors to return. Washington would promise not to attack Pyongyang as long as its nuclear activities remained frozen and talks continued.

If the North Koreans accepted the above package, the United States would offer a nonaggression pledge, sign a peace treaty, and open diplomatic relations. The allies would also begin to provide large amounts of economic aid. Japan is eventually expected to provide up to $10 billion as a form of compensation for its colonization of North Korea in the first half of the twentieth century. But other countries, including the United States, would have to increase assistance as well, and China would have to provide much of the technical assistance, given its experience in building enterprise zones within a command economy. This approach would not envision a massive influx of funds to temporarily raise the North Korean standard of living (effectively the approach tried in the former East Germany after the Cold War) but rather an intensive development program. As such, while the price tag would be substantial—perhaps $2 billion a year for a decade—it would not be astronomical.

The United States would also lead efforts to help North Korea develop new energy sources. However, given what is now known about North Korea's trustworthiness, those sources must not involve nuclear-capable facilities of any kind.

This plan would be presented as an integral whole. Only in that way would it provide North Korean leaders a clear alternative vision for the future, as well as public and concrete promises about steps the outside world would be willing to take to help achieve that more peaceful future. In practice, however, it could be adopted in stages if that proved most feasible. It would be phased in incrementally in any event, because it would take time to work out the details of various arms accords and considerable time to implement an effective aid program for North Korea. But the expansion of North Korea's nuclear arsenal would have to be verifiably stopped right away.

What if this approach does not work? First, given past North Korean negotiating behavior, there is good reason to think it will work. The negotiation of the 1994 Agreed Framework, for example, showed that North Korea was willing to trade away a substantial nuclear capability for a package of benefits that included alternative sources of energy and the hope of gradual diplomatic engagement and economic recovery.

Since that time, North Korea's economic problems have gotten even worse. Accordingly, Kim Jong Il has demonstrated at least a limited interest in trying economic reform, as attested by his numerous visits to China's special enterprise zones and tentative but frequent efforts to test new economic ideas within North Korea. North Korean leaders seem to want to change; they just cannot figure out how to do so successfully while also holding onto power.

If a grand bargain cannot be negotiated with North Korea, a tougher policy of coercion coupled with tighter economic sanctions may have to be seriously considered. Military strikes against the uncompleted North Korean nuclear reactors, as well as the existing small reactor and reprocessing facility and any remaining spent fuel rods, may ultimately have to be contemplated as well. Strangulation may be America's only hope at that point, short of all-out war or the opening of a nuclear Pandora's box in Northeast Asia and beyond.

An additional advantage of trying this broad road map for future relations with North Korea is that it could help the United States implement a hard-line policy if truly necessary. Regional support for such an option, especially critical in regard to South Korea and China, might be more obtainable if Seoul and Beijing recognized that other options had been tried and had failed. But it is premature to fall back on that undesirable approach today.

CONCLUSION

Some would consider any offer of further aid to North Korea a reward for blackmail. But the package deal proposed here would be one with tough conditions. North Korea would not get half the aid by making good only on the nuclear and missile programs, for example. Such an approach would perpetuate its penchant for viewing dangerous arms programs as a way to gain money from the international community. It would also do little to fix its economy or address other acute security and human rights issues. By adding conventional force reductions to the package, as well as the return of Japanese kidnapping victims and gradual improvement in North Korean human rights practices, the United States and allies would be setting much of the agenda. They would also be pushing North Korea to begin to make fundamental choices about its future relationship with the outside world and about economic reform and gradual political liberalization.

This plan should have a good chance of succeeding. Yet if it failed, the United States would be much better positioned to adopt a tougher line in conjunction with its regional security partners than it is today. Proposing a broad road map requires imagination and hard diplomatic work but has few if any other drawbacks.

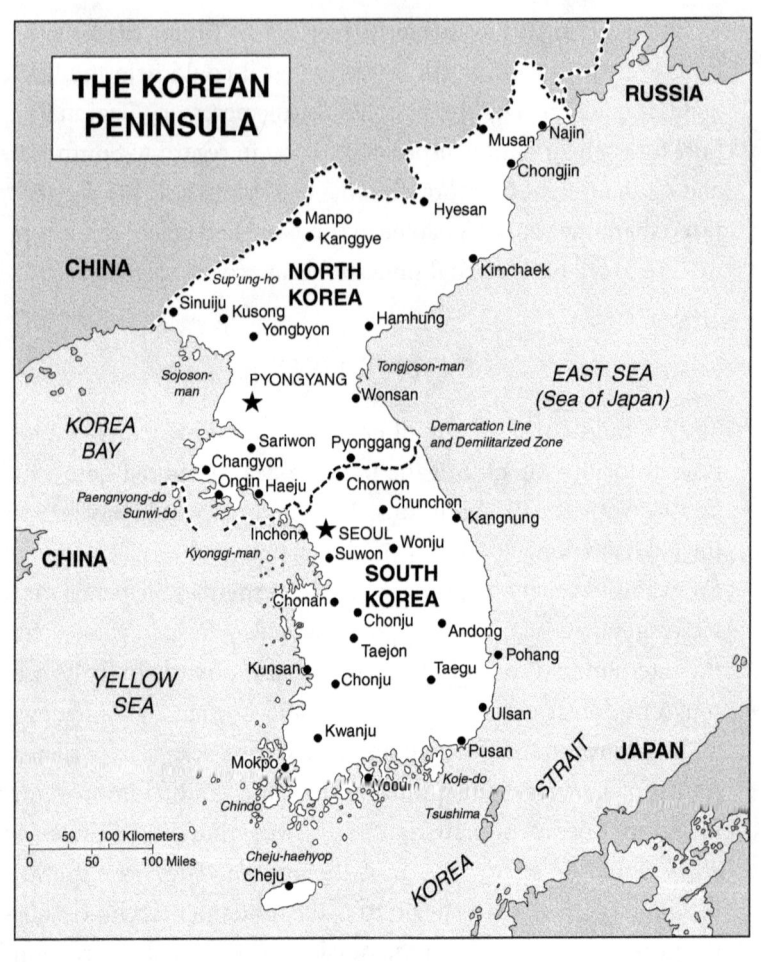

CHAPTER 1

THE HERMIT KINGDOM

North Korea, often known as the "hermit kingdom," is a strange, secretive, dangerous, and deeply troubled small country. Created when the Korean peninsula was divided at the end of World War II, it is an old-fashioned communist state dominated by a ruthless dictator but with its own brand of eccentric ideology mixed in as well. Its official name, the Democratic People's Republic of Korea (DPRK), could not be more misleading. It is as badly out of place in today's world as Castro's Cuba but a far worse place to live and much more threatening to the international community.

Internally, North Korea is very poor and very repressive. In some ways, it resembles Stalin's Soviet Union, with its widespread human rights abuses and gulag system. This is not just the view of the United States; in April of 2003, the United Nations Commission on Human Rights overwhelmingly passed a resolution criticizing North Korea for "all-pervasive and severe restrictions on the freedoms of thought, religion, opinion, expression, assembly and association . . . torture and other cruel, inhuman or degrading treatment . . . and imposition of the death penalty for political reasons."

North Korea may resemble Mao's China as much as Stalin's Soviet Union. To begin with, there is the history of failed agricultural collectivization efforts and resulting famine. At least hundreds of thousands of North Koreans died of starvation in the 1990s, mirroring earlier tragedies in both the Soviet Union and the People's Republic of China (PRC).

Also striking is the cult of personality that has been created for North Korea's supreme leaders. Combined with the country's Confucian traditions, this has produced a remarkable reverence for the political leadership. Today North Korea glorifies Kim Jong Il, (who holds the official title of chairman of the National Defense Commission) and is often referred to as "respected and beloved general," just as it glorified his father, the country's first president, Kim Il Sung (the "Great Leader"), until the latter's death in 1994.

The state's propaganda machine constructs and repeats absurd myths about these two. Sometimes the myths are built on a kernel of truth; sometimes they are pure fabrications. The military accomplishments of the father during World War II are at least loosely grounded in historical fact, if generally exaggerated, though his supposed scientific and political genius and devotion to his people were gross distortions at best. In fact, he created one of the world's worst police states during his half century in power. He also created as many as 34,000 monuments to himself, required his photograph to be displayed virtually everywhere, and went so far as to require his subjects to pin his image to their clothing every day.

Kim Jong Il is officially revered in a similar way. However, the cult of personality is even more warped in his case; while his father truly had been a warrior in World War II, official stories about the younger Kim are almost all pure fantasy. He was allegedly born in a modest cabin on sacred Mount Paektu in northeastern Korea, accompanied by the appearance of bright stars and double rainbows in the sky, as well as magical carvings in nearby trees commemorating his arrival into the world. (In fact, the younger Kim was born as a war refugee in Siberia in 1942.) His supposed exploits go well beyond politics and economics. One of the tallest yarns is that Kim Jong Il wrote over 1,000 books during college alone. Later in life, he supposedly directed, wrote, or commissioned scores of films, according to state propaganda.

The truth is of course much uglier. Kim's most notable accomplishments in the film business, for example, include kidnapping two famous South Korean actors and forcing them to make movies for him (they ultimately escaped on a trip to Eastern Europe). His personal habits involve rampant womanizing and drinking more than artistic endeavor. Those who have met him report a man capable of intelligence, seriousness, and even charm. But he has presided during a period of mass starvation in North Korea and the continual, gradual collapse of his country.

From what is known about North Korean attitudes, this state-sponsored brainwashing has succeeded remarkably well with its captive and isolated audience, which blames the outside world for most of its problems and reveres its leaders (especially the late Kim Il Sung). However, it is probably also true that the hundreds of thousands who have lost family members due to state terror and famine probably do not consider the person once known as the "Dear Leader" quite so dear. In addition, while Kim Jong Il's extravagant tastes and affection for race cars and movie stars and other such indulgences may not be well known within North Korea, his aloofness is noted, and he is not cherished by his people as his father was.

Externally, North Korea is dangerous despite its economic weakness and small size. It is a major military threat to South Korea, also known as the Republic of Korea (ROK), a country that it has invaded once, in 1950, and to the Northeast Asia region more broadly. It has a huge military—1 million troops out of population of 22 million, in per capita terms the highest percentage in the world and ten times the global average. It also devotes a far greater share of its gross domestic product (GDP) to its armed forces than any other country on earth. Its forces arrayed near the demilitarized zone (DMZ) separating it from South Korea represent the densest concentration of firepower in the world by far. It also exports arms such as ballistic missiles to other radical states.

North Korea's miserable circumstances contrast starkly with those of South Korea, which has advanced as far in the last fifty years as any other country on the planet. A country known for subsistence farming and an autocratic government at the time of the Korean War, it is now a healthy democracy with per capita income approaching $15,000 a year—nearly comparable to living standards in Portugal or Spain. South Koreans can be enormously proud of their accomplishments. Americans can be proud too, especially those who have helped protect the Republic of Korea militarily and those who have helped it develop its economy over the past half century.

By contrast, although the DPRK gained some temporary success as a planned industrial economy after the Korean War, that model ultimately worked no better in East Asia than it did in the Soviet Union. Today, North Korea's 22 million inhabitants must each get by on the equivalent of just $1,000 a year (and even that is a generous estimate based on so-called purchasing power parity measures; $500 may be a fairer estimate). North Korea's current economic growth rate, after a decade of sustained decline, is estimated at negative three percent a year. Its terms of trade generally deteriorated throughout the 1990s and have continued to produce poor results in recent years.

Meanwhile, despite being heirs to a rich history, strong religious tradition, and wonderful culture, North Koreans are denied the right to practice their faiths and many other aspects of their traditional way of life. They now must pay homage to Kim Jong Il and the memory of his father, Kim Il Sung. They must also participate economically and socially in the DPRK's *juche* system of national self-reliance and extreme isolation. What began half a century ago as an attempt to merge the egalitarianism of Confucianism with the economic science of industrial age communism deteriorated into a state ruled by an insular, self-indulgent, and self-aggrandizing regime that has totally failed to meet its responsibilities to its own people. The experiment simply did not work.

Thus, it was at least partially understandable that, in his State of the Union address in early 2002, President George W. Bush would describe North Korea as part of an "axis of evil." One can challenge Mr. Bush's suggestion of an alliance involving North Korea, Iran, and Iraq, as well as the strategic wisdom of such blunt presidential language. But one cannot dispute the facts. North Korea's government has created one of the most miserable places on Earth to live, even as its leaders thrive in luxury, and it is in no apparent hurry to change its system for the good of its people. It threatens South Korea, as well as American forces in the ROK, Japan's nearby population centers, and the region as a whole with the possibility of a second unprovoked war, including massive artillery and missile attacks. The risk is made far worse by the likelihood that it possesses nuclear weapons and the virtual certainty that it possesses chemical arms.

IS NORTH KOREA TRYING TO MEND ITS WAYS?

Despite all of the above, North Korea has also spent the last decade trying to change, at least within certain bounds. Its leaders have not offered to give up their totalitarian hold on power, and their motivations for wishing to change are not altruistic. Kim Jong Il is no Mikhail Gorbachev or Deng Xiaoping. Rather, he appears to be a leader who sees his country falling apart and wants to hold it together to protect his own power and privilege.

Kim's motivation might well be less to reform than to avoid a fate like that which befell the Shah of Iran in 1979—or, worse yet, Romania's Nicolae Ceausescu in 1989, killed by his own people in a mass uprising. Kim does not have the oil wealth that propped up Saddam Hussein; he no longer receives subsidies and aid of many hundreds of millions of dollars a year from the Communist Bloc, as he did during the Cold War. Should hostilities again erupt on the peninsula, he almost surely cannot count on Chinese soldiers to fight alongside his troops as they did during the Korean War half a century ago. Meanwhile, his heavy industries are falling into disrepair, a half century of abuse has destroyed much of his country's farmland, and a half century of brainwashing and suppression have left the North Korean people ill-equipped to compete in the modern global economy.

Kim Jong Il's situation is dire enough, and his personality unpredictable enough, that North Korea might still follow extreme policies. That could possibly mean a conventional invasion of the South, even if he thinks the prospects for success to be relatively poor (as Japan did when attacking the United States in 1941). But more likely are efforts to continue his recent patterns of using weapons programs to acquire foreign currency. That could be attempted through overseas arms sales in some cases. Or it could be done through what increasingly amounts to a policy of blackmail and extortion, in which North Korea tries to convince other countries to buy out its nuclear capabilities and missile forces and other threatening weaponry.

But despite this terrible record of governance, North Korea has been changing many of its ways for the better. It still frequently resorts to its traditional tools of threat, brinkmanship, bluster, and intimidation. But it has also done things that would have been unthinkable just a few years ago. Kim Jong Il has participated, even if haltingly, in the beginnings of a détente policy with South Korea, particularly in response to former President Kim Dae Jung's "sunshine policy." This policy has been public and prominent, in contrast to the inter-Korean talks of past eras, and was a major step forward even if it was motivated in part by the short-term pursuit of cash. Kim also welcomed U.S. Secretary of State Madeleine Albright to Pyongyang in 2000, the year after a visit by former Secretary of Defense William Perry. South Korean tourists have recently visited the North; some family reunions have taken place between people separated for half a century by hot war and then cold war. (The Koreas still have no normal diplomatic relations and no peace treaty between them.) Some change has also occurred in North Korea's command economy. Free economic zones, partially modeled after China's reforms under Deng Xiaoping, have been introduced in a few small regions of the country and farmers' markets have emerged.

Indeed, the partial thaw in North Korea's behavior toward the outside world continued right up until the recent nuclear crisis began in October 2002. In the two-month period just before U.S.

Assistant Secretary of State James Kelly confronted North Korea with evidence that it was secretly attempting to develop a uranium enrichment capability (based on information about technologies North Korea was trying to obtain abroad), Pyongyang took a number of positive steps. At home, it lifted price controls and increased wages. In foreign policy, it agreed to reestablish road and rail links with South Korea and began work on the project. It sent more than six hundred athletes to the Asian Games in South Korea (the first time it had ever sent athletes to an event in the ROK). It resumed high-level dialogue with the United States and South Korea. It also held a summit with Japanese Prime Minister Junichiro Koizumi, during which it admitted to having kidnapped at least thirteen Japanese citizens years ago. While claiming that eight of these abductees had died, it then allowed five to return home for a visit.

Improvements continued on the security front as well. By the mid-1990s, North Korea had reduced its overseas arms sales by a factor of five—from an average of about $400 million annually in the late 1980s to less than $100 million a year (in constant 2003 dollars). That may have had more to do with the drying up of the market than with any restraint on Pyongyang's part, but it still meant that North Korea was doing less to threaten U.S. global interests.

Even more important, North Korea's support for terrorism declined drastically. After having brought down a South Korean airliner and assassinated part of the ROK cabinet in the 1980s, North Korea essentially got out of the terrorism business. Although technically still included on the State Department's list of state sponsors of terrorism, North Korea is now accused only of harboring a few aging Japanese who hijacked a plane in 1970 and of possibly selling modest quantities of small arms to terrorists (almost surely not al Qaeda). The last time it may have kidnapped a Japanese citizen appears to have been 1991.

And of course, North Korea entered into the 1994 Agreed Framework with the United States, which capped its fledgling nuclear capabilities. Even with the discovery in 2002 of the secret and illegal North Korean uranium enrichment program, which appears to have been begun by 1997, the DPRK's maximum nuclear arsenal was believed to have been two weapons as of early 2003. That number stands in stark contrast to the 50 or more it might otherwise have had by then, absent the 1994 accord. Given the security benefit, the costs to outside powers of providing fuel aid and funds for new reactor construction under the Agreed Framework have been quite modest—a total of $1.4 billion through 2001 ($600 million from South Korea, $300 million apiece from the United States and Japan, almost $100 million from Europe, over $10 million from Australia, and more modest sums from a host of other countries).

THE RECENT NUCLEAR CRISIS

But the U.S. discovery of that uranium enrichment program, which North Korea first denied but then admitted to possessing, changed everything. It did more than set back the détente process; it led to a crisis on the peninsula unlike anything since at least 1994. That program is a clear violation of North Korea's obligations under the 1968 Nuclear Non-Proliferation Treaty (NPT), which it signed in 1985, and hence of the Agreed Framework as well. It also violates a 1991 accord between North Korea and South Korea, an agreement that was facilitated by a U.S. decision to remove its nuclear weapons from the ROK, that banned any and all nuclear weapons capabilities on the peninsula.

Those are solemn commitments, and violations are serious. Unlike, for example, the Anti-Ballistic Missile (ABM) Treaty, which was designed for the specific circumstances of Cold War superpower arms competition and thus naturally had less relevance when the Bush administration decided to withdraw from it in 2001, the NPT is a treaty of continued relevance and indefinite duration given the ongoing need to control the most dangerous technology ever invented by humankind. Moreover, North Korea is a country with a past of aggression, a very poor human rights record, and an extremely oversized and threatening military. Under such circumstances, its violations of its international commitments not to obtain weapons of mass destruction (WMD) are especially serious.

After Assistant Secretary Kelly confronted North Korea with the evidence about its uranium program in October 2002, Pyongyang declared that it had "nullified" its commitments under the Agreed Framework, though it later retracted some of its words. But overall, things got even worse in ensuing weeks and months. After the United States and its East Asian and European allies in the Korean Energy Development Organization (KEDO) cut off fuel shipments to the DPRK in December, shipments they had begun under the terms of the Agreed Framework, North Korea escalated in turn. It expelled International Atomic Energy Agency (IAEA) inspectors on December 31. Then, on January 9, it announced its withdrawal from the NPT.

In late January, North Korea evidently began to move some of its eight thousand spent nuclear fuel rods out of storage in an apparent attempt to prepare them for chemical reprocessing (basically a process of extraction and purification to separate the plutonium from the nuclear waste in which it is embedded). After being irradiated in North Korea's small "research reactor" in the late 1980s and early 1990s, they could provide enough plutonium for about half a dozen bombs once reprocessed. In early February of 2003, North Korea claimed to have restarted that small research reactor (with a power output of 5 megawatts, or MWe), as confirmed by U.S. intelligence later in the month. It thus appeared that North Korea's nuclear arsenal, which may have already consisted of one or two bombs (using plutonium from spent fuel rods taken from the reactor in 1989, 1990, and 1991), might grow to about eight warheads by the end of the year.

Then things slowed down a bit. North Korea may have had technical trouble restarting the plutonium reprocessing facility. It may also have been influenced by international pressure. While China and Russia made it clear that they did not support a tightening of sanctions against North Korea anytime soon, they also opposed North Korea's nuclear efforts. In mid-February, Chinese Vice Foreign Minister Wang Yi reportedly told North Korean Foreign Minister Paek Nam Sun to stop "playing with fire." Similarly, Russia stated that a nuclear-armed North Korea was not in its interest and suggested it might ultimately support U.N. sanctions on North Korea if Pyongyang continued to pursue nuclear weapons. This type of language continued through the spring, with China, Russia, Japan, and South Korea all repeatedly making their views clear—even if they also resisted adding any of the more threatening words that the United States advocated in case diplomatic pressure alone did not work.

North Korea may also have been intimidated by the U.S.-led war against Iraq. Reportedly, Kim Jong Il was not seen for many weeks in early 2003, disappearing after a meeting with visiting Russians on February 12 and resurfacing only for a military ceremony on April 3. Some Bush administration insiders speculate that his absence was attributable to fear for his own personal safety.

But some combination of technical troubles, Chinese cajoling, and greater fear for U.S. power may only produce a temporary delay in North Korea's provocative course of action. Indeed,

North Korea stated that the Iraq war proved its case for acquiring a "tremendous deterrent" to invasion. In early April, its withdrawal from the NPT became official. Even as Pyongyang prepared for talks with the United States in Beijing in late April, it suggested that it was poised to restart its reprocessing efforts. At those talks, it reportedly claimed that it already possessed nuclear arms. At various times it also seemed to suggest that it had already reprocessed additional plutonium, or that it was about to do so soon. Meanwhile, U.S. intelligence independently reached the conclusion that North Korea had recently reprocessed at least modest additional amounts of the spent fuel.

North Korea hinted as well that it might even take the extreme step of testing a nuclear weapon or, worse yet, selling some plutonium abroad. Mr. Bush apparently took the latter worry seriously enough to discuss means of interdicting possible DPRK nuclear exports with visiting Australian Prime Minister John Howard the following week, and then again with the world's major industrial powers at the G8 summit in France in early June. (That would be a daunting task given the fact that a bomb's worth of plutonium is as small as a grapefruit, that plutonium does not give off a powerful radioactive signature, that even a country with as weak an economy as North Korea sends out thousands of cargo ships a year, and that the China-North Korea border is difficult to police.) The administration also devised a "proliferation security initiative" with allies, to stop and search certain North Korean vessels when they are in the coastal waters of participating countries.

There were other related problems. In early May, North Korea annulled the agreement it had reached with South Korea to keep the peninsula free of nuclear weapons. To justify the action, Pyongyang cited a December 2002 Bush administration document insisting that the United States retained the right to use all options—including nuclear weapons—to respond to a chemical or biological attack against its interests, and claimed that statement violated the earlier accord.

Nor would the DPRK be limited to a maximum of six or eight nuclear weapons over time. It is also capable of producing another bomb's worth of plutonium annually from the plutonium research reactor. In a March 2003 statement to Congress, Assistant Secretary of State James Kelly estimated that within a year North Korea might also be able to enrich enough uranium for two bombs annually with its secret underground program. Should it also finish its 50-MWe and 200-MWe reactors at the Yongbyon site, the floodgates would truly open. At that point, it might be able to produce anywhere from thirty to fifty-five bombs a year. (North Korea might need two years to complete the smaller reactor, three or more for the larger one.)

North Korea's provocative actions have not been limited to the nuclear domain. In mid-February of 2003, in response to reports that the United States was considering a naval blockade if the DPRK nuclear program continued, Pyongyang even threatened to abandon its commitment to the 1953 Korean War armistice. A week later, it fired an antiship cruise missile into the Sea of Japan, an action it repeated shortly thereafter. On March 2, its fighter jets menaced a U.S. reconnaissance aircraft in international airspace over the Sea of Japan, perhaps intending to take its American crew hostage. (If so, the attempt failed.) At about the same time, North Korea fired a dangerous laser at two U.S. Army helicopters patrolling just south of the DMZ.

What were U.S. actions over this time period? Although it did cut off fuel oil shipments late in 2002, the United States initially tried to maintain a semblance of calm in responding to Pyongyang. Part of its motivation was probably to avoid distracting the world's attention from preparations for war in Iraq; part of it was to avoid rewarding North Korea with attention after such blatant provocations. Perhaps another element of Washington's calculus was hope that Pyongyang would eventually think better of its recent decisions or be convinced to reverse course by Beijing or Seoul.

Indeed, for a time the Bush administration took a softer line than the Clinton administration had in 1994. Specifically, on December 29, Secretary of State Powell stated that the United States was not considering the use of force to address the Korean nuclear standoff. At about the same time, other administration statements indicated an openness to diplomacy. Powell also said in early January that the United States would consider making a pledge that it had no aggressive intent toward the DPRK, thereby providing the nonaggression promise Pyongyang had been demanding. Assistant Secretary Kelly also suggested a willingness to help North Korea with its energy problems if the nuclear issue could first be addressed.

The president's own words were mixed. In early January, he stated in regard to Kim Jong Il that "I have no heart for somebody who starves his own folks"—following even stronger language the previous year when he stated that he "loathed Kim Jong Il" for the same reason, and referred to him as a pygmy (the North Korean president stands only slightly over five feet in height). But then on January 14, the president suggested the possibility of a bold initiative involving aid, energy, and diplomatic and security benefits if North Korea first arrested its nuclear ambitions. In his state of the union speech on January 28 he returned to a harder line, describing the DPRK regime as one that "rules a people living in fear and starvation," and refusing to allow the United States to be blackmailed. In early March of 2003, President Bush stated that the United States had not ruled out military options for addressing the Korea problem, though South Korea's new president, Roh

Moo Hyun, had earlier dismissed the option categorically. Their difference of opinion on the potential need for a military option persisted even after their brief visit—more of a "getting to know each other" session than a substantive meeting—on May 14 in Washington.

On balance, Mr. Bush clearly continued to lean toward a hard line with North Korea, just as he had since the early days of his presidency. Shortly after taking office, President Bush cast cold water on Kim Dae Jung's sunshine policy and any continuation of Clinton-style engagement with Pyongyang, even after Secretary of State Colin Powell had indicated that the administration would pick up diplomacy where its predecessor had left off. A year later, President Bush gave his "axis of evil" speech, in which he lumped North Korea with Iran and Iraq and suggested that stern policy measures would be needed to deal with all.

By April 2002, Powell was telling Congress that the United States was willing to talk with North Koreans anytime, anyplace, even in a bilateral context, perhaps reflecting a temporary softening of the administration's position. But the discovery of the uranium enrichment program hardened President Bush's thinking again. Although still willing to support U.S. participation in multilateral diplomacy with North Korea, President Bush reportedly feels that accepting DPRK demands for bilateral negotiations between Washington and Pyongyang would be relenting to blackmail.

Mr. Bush reportedly has some liking for the highly coercive strategy recommended by several members of his administration. For example, in the spring of 2003, Secretary of Defense Donald Rumsfeld was said to favor joining with the Chinese to use economic and diplomatic pressure to force regime change in Pyongyang. Beijing would almost certainly not accept such a proposal, but if the report of Rumsfeld's thinking is true, it is interesting nonetheless for what it may reveal about the views of administration hard-liners. President Bush did not adopt this policy but appears not to have ruled it out either; indeed, he is partly adopting Rumsfeld's suggestions for a prompt crackdown on North Korean counterfeiting and drug trafficking operations as part of the proliferation security initiative.

Just where North Korea's nuclear weapons program will go in the months ahead is unclear. There will likely be many ups and downs in the process of negotiations; indeed, the April 2003 Beijing talks between North Korea and the United States had promising and menacing elements all in the space of a couple of days. But in any event, it seems unlikely that the basic problem will be solved—even if the nuclear crisis can be contained for the moment, North Korea will likely still have a broken economy, a highly threatening military posture near the DMZ, and the continued capability to develop nuclear weapons. Even if the nuclear crisis cools temporarily, it could easily worsen again, as it has before. North Korea could even test a nuclear device or, worse yet, export nuclear materials abroad, perhaps even to a terrorist organization like al Qaeda.

These facts mean that the grand bargain laid out in this book will be relevant regardless of the precise state of North Korea's nuclear programs in the coming months. Only a truly extreme development such as all-out war on the peninsula could change the situation so drastically as to make a major new diplomatic strategy unnecessary. Under these circumstances, the United States and its regional partners need to develop a comprehensive plan, not just a set of short-term negotiating tactics, for addressing the North Korea problem. Depending on where things stand in late 2003 and thereafter, they may still need a short-term fix to the crisis. In any event, they will surely still need a longer-term strategy.

Now that the 1994 Agreed Framework is clearly inoperative, there is considerable dispute over who violated it first. Even before it fell apart in late 2002, the accord was beset by numerous problems. Shortly after it was concluded, Pyongyang was insistent that the new nuclear reactors promised to it not come officially from South Korea. That led to a delay in working out acceptable diplomatic niceties in the description of the new reactors.

Other events produced delays as well. In 1996, a North Korean submarine came aground in South Korea, and twenty-five commandos came ashore. Half were subsequently killed by each other and the other half by South Korea. As a result, Seoul temporarily suspended cooperation on the reactor deal. The above events, as well as suspicions that North Korea was developing an underground nuclear-related site in the late 1990s (these particular fears turned out to be unfounded, even though we now know that North Korea did have a hidden uranium program elsewhere) and its long-range missile launching in 1998, led the Clinton administration to delay lifting economic sanctions on North Korea as required by the 1994 accord. It is hard to blame Seoul and Washington for their reticence under such circumstances. Yet North Korea turned around and cited these examples as proof that it was not the first to violate the 1994 accord. North Korea also claimed that the United States failed to live up to its pledge to forswear formally the threat or use of nuclear weapons in a conflict on the peninsula.

The fairest assessment of this troubled history is that each side has a basis for criticizing the other, yet neither had fundamentally broken out of the Agreed Framework until North Korea developed its uranium enrichment program. That program constitutes a clear and extremely serious violation of the NPT and thus of the Agreed Framework itself. Among its other lessons, this history means that any future accord with North Korea must be very well verified.

"THE MOST SERIOUS CHALLENGE TO U.S. REGIONAL INTERESTS IN A GENERATION"

However one explains the dynamics, the nuclear situation in Korea constituted a major crisis by early 2003. According to Vice Admiral Lowell Jacoby, head of the U.S. Defense Intelligence Agency, "Pyongyang's open pursuit of additional nuclear weapons is the most serious challenge to U.S. regional interests in a generation." Even if Pyongyang can be convinced to step back from the brink for now, the basic situation seems likely to remain precarious for some time to come.

The United States must make it a top national security priority not to allow North Korea to develop a nuclear arsenal. There are several reasons why such an arsenal would pose a grave risk. First, if it develops substantial amounts of fissile material, North Korea might sell it to terrorists. Second, if its government someday collapses, its nuclear materials could then fall into the hands of those who would sell them to the highest bidder. Third, U.S.-ROK deterrence could be weakened if North Korea thought it had a nuclear trump card. Should war result, the more bombs North Korea possessed, the greater would be its odds of successfully delivering a nuclear warhead against Seoul or another population center. Finally, North Korean nuclear weapons could start a nuclear domino effect in Northeast Asia and weaken global nonproliferation efforts more broadly.

So the situation with North Korea is very serious. Complicating it still further is the fact that U.S.-ROK relations are now in mediocre shape. This is not the first time the alliance, South Korea's only formal security relationship, has faced challenges. Decades ago, Washington sometimes chastised Seoul for repressive internal practices. At the same time, many South

Korean reformers and students felt that Washington was too close to their autocratic leaders, notably around the time of the so-called Kwangju (sometimes written Kwanju) massacre of 1980.

But today, the problems are perhaps even harder to solve. The United States is seen by many in South Korea as an insensitive and patronizing great power. This image was worsened greatly in the last two years. The first cause was President Bush's dismissive attitude toward President Kim's sunshine policy early in 2001. Other problems contributed as well. A tragic accident, in which two young South Korean girls were killed by a U.S. armored vehicle in 2002 yet the American soldiers in it were acquitted of wrongdoing by an American court, inflamed South Korean sentiments. More gradually, increasing tensions have also developed over a large U.S. military base complex in Seoul that keeps increasingly valuable land from South Korean use. The United States plans to relocate the forces at this base and certain others in the ROK to different parts of the country but has not yet done so. President Bush's "axis of evil" concept, as well as his administration's stated willingness to consider military preemption against threatening states more frequently than American governments have in the past, have further exacerbated tensions between Seoul and Washington.

South Korea's new president, Roh Moo Hyun—not believed to have been Washington's preferred candidate in late 2002 elections, when he narrowly beat the more conservative candidate, Lee Hoi Chang—endorses a continuation of the sunshine policy. As noted, he also opposes military threats against the DPRK, even if its nuclear program accelerates. President Roh has recently taken steps to prevent a further deterioration in U.S.-ROK relations, including convincing his country's National Assembly to approve deployment of ROK noncombat troops to support the U.S.-led war against Iraq. But the possibility that presidents Bush and Roh can develop a common policy toward North Korea and work together productively remains unsupported.

The fundamental difference between South Korean and American views on future policy toward North Korea should not be overstated. For example, just a few years ago, under the administration of Bill Clinton in the United States and Kim Young Sam in South Korea, it was often Washington that supported engagement with North Korea and Seoul that resisted. Had their respective razor-close presidential races each gone differently in 2000 and 2002, moreover, the United States and South Korea might have reversed roles on which favored more ambitious efforts to give Pyongyang incentives to build a new relationship. But given the current governments in Washington and Seoul, the rift is rather serious. And South Korean pride has been sufficiently injured by Bush administration actions that even many conservative Koreans no longer feel as comfortable about the United States as they once did.

TOWARD A GRAND BARGAIN WITH NORTH KOREA

So where do Washington, Seoul, and Tokyo go from here? How do they work with Beijing, probably North Korea's closest friend and its only treaty partner, to prevent a humanitarian catastrophe and a worsening nuclear crisis in Northeast Asia? This issue is perhaps even more important for future U.S. security than the war with Iraq, since Saddam Hussein was almost surely years away from a nuclear capability when he was overthrown, whereas North Korea already has one.

In this book, we propose an answer—a "grand bargain" with North Korea. It would be worked out and implemented over time, of course. It might even be negotiated in pieces (though there is good reason to aim for a single, large deal). But in any case, it would be big and bold in scope so as to provide a vision and a road map for the allies and for North Korea. Such visions help countries stay focused on the potentially great benefits of a fruitful diplomatic process, reducing the odds that their negotiations will bog down in pursuit of marginal advantages on specific issues. Visions or road maps are often especially useful in guiding negotiations between countries that do not know each other well or mistrust each other, as Richard Haass and Meghan O'Sullivan have observed.

This broad plan would be tough and demanding on North Korea. It would also offer generous incentives. The use of both carrots and sticks is not contradictory. The outside world should not give Pyongyang substantial aid and other benefits simply to appease a dangerous leader or solve an immediate security crisis. But if North Korea is prepared to eliminate its nuclear weapons programs, transform the broader security situation on the peninsula, reform its economy, and even begin to change its own society, outside countries can and should be generous. Doing so would not be weakness; it would be a promising way to truly solve an important security problem by changing the fundamental nature of the adversary. If North Korea did not verifiably cooperate with this effort, the United States and its partners could then get tougher.

The last decade of U.S. policy has not followed a broad vision. It has been more narrow and tactical, focusing on the crisis du jour rather than a broader game plan. Such a tactical approach was perhaps inevitable in the early Clinton years, when the administration was focused on domestic matters and experiencing difficulty in its foreign policy from Somalia to Haiti to Bosnia. As a result, it had a hard time focusing strategically on North Korea at the highest levels of government and on developing an integrated approach for dealing with Pyongyang that combined incentives with threats and deterrence.

A tactical, nuclear-specific focus could also be defended as a reasonable approach in the early 1990s. Indeed, until stopped by the first Bush administration, Israel had reportedly been pursuing a deal to compensate North Korea for not selling missiles to Iran just a short time before. If it made strategic sense for a security-conscious and hard-nosed country such as Israel to consider buying out North Korea's missile program, why did it not make sense for the United States and regional allies to buy out North Korea's even more dangerous nuclear program—especially if the deal involved not cash but simply the replacement of dangerous energy technologies with safer ones?

In addition, many American policymakers expected that, given the dissolution of the Soviet bloc, North Korea would no longer enjoy the aid or favorable trading arrangements it needed to survive and would soon collapse. That would have amounted to a long-term solution. Others may have expected that working out a deal on nuclear weapons would naturally lead to a quick thaw in relations on the peninsula without any need for articulation of a broader vision. In any event, even if some had wished to articulate such a vision, domestic politics in the United States and South Korea stood in the way. And a tactical, crisis-driven approach to dealing with North Korea did produce some temporary successes, most of all in regard to the Agreed Framework.

There is nothing inherently wrong with this type of incrementalist approach, focusing first on North Korean nuclear and missile capabilities. Nor should it be confused with appeasement if pursued carefully. For example, in a 1999 government review, former Secretary of Defense Bill Perry suggested that step-by-step engagement be attempted, with continued progress conditional on improved behavior by Pyongyang. Perry suggested that a policy of pressure be prepared as well, should the conciliatory approach fail. This approach would amount to "testing" North Korea and reverting to a hardline policy should engagement fail. A number of scholars and former policymakers have continued to promote such a policy during the Bush presidency.

But despite its reasonable logic, this approach does not look particularly promising. President Bush has made it clear he is opposed to this approach. Nor is North Korea likely to agree to the type of relatively narrow deal envisioned in most plans that emphasize resolution of the nuclear and missile issues. Prior to the recent crisis, the DPRK already was receiving most of the benefits that the nuclear/missile engagement school proposes offering now (except the nonaggression pledge). It also received some shadowy cash payoffs from South Koreans that have tainted the reputation of former President Kim Dae Jung and the détente process he initiated with Kim Jong Il. Yet North Korea chose to ignore some of its key commitments under the 1994 Agreed Framework and NPT anyway. There is nothing logically wrong with what nuclear/missile engagers tend to propose. But it no longer seems a promising route, and in fact it may have inadvertently encouraged the DPRK to develop a worsening habit of using its dangerous weapons programs to gain money and diplomatic attention. Whether one views that as extortion or the desperate actions of a failing regime, the outcome has been the same.

In addition to its other advantages, a broader approach would also respond to the recent suggestion of the government of South Korean President Roh that the United States offer a bold initiative to Pyongyang. Without strong cooperation between Seoul and Washington, no plan for dealing with North Korea can work—and if it senses dissension and discord in the U.S.-ROK alliance, Pyongyang will probably succumb to its traditional temptation to try to split apart the two allies.

Like other plans, our proposed grand bargain would denuclearize North Korea. The most important, and vital, goal would be to prevent any further development of North Korea's nuclear inventory. Almost as important, though somewhat less urgent, would be to eliminate the small quantities of separated plutonium, possibly already in the form of one or two bombs, that North Korea possessed throughout most of the 1990s.

Such a plan would begin with rapid restoration of fuel oil shipments as well as a freeze on North Korea's nuclear activities—particularly plutonium production and reprocessing at Yongbyon—while negotiations proceeded. Our proposal would replace North Korea's Yongbyon nuclear facilities with conventional, not nuclear, power sources. It would include rigorous monitoring of North Korean nuclear-related sites and short-notice "challenge" inspections at places where outside intelligence led to suspicion of possible nuclear-related activities. All North Korean nuclear activities nationwide would have to cease permanently and verifiably.

Given North Korea's worries about the Bush administration's doctrine of preemption and recent initiation of military operations against Iraq, it might not be feasible to convince the DPRK to give up all of its nuclear capabilities immediately. In fact, it might take several years to reach that final goal, perhaps even until the end of the decade. But as long as any deal immediately and verifiably froze the DPRK's nuclear activities and then quickly began to get fuel rods out of North Korea, the United States could be patient in seeing the last kilograms of plutonium accounted for and the uranium enrichment program put under monitoring.

Depending on circumstances at the time negotiations occurred, this approach would retain the threat of a military strike against Yongbyon as a last resort. Although Washington has been unable to convince Seoul about the need for such a threat today, that could change. By seriously trying diplomacy first, including an offer of numerous inducements for North Korea, the United States would have a better chance of getting its regional allies to support a threat should diplomacy fail. By providing more carrots, it might gain greater support for the possible use of a stick as well.

Any such military strike at Yongbyon, though unlikely to spread much radioactivity, according to studies done at the Pentagon in the early 1990s, would be extremely risky given the possibility that a larger war would result. (More specifically, radioactive release would probably be quite limited unless an operational nuclear reactor with heavily irradiated fuel were struck.) And it would probably fail to destroy or render unusable many of North Korea's spent fuel rods, meaning that the DPRK might still manufacture one or more weapons even after an attack. That said, in our judgment it would be preferable to an unchecked, large-scale DPRK nuclear program, if someday that were the only alternative outcome.

However, in our view preemption should not be needed, given our strong conviction that this type of grand bargain proposal will convince the DPRK to give up its nuclear aspirations—at least over a gradual implementation period. True, North Korean hardliners may fear the Bush administration enough that they will argue against giving up their nuclear program at present. Perhaps they would also have done so under the Clinton administration.

But Kim Jong Il runs North Korea. And he has demonstrated sufficient interest in engaging with the outside world and in exploring economic reforms that the United States and other countries should seriously test his willingness to go further. Moreover, his position within North Korea now appears rather strong. He has used purges and promotions to produce a top officer corps loyal to him. In addition, military commanders probably do not believe they have any better ideas for how to fix North

Korea's economic problems. If a proposed package deal addressed North Korea's core security worries while also opening up real prospects for recovery and greater international engagement, North Korea might very well take the idea quite seriously.

If a grand bargain allowed North Korea to surrender its nuclear capabilities gradually and also allowed it to keep some of its conventional weaponry near the DMZ, Pyongyang might well be persuadable. It might prefer to have both aid and nuclear weapons—but we should try to force it to choose. Moreover, there is little harm in testing this proposition; no irrevocable harm would be done as a result of a failed experiment, and the allies would never let down their military guard at any point in the proposed process.

Our approach would not stop with the nuclear and missile issues. Notably, it would also mandate cuts in conventional forces on both sides of the DMZ and would accompany those cuts with a commitment to help North Korea gradually restructure its economy. Cuts of 50 percent or more in large conventional weapons would reduce the threat North Korea poses to South Korea, and in particular to nearby Seoul, with its artillery and rocket forces. But unlike some proposals, our approach would not *require* North Korea to withdraw all of its conventional capabilities from the DMZ region. North Korea almost surely considers its forward-deployed forces necessary to deter South Korea and the United States. Hence it cannot realistically be expected to surrender both its weapons of mass destruction (including nuclear, chemical, and biological capabilities) and its conventional deterrent. Since our proposal would not require that it do so, it is possible that North Korea's military—an important constituency for Kim Jong Il—might be persuaded to support the plan.

Indeed, the purpose of these conventional reductions would actually be economic as much as military. Secretary of Defense

Rumsfeld recently argued that the real solution to North Korea's problems is to move toward a market economy, and that view is convincing. Conventional arms reductions could help significantly. If Pyongyang agreed to them, its economy would benefit twice—first by a reduction in the size and cost of its military, second by gaining greater technical and economic aid (as well as a lifting of trade sanctions) from Japan, South Korea, the United States, and China.

Given this economic logic to the grand bargain, it would make sense to keep giving aid only if North Korea continued down the path of economic reform. China could provide technical help, given its experiences of the last twenty-five years in gradually introducing entrepreneurial activity into a communist system.

If North Korea was planning to make conventional cuts anyway, as some have suggested, that would pose no problems. (Indeed, North Korea has stated it wants nuclear arms so it can cut its expensive conventional forces; the second part of this idea is a good one.) Washington and its partners should care about results, and a combination of DPRK force cuts and economic reforms stands the best chance of producing stabilizing and desirable results. External aid can help in that process whether North Korea insists on it as a precondition to reducing its forces or not. Similarly, if the United States considers or even carries out conventional force realignments in South Korea, as Secretary of Defense Donald Rumsfeld is planning, no harm would be done either. We would argue against announcing any significant U.S. cutbacks before a grand bargain could be proposed and negotiated, but force redeployments from one part of the peninsula to another would not weaken deterrence or the allies' bargaining position.

China could also offer reassurance, surely important to North Korean leaders, that it is possible to reform a command economy without losing political power in the process. While most Americans would probably prefer to see North Korea's corrupt and ruthless government fall, that outcome does not seem realistically obtainable without incurring huge security risks and exacting an enormous humanitarian toll on the North Korean people. Moreover, if North Korea accepts this grand bargain proposal, it will be agreeing to at least a gradual, soft, "velvet" form of regime change—even if Kim Jong Il holds onto power throughout the process.

Other elements of the grand bargain would include a continued North Korean commitment not to resort to terrorism, the permanent return to Japan of all kidnapping victims, and initiation of a human rights dialogue designed to gradually coax North Korea into certain internal reforms. North Korea would end its counterfeiting and drug smuggling activities. Pyongyang would also sign the chemical weapons and biological weapons conventions and fulfill its obligations under them, including the complete destruction of its existing stocks of such weapons.

The United States would offer numerous benefits beyond economic and energy aid. But none would require a change in its fundamental regional policies. It would provide a nonaggression pledge (and perhaps even an active security guarantee if North Korea wished, akin to what it provides its allies) and a no-first-use pledge regarding weapons of mass destruction. It would also end economic sanctions, remove North Korea's name from the list of state sponsors of terrorism, sign a peace treaty, and open up diplomatic relations.

It may seem counterintuitive to aim for a big, multifaceted deal if Washington and Pyongyang cannot even sustain a narrow agreement on a specific issue. Why run when you can't even walk? Accordingly, a recent Center for Strategic and International Studies (CSIS) report explicitly recommended *against* any proposal including ambitious conventional arms reductions in Korea on the grounds that it would probably be a recipe for stalemate and failure. The Perry report also took aim at broad proposals, suggesting that they would meet resistance in Pyongyang, which would see any attempt at major reforms as designed to undermine the regime. But in fact, there are several very good reasons to think big:

- **First, the current situation is at an impasse.** A new idea is needed. Coercion is unlikely to cause North Korea's collapse or convince Pyongyang to change policy quickly enough to prevent a major nuclear crisis in Northeast Asia. The Bush administration's proposal, by which broad concessions are demanded of North Korea without an offer of concrete incentives, stands little chance of convincing Pyongyang to change course—and elicits little support from key U.S. security partners in the region. On the other hand, while limited engagement like that seen in the 1990s worked for a time, capping North Korea's nuclear program, it later lost relevance when the DPRK blatantly violated the 1994 Agreed Framework. Those, like the CSIS scholars, who currently argue that an ambitious plan would be unattainable fail to recognize that limited deals may now be even harder to reach.

- **Second, aiming for a larger bargain, in which more is offered to North Korea but more is also demanded may break the impasse.** Other peace negotiations, such as those in the Balkans and the Middle East, have been guided by broad visions or road maps. Korea's should be too. The grand bargain approach has the potential to give both sides in the negotiations what they want. The United States and its allies can reduce the DPRK threat across the board and begin to turn that police state away from a policy of reflexive confrontation and blackmail. North Korea can gain much greater levels of assistance over time and perhaps begin to reform its economy in the way China and Vietnam have successfully done—as it at least occasionally seems to desire.

- **Third, studies of North Korean negotiating behavior suggest that broader deals may work better than overly narrow proposals on specific issues.** This seemed to be the pattern in the 1993–1994 negotiations leading to the Agreed Framework. Those talks went slowly for a long time but succeeded once broadened beyond the nuclear weapons issue to include energy, economics, security, and diplomatic incentives (even if most of those features of the deal were not spelled out in detail and not successfully implemented in later years, as discussed above).

- **Fourth, offering aid tied to conventional arms cuts makes more economic sense than buyouts of nuclear and missile programs.** Specifically, such a deal should reduce North Korean military expenditures substantially, helping reform the DPRK economy and making it more likely that any aid would be well used. North Korea's conventional military forces comprise one million individuals and are backed up by large reserve forces and a large arms industry; what is known of North Korean nuclear, missile, biological, and chemical programs suggests corresponding efforts involving perhaps tens of thousands of individuals. This suggests that the lion's share of North Korea's defense budget, which represents 20 to 30 percent of its GDP, is gobbled up by conventional forces, so these should be a main focus of any reform proposal. Indeed, North Korea has itself recently recognized the excessive strain that conventional forces place on its economy, claiming it needs nuclear weapons in order to provide for its security at lower cost by facilitating reductions in the size of its military. Ideally, heavy forces on the Korean peninsula would decline by 50 percent or more under this type of plan.

- **Fifth, while couched in broad and ambitious terms, this road map could be put into effect gradually.** In fact, even if negotiated as a single package, it would have to be implemented over time and not instantaneously. Intrusive nuclear inspections typically take months or longer; conventional force reductions take at least a couple of years; economic development programs take longer still. So the concept is grand in its intent and scope but need not be rushed in its implementation. In fact, the need for gradual implementation would provide each side with leverage over the other. The United States and its partners would continue to provide aid and economic help only if North Korea upheld its end of the bargain, and security guarantees would be contingent on complete compliance with denuclearization demands as well as with other elements of the proposal. Likewise, North Korea would not have to give up all of its nuclear potential until it gained a number of concrete benefits, and it would not have to keep reducing conventional forces unless outside powers continued to provide assistance.

- **Sixth, this type of broader agenda can unite the United States with other key players—South Korea, Japan, and China.** These four countries need to be united in their basic approach to the North Korean problem, so that Pyongyang will not be tempted to play one off against the others as it often has in the past, and so that they can work together to pursue their common goals. But these four countries will not unite behind a policy that begins with hard-line measures; in particular, South Korea and China will consider a tough line against Pyongyang only if serious diplomacy has clearly first been attempted and failed. Uniting the four players is thus the best way to improve the prospects both for diplomacy and for a successful coercive strategy should diplomacy fail.

Our proposal is the first one of its kind to be presented in detail. But it is not entirely without precedent. Most notably, the sunshine policy of Kim Dae Jung hinted at broader policy changes designed to produce a much different Korean peninsula, a concept recently reiterated by U.N. special advisor Maurice Strong.

There have also been suggestions of a similar approach in the American debate. A recent article coauthored by a former U.S. ambassador to Korea, James Laney, briefly mentions conventional arms drawdowns along the DMZ as an element in a broader bargain, though with little detail. So does a recent paper by a former South Korean defense minister. A previous proposal by a Council on Foreign Relations task force also raised the conventional force issue, but again, quite vaguely. (A more recent Council on Foreign Relations task force did not emphasize it.)

Conventional force reductions have been mentioned in passing over an even longer period. A 1991-1992 accord between the DPRK and the ROK that resulted from an initial attempt at détente on the peninsula paid lip service to the idea. In a broader sense, ideas for cutting conventional forces have been floated for years in Korea; North Korea has proposed cuts to 100,000 personnel on a side, for example. But such a proposal was not serious, because no verification mechanisms were proposed and because spy satellites and reconnaissance aircraft cannot verify reductions in personnel but only in large military equipment.

Although conventional force reductions are the linchpin of our proposal, there are other key elements. The most important is a broad notion of what type of economic reform approach might work in Korea. In broad strokes, although the cases are different, there is reason to think that what worked in China starting about a quarter century ago (and Vietnam somewhat more recently) can work now in North Korea. If so, a grand bargain could do much more than address an acute security problem; it could begin to transform what has been one of the world's most troubled and dangerous regions for decades.

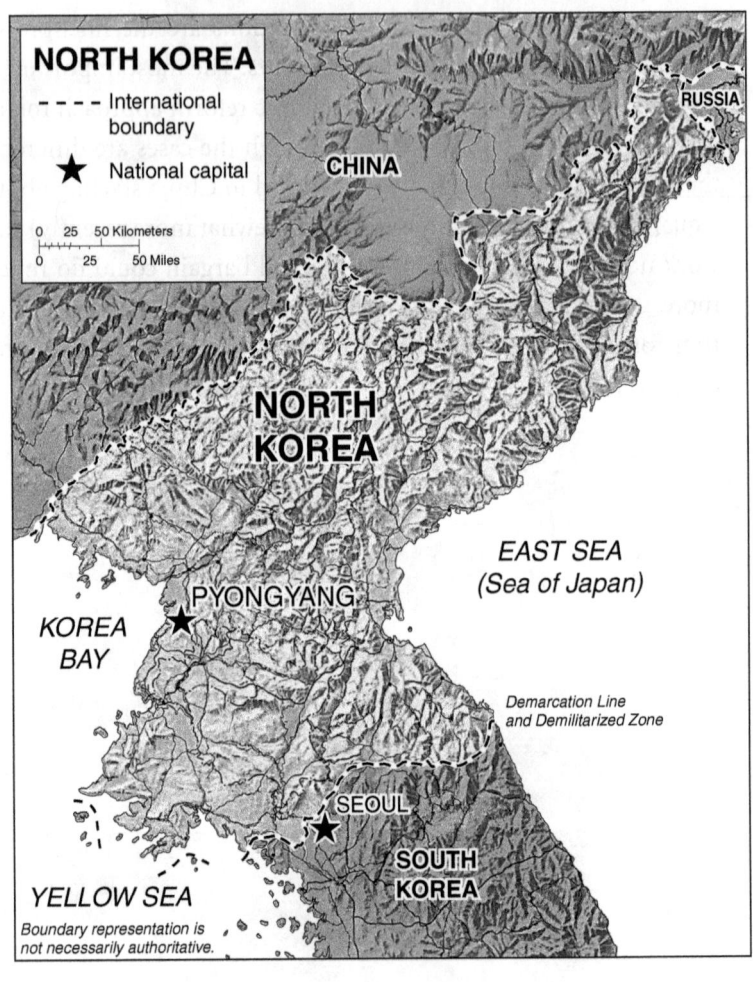

CHAPTER
2

THE CRUX OF THE CONFRONTATION

Conventional forces are the crux of the Korean confrontation and have been for half a century. True, they are not the most urgent and direct security threat that the DPRK poses to U.S. interests today; North Korea's nuclear program represents the greatest risk. Moreover, the DPRK has weakened in relative terms over time compared with allied forces and no longer has as credible an invasion option as it once did.

But it is conventional forces that keep Seoul at imminent risk of widespread devastation should war erupt, and in recent decades, North Korea has increased the density of its forces near the DMZ to drive home that threat. It is chiefly conventional forces that result in North Korea's spending perhaps a quarter of its entire GDP on its armed forces. And to the extent DPRK leaders still harbor any hopes about forcibly reunifying the peninsula, it is conventional forces that would be their primary instrument for doing so.

This chapter therefore focuses on the conventional military threat, and the conventional military balance, in Korea. This aspect of the Korean confrontation has received considerably less analysis in recent years than nuclear and missile issues have, so the background material may be useful for many readers and policymakers. In addition, a clear baseline is needed against which to evaluate proposals for conventional arms reductions, as we proceed to do in subsequent chapters.

A KOREAN CONFLICT AND THE U.S. TWO-WAR SCENARIO

For much of the post–Cold War period, the United States has focused intently on Korea as a place where war might well occur. Indeed, the peninsula was often specified as one of two possible regions, in addition to the Persian Gulf in general and Iraq in particular, where U.S. combat forces might be called upon in large numbers to help defend a threatened ally. This scenario was therefore at the heart of the Pentagon's two-war framework, a philosophy toward force planning used in one way or another by every secretary of defense—Cheney, Aspin, Perry, Cohen, Rumsfeld—since the Berlin Wall fell.

Many at the Pentagon believed a surprise North Korean attack on South Korea could achieve important successes, quite possibly including the capture of Seoul, before U.S. reinforcements arrived in sufficient numbers to work with surviving ROK troops to stop and then reverse the onslaught. Even as the capabilities of the DPRK for such an attack atrophied along with its economy as the 1990s wore on, the Defense Intelligence Agency still considered a Korean war scenario to be the primary near-term military concern of the United States. And even if the attack failed, casualties would likely be enormous, given certain characteristics of the conflict: no allied defenses against North Korean artillery, extremely high densities of forces, difficult terrain, urban fighting, and the likelihood of chemical weapons use by the DPRK. U.S. forces needed for the defense and ultimate liberation of the ROK have been estimated by Pentagon planners at roughly six ground combat divisions, including Marine and Army units, ten wings of Air Force aircraft, and four to five Navy aircraft carrier battle groups.

It is argued below that allied prospects for successfully defending ROK territory, even against an initial massive DPRK onslaught, are actually rather good today. This is a point with which Secretary of Defense Donald Rumsfeld may concur. He is now planning to redeploy many of the over 37,000 U.S. forces presently in the ROK southward from their current positions near the DMZ; he would be unlikely to consider such ideas unless convinced that South Korean forces were largely capable of the initial defense.

This analysis should further deter leaders in Pyongyang. Any hope they may now harbor of completing a rapid military thrust before the allies could fully respond is ill-founded. North Korean leaders probably already know that large-scale war would be an unwise gamble but may not have entirely ruled it out as a desperation option. They should. Getting the baseline right is also critical for considering arms control options. If the allies today really are hopelessly outgunned, as some argue, any arms control proposal would have to make highly disproportionate demands on DPRK forces. But if, as we argue, the balance is less unfavorable and indeed largely in the allies' favor, somewhat more equitable—and thus diplomatically feasible—possibilities can be considered.

A U.S. PREEMPTIVE OPTION?

Does the United States, together with its South Korean ally, have a realistic capability for waging offensive war against North Korea? This is a natural question to ask in light of the severity of the North Korean threat, together with the successful 2003 campaign in Iraq following on the heels of the generally successful war against the Taliban in Afghanistan. It is also especially relevant in light of the Bush administration's stated willingness to consider preemptive uses of force against extremist groups or states involved in terrorism and/or having weapons of mass destruction. Although North Korea has virtually ended any and all support for terrorism, it is still an extremist state with active and advanced weapons of mass destruction programs. Certainly, North Korean leaders and military planners have to be asking themselves if combined allied forces would ever consider striking at them first, and how they might do so.

Such a preemptive use of force by the ROK and the United States seems very unlikely, however. For there is another broad reality about the Korean conventional military balance today: even though U.S.-ROK forces enjoy superiority and could increase their superiority quickly through a U.S. military buildup, they could not be confident of winning an offensive war against the DPRK with low casualties to themselves and surrounding civilian populations. Preemption to overthrow the regime, along the lines of what occurred in Iraq and what the Bush administration discussed in its 2002 National Security Strategy, is not an appealing option. Even with the U.S. military's recently demonstrated prowess in using overpowering and sometimes innovative concepts such as special forces raids, rapid mechanized movements of heavy forces, air-ground combined arms attack, and sophisticated urban operations, North Korea would likely be much harder to defeat than Iraq.

There are several main reasons. First, so many North Korean weapons are near Seoul, many in protected locations, that even a well-timed surprise attack could not prevent thousands of explosive rounds launched by artillery tube or missile from landing in Seoul. Our proposal would require reductions of roughly half in weapons such as artillery, as well as the verifiable elimination of North Korean chemical stocks. But an overwhelming capability to wreak devastation would remain in DPRK hands.

Second, many North Korean military and political headquarters are deep underground, making it hard to attack them even with a "shock and awe" type of air campaign. U.S. special forces would also have a harder time infiltrating into North Korea and locating such sites for aerial attack than in Iraq, given the degree to which the country is cut off from outsiders. (More outsiders would be in North Korea under a grand bargain deal, largely to verify compliance with North Korea's arms control obligations, but they would still number far fewer than in Saddam's Iraq.)

Third, there is no easy axis of approach to Pyongyang similar to the open desert used by coalition forces to race to Baghdad in March and April of 2003. Terrain in Korea is difficult and complex. Among its other implications, this means that the enemy harassment of supply lines like that which coalition forces faced at a few specific sites in Operation Iraqi Freedom could be a much more pervasive problem in any invasion of North Korea.

Fourth, North Korea's military, with total active-duty strength over (or at least near) one million, is much larger than Iraq's. And for all the talk of small coalition forces prevailing in Iraq, they actually numbered well over 250,000 to Iraq's 400,000-man armed forces. (Moreover, three-fourths of Iraq's troops were believed unlikely to fight hard before the war began; few make a similar assumption about North Korea's military.) Winning decisively in Korea would likely require hundreds of thousands of U.S. troops in addition to the large ROK armed forces.

Fifth, North Korean troops are believed to be even more thoroughly indoctrinated by their leadership, and hence more dedicated to their nation's defense, than were Saddam's forces. Indeed, most North Korean soldiers would probably be more dependable, and fiercer in battle, than were most of Saddam's elite units, such as his Republican Guard, Special Republican Guard, presidential guards, and Fedayeen Saddam. Similar conclusions follow for North Korea's top military and political leadership, which would probably fight on even if somehow Kim Jong Il were targeted and killed in a "decapitation attack" of the type attempted against Saddam Hussein at the beginning of Operation Iraqi Freedom. It is for these reasons that Pentagon war simulations, even if inexact, predict hundreds of thousands of deaths in any future Korean war regardless of how it might start.

So all-out preemption to overthrow the North Korean regime is very much a last resort under the most extreme of circumstances, and not one likely to appeal even to hard-liners in the Bush administration. The most salient questions, therefore, are how to measure the Korean military balance and how to reduce forces so that peninsular security is improved and military expenditures are reduced. A good place to begin this discussion is with the basic facts and figures on the Korean military balance today.

MILITARY FORCES AND MILITARY GEOGRAPHY ON THE PENINSULA

Although U.S. defense reviews in the 1990s lumped Korea with Southwest Asia conceptually, the peninsula is much more like a cross between the former intra-German border and Bosnia than like Kuwait, Saudi Arabia, or southern Iraq. That image applies to both the nature of the terrain and the nature of the fighting forces deployed in the vicinity. The Korean peninsula as a whole is roughly 250 kilometers wide at its waist and about 1,000 kilometers long. It is characterized by very hilly topography; much of what flat land exists is marsh or rice fields.

Korea's central region is also one of the most heavily militarized zones in human history. Significantly more than 1 million troops and 20,000 armored vehicles or artillery pieces, as well as more than 1 million land mines, abundant chemical weapons, and fortified defensive positions, are found between Pyongyang and Seoul. (The distance from the 4-kilometer-wide DMZ to Seoul is roughly 40 kilometers and that from the DMZ to Pyongyang about 125 kilometers.) Forces in Korea are more densely concentrated than Warsaw Pact and NATO units were in Central Europe during the Cold War. For North Korea, in fact, roughly 70 percent of its total units and up to 80 percent of its estimated aggregate firepower are within 100 kilometers of the DMZ, significantly greater fractions than in the 1980s. (See Table 2.1 for background information on the Korean military balance.)

There exist only two main natural axes of potential attack in the (relatively) flat western part of the peninsula, near Seoul. Known as the Chorwon and Munsan corridors, they each are about 15 kilometers wide in some places and branch out and interconnect in others. Another three to four attack corridors could be imagined in the central and eastern parts of the country,

TABLE 2.1 US/ROK/DPRK VITAL STATISTICS

	DPRK	ROK	USA
Population (millions)	22	48	281
Land Area (square kilometers)	121,000	98,000	9,629,000
GDP (billions of dollars)	15	865	10,082
Defense Budget (billions of dollars)	4	14	396
Defense Spending as % of GDP	25	3	3.3
Active-Duty Troops (millions)	1.1	0.685	1.4
Reservists (millions)	6	4.5	1.0

Notes: ROK = Republic of Korea (South Korea)
DPRK = Democratic People's Republic of Korea (North Korea)
Source: International Institute for Strategic Studies, *The Military Balance 2002/2003* (London: Oxford University Press, 2002); and Central Intelligence Agency, *CIA World Factbook* (2003), available at www.cia.gov.

given the existing road networks and terrain, although the Sea of Japan (known in Korea as the East Sea) coastal route would be the most accessible to vehicles.

North Korea would probably begin any war with a massive artillery barrage of South Korean and U.S. positions below the DMZ, and likely of Seoul itself. Chemical weapons might well be used. Infantry and mechanized forces would then try to take advantage of the carnage and chaos to penetrate U.S.-ROK defenses and reach Seoul quickly. They would be aided by about one hundred thousand special forces, some predeployed into South Korea if possible, that would move by tunnels, small planes, mini-submarines, and more conventional means. North Korea would probably try to catch the allies by surprise, profit from cloud cover that would reduce (somewhat) the effectiveness of U.S. airpower, and seize Seoul before U.S. reinforcements (or South Korean reserve soldiers) could arrive en masse. It then might try to take the rest of the peninsula; perhaps more likely, given its limited capabilities for long-range mechanized movement, it might try to use Seoul as a "hostage" to negotiate favorable surrender terms.

The following summaries of the forces possessed by the two Koreas and the United States give a general perspective on the nature of the peninsular military balance. They also provide information that is employed in the analyses that follow.

NORTH KOREAN MILITARY CAPABILITIES

Although it is difficult to know its intentions or aspirations, North Korea is still very much postured for a possible invasion of South Korea. The regime may even still harbor remote hopes of reunifying the peninsula under its rule; certainly its military doctrine appears to be based on such a plan. Its forces are generally not postured or prepared to fight defensively; its forward-deployed forces within 100 kilometers of the DMZ have increased from 40 percent to 70 percent of total troop strength over the past two decades.

North Korea's forces are large and heavily armed. It has nearly 1.1 million troops in its active duty forces, according to official numbers, and about 6 million in its reserves. Actual troop levels may be somewhat lower but probably not dramatically so. Nearly 90 percent are ground forces. The International Institute for Strategic Studies estimates that defense spending levels of about $2 billion support these forces, though that number is highly uncertain given the paucity of statistics on North Korea and the difficulty of converting prices in a poor, command economy into dollar terms. Indeed, most estimates are fully twice as high, or around $4 billion a year. That would translate to about 25 percent of a North Korean GDP now estimated at about $15 billion (having been more than $20 billion in the late 1990s and perhaps as much as $30 billion in the 1980s).

North Korea's armored forces include about 3,500 main battle tanks, 3,000 armored personnel carriers and light tanks, and more than 12,000 large-bore artillery tubes. Some 500 of its artillery pieces can reach Seoul, 40 kilometers away, from their current positions. It has about 620 combat aircraft and 24 armed helicopters, as well as 26 full-size submarines and about 55 minisubs for special operations. In addition, it possesses about 7,500 mortars, 500 ballistic missiles, 11,000 air defense guns, 10,000 surface-to-air missiles, and numerous variants of antitank guided weapons. It probably possesses one million tons of conventional ammunition, 5,000 metric tons of chemical agents (produced in a total of eight factories), and quite probably biological arms as well. It also has 4,000 underground facilities near the DMZ and probably twenty tunnels under the DMZ, of which four have been found.

The DPRK's order of battle comprises about 150 active duty brigade equivalents. That number includes those associated with North Korea's 27 infantry divisions, as well as some 15 independent armored brigades, 14 infantry brigades, and 21 artillery brigades. There are also more than 20 brigades in the special forces, totaling about 100,000 troops. The special forces would attempt to deploy by air, sea, land, and the famous sub-DMZ tunnels to spread mayhem throughout much of South Korea and disrupt U.S.-ROK combat operations. The 620 or so North Korean combat aircraft are organized into 18 main combat regiments.

The various naval vessels can be divided into seven main groups: frigates (numbering just 3), missile craft (numbering 43), torpedo craft (about 100), patrol craft (roughly 158, of which 133 are for coastal and river operations), submarines (as noted, about 26, of old Soviet designs as well as some 55 miniature subs for special forces as noted), amphibious ships (a total of 10), and mine warfare ships (23).

Given the obsolescence of most North Korean equipment, however, the actual capabilities of most forces would be notably less than the raw numbers suggest. About half of North Korea's major weapons are of roughly 1960s design; the other half are even older. The U.S. Army's Cold War system for comparing the capabilities of equipment suggests that ground-combat units equipped with modern Western weaponry are perhaps only 20 to 40 percent better than those of comparable size with obsolescent equipment like North Korea's. But the Gulf War and Operation Iraqi Freedom should have done much to discredit that methodology. A reputable defense contractor, the Analytical Sciences Corporation, developed a more up-to-date and realistic "TASC-FORM" approach, utilized in the 1990s by the Office of Net Assessment at the Pentagon. It evaluates modern Western weaponry as generally two to four times better than older Soviet-vintage systems.

This means that North Korea's heavy forces, possessing enough raw combat equipment to fill out perhaps ten U.S. divisions, are estimated to have the overall capability of only about 2.5 modern U.S. armored divisions. Adding in the calculated scores of equipment operated by light infantry, the North Koreans have the overall firepower of nearly five modern U.S. heavy-division equivalents in their force structure. That is nearly equal to the six modern-division equivalents that Iraq possessed in 1990, according to the same TASCFORM scoring metric. This North Korean firepower is configured in a more potent way than the comparable amount of Iraqi armor and artillery, as discussed below, but remains limited in overall effectiveness. North Korean airpower, though about six U.S. wing equivalents in size, corresponds to only about two F-16 wing equivalents in estimated net capability.

So much for hardware; what about North Korean doctrine and military readiness? Here the DPRK makes out even less well. Associated for half a century with highly inflexible Soviet military practices, it places great stock in top-level leadership and scripted war plans. Thus, it is doubtful that North Korea has produced many good mid-level officers. Nor has it been able, particularly of late, to afford the types of large-scale combined-arms training that characterize the U.S. and South Korean militaries. On the other hand, North Korea's artillery capability does not for the most part depend on sophisticated tactics or operations, at least not in order to pose a terrorist-like threat to Seoul. Certain other capabilities could also be of acute concern to allied forces. For example, although the U.S. Office of Naval Intelligence characterizes the overall DPRK submarine force as being obsolescent and "only modestly proficient in basic operations in its own coastal waters," it points out that it could have some effectiveness in missions such as mining, attacks against ships, and insertion of ground forces.

SOUTH KOREAN MILITARY CAPABILITIES

South Korea has a military of about 685,000 active duty troops and 4.5 million reservists. Indeed, its armed forces in general are something more than half the size of North Korea's, whether one thinks in terms of personnel, major equipment holdings, or force structure. Its air and naval forces are comparable in number to North Korea's.

Overall, South Korea's military has become a very good institution in modern times. It is probably one of the stronger militaries in the world, in fact—quite possibly belonging on any top ten list of international armed forces. It has its limitations and its problems but at this point in history is probably better than North Korea's. It also presents a formidable forward-defense capability against any possible North Korean attack.

To be more specific, South Korea deploys about 2,300 main battle tanks, about 2,500 armored personnel carriers and light tanks, about 5,000 large-bore artillery pieces, 538 combat aircraft, 115 attack helicopters, 39 major surface combatants in its navy, and 20 submarines. In addition, it fields about 6,000 mortars, almost 1,000 air defense guns, just over 1,000 surface-to-air missiles, and a dozen surface-to-surface missiles. Finally, it also possesses 84 patrol and coastal ships, as well as 15 mine warfare ships, 12 amphibious vessels, and 60 naval combat aircraft.

South Korean defense expenditures are about three times as great as the DPRK's. (South Korea spent an average of $12 billion in 2000–2001 and had a defense budget of about $14 billion in 2002.) But the ROK has a much bigger GDP, of which these expenditures amount to just 3 percent—hardly a major strain on the country's economy. Indeed, Seoul now actually comes under gentle criticism from the United States for not spending quite enough on its armed forces, though it may increase its budget by several billion dollars in 2004. While it does cover almost half of nonpersonnel costs incurred by U.S. forces in Korea (or about $700 million a year), this amount falls short of what the United States would like.

South Korea's major combat equipment, as evaluated by the TASCFORM scoring system, is roughly equal in aggregate to North Korea's. Better quality makes up for lower quantity. Specifically, the ROK's ground combat weapon capabilities are estimated to be roughly three-fourths as great as the DPRK's. Factoring in attack helicopters, its aggregate air capabilities are slightly greater than the North's, totaling about 2.5 F-16 wing equivalents by the TASCFORM system.

South Korea would appear to have outright superiority, as measured by these types of static indices, once one factors in the effects of superior training, equipment maintenance, logistics, and support equipment like reconnaissance and communications gear (to say nothing of the advantage of fighting from prepared positions, should North Korea be the attacker). Quantifying the importance of these effects is difficult, but those who have attempted to do so have found impressive results. Trevor Dupuy's assessment of the military outcomes of the Arab-Israeli wars, for example, suggests that excellence in these dimensions of military capability may double combat effectiveness. Indeed, the Pentagon's official assessment of the Korean military balance now suggests that, due to qualitative advantages, South Korean forces are superior to those of North Korea.

Still, there are areas in which South Korea should clearly improve. A number of programs have been slowed or canceled due to recent financial troubles. According to the United States, South Korea's principal shortcomings are in the areas of command, control, and communications; chemical and biological defenses; and precision munitions.

THE UNITED STATES' FORCES

No one doubts that another war in Korea would be demanding on U.S. forces. As envisioned under all post–Cold War defense plans—the first Bush administration's "base force," the Clinton administration's 1993 Bottom-Up Review (BUR) and 1997 Quadrennial Defense Review, and the second Bush administration's 2001 Quadrennial Defense Review—the United States would deploy almost half of its combat forces there in a possible war. Associated troop numbers would probably be in the vicinity of 500,000, comparable to the 550,000 who fought in Desert Storm. Indeed, some reports suggest that more than 600,000 U.S. troops could ultimately be deployed.

The United States normally bases about 300 fixed-wing combat aircraft in the immediate vicinity of Korea. (That tally counts forces in Japan, including about 75 fixed-wing aircraft on an aircraft carrier that are generally nearby.) In addition, it added modest numbers of F-117 stealth fighters and F-15E Strike Eagle fighters early in 2003, when they were deployed for an annual exercise and then kept in place given the state of tension over North Korea's nuclear program. (A modest additional ground force element of perhaps 1,000 troops was added then as well, and B-52 and B-1 bombers were stationed on Guam for the same reason.) It could easily double its available combat planes in the region within a week, and double them again in another couple of weeks. U.S. Army and Marine Corps forces in Northeast Asia also have roughly 100 attack helicopters associated with them. Airfields available for U.S. combat aircraft would number at least half a dozen at the outset of hostilities and could quickly be expanded to a dozen or more locations in Japan and the ROK.

The United States stations two brigades of the Army's Second Infantry Division in South Korea. Distributed roughly halfway between Seoul and the DMZ, they are based in a total of seventeen camps astride the two main potential attack corridors in the western half of the country. They are now expected to be redeployed southward on the peninsula under a new plan approved by the U.S. and ROK governments, but it will take time for that to happen. U.S. ground forces in Korea might be roughly tripled in size within ten days in a crisis. (That is relatively fast by the standards of normal military logistics, but a great deal could happen in any war in Korea before they arrived. For that reason, Secretary of Defense William Perry considered options for preemptively strengthening the U.S. presence in South Korea by tens of thousands of forces during the 1994 nuclear crisis, though those options ultimately were not employed.)

Notably, Marine Corps pre-positioned ships at Guam and Army pre-positioned equipment in Korea, each representing about a brigade's worth of capability (enough for 3,000 to 5,000 troops), could quickly be filled out with troops airlifted from the United States to Korea. The Twenty-fifth Infantry Division from Hawaii could deploy within the first ten days as well. A brigade's worth of Army equipment and a second brigade of Marine equipment pre-positioned on ships in the Indian Ocean could arrive shortly thereafter.

After several weeks, a variety of ships could arrive from the United States. Eight SL-7 fast sealift ships carrying a U.S.-based heavy Army division could reach Korea after some twenty to thirty days, as could an even greater number of large, medium-speed, roll-on/roll-off (LMSR) vessels. More light ground forces and Marines could arrive in that time frame as well, as could aircraft carriers and other ships from the Mediterranean, the Persian Gulf, or the west coast of the United States. Within seventy-five days, according to official plans, the entire transport operation would be completed. As a practical matter, given the inevitable complications of actual deployments and the potential need to clear DPRK mines and submarines from ROK waters before unloading supply ships, it might take one hundred days.

In all, using the TASCFORM metric referred to earlier, these U.S. forces would correspond to at least 5 modern heavy ground-division equivalents and more than 15 modern fighter wings. The former capability would easily exceed those of either the DPRK or the ROK; the latter would exceed the sum of all Korean air forces by a factor of three.

U.S. forces also train hard, both on their own and in conjunction with the ROK military. The allies used to conduct a huge exercise known as Team Spirit. It involved about 200,000 troops in field operations, but it was canceled as part of the Agreed Framework as a gesture of reassurance to North Korea. The allies still conduct a number of smaller exercises, including the annual "Ulchi Focus Lens" effort—primarily a computer-based simulation involving 75,000 allied troops.

MILITARY ANALYSIS OF AN ATTEMPTED NORTH KOREAN INVASION

Were North Korea again to attack South Korea with the intent of capturing Seoul and reunifying the peninsula by force, its prospects for success would be very poor—even worse than commonly believed. Not only would the eventual outcome of the war be in little doubt, a point most agree on, but the chances of an initial North Korean breakthrough and approach to Seoul are also very low.

North Korea could, to be sure, seriously harm the South Korean people and economy. Notably, it could pose threats through long-range artillery attacks against Seoul, surface-to-surface missile strikes, and commando raids. Consider the artillery, for example. As noted, about 500 of North Korea's roughly 12,000 artillery tubes are within range of Seoul in their current positions. Most artillery can fire several rounds a minute. Also, the initial speeds of fired shells are generally around half a kilometer per second. That means that even if an ROK counterartillery radar some 10 kilometers away picked up a North Korean round and established a track on it within seconds, a counterstrike would not be able to silence the offending DPRK tube for at least a minute (and probably closer to two minutes). On average, such a tube could therefore probably fire two to five rounds, and quite possibly a dozen or more, before being neutralized or forced to retreat fully into its shelter. Some tubes may even be able to fire from protected positions, permitting them to keep up the barrage until they suffer either a near-direct hit by an artillery round or an attack from a laser-guided or satellite-guided bomb.

That means that at least several thousand rounds could detonate in Seoul no matter how hard the allies tried to prevent or stop the attack. An average round could cause tens of casualties and considerable physical destruction. The end result could be many tens of thousands of civilians dead and many tens of billions of dollars in damage. Attacks against Seoul would probably be much worse if they involved chemical weapons.

Such inevitable carnage in the nation's capital explains why the South Korean government cannot consider war an acceptable outcome and why all-out military preemption to overthrow the North Korean regime cannot appeal very much even to a U.S. administration that has emphasized the potential need for more preemptive action against extremist states in its recent National Security Strategy. But the ability of the allies to prevail militarily can hardly be doubted, and the probability that they would lose substantial amounts of territory even temporarily is very low.

To understand why the North Korean battle plan is so unpromising, consider the following nine points:

First, although attackers do not necessarily require a three-to-one local combat power advantage over defenders to prevail in combat, they rarely can achieve rapid breakthroughs when attacking prepared defenses of strength comparable to their own. When armies tried to drive directly through prepared defensive positions in World War II, for example—what North

Korea would have to do in a future war on the peninsula—they rarely advanced more than 4 or 5 kilometers a day. Indeed, advance rates were usually less than that. They were as low as about 1 kilometer a day in campaigns against very well prepared defenses, such as the allies' attack against Germany around the Siegfried Line.

With such slow initial progress, North Korean forces could not succeed. Over time, they would become increasingly vulnerable to U.S. tactical aircraft reinforcements and lose whatever protection attacking in bad weather might initially give them vis-a-vis advanced munitions dependent on laser homing or infrared guidance. They would also probably run out of supplies after a few days, because allied artillery and air attacks as well as road obstacles would prevent significant movement of trucks and other resupply vehicles down key invasion corridors. By way of perspective, successful breakthrough operations by the North Koreans in 1950 benefited from a number of major conditions that would not apply again. Among them are that combined South Korean and U.S. forces were nearly a factor of ten smaller than they are today and essentially absent from key attack corridors; that they did not possess effective antitank weapons at first; and that their units were in very poor condition.

Second, not only are ROK defenses prepared, and comparable in firepower to North Korea's military, but they are also dense. Across just 250 kilometers of front, much of it unusable by armored vehicles, is deployed most of the South Korean army. The resulting force-to-space ratio of about one division per 10 kilometers is excellent. Modern ground forces are generally designed to cover more than twice that much front.

Third, rivers, marshes, demolitions, and other impediments to movement are present in the DMZ region. DPRK movement by road would be nearly impossible, because it would channel attackers into a killing zone and also require use of prechambered bridges that would certainly be destroyed by the allies early in any war. Even assuming an attack in the winter that allowed forces to traverse frozen rice fields, either the Han or the Imjin river would need to be crossed in any attack in the western half of the country near Seoul—and those rivers might not be frozen hard enough to support tanks.

The combined effects of terrain, demolitions, and artillery in slowing armored vehicles would greatly increase their vulnerability to direct fire from tube-launched, optically tracked, wire-guided (TOW) antitank weapons, tanks, and other antitank guns. In quantitative terms, the vulnerability of armor can increase two to twenty times when it is slowed down appreciably. North Korea might attempt to obstruct the view of U.S. and ROK forces by heavy use of smoke-generating artillery rounds and grenades in the vicinity of an attempted breakthrough. But allied forces would still enjoy the advantage of being able to fire from protected positions, even if they lost some of the range of their advanced sensors and optics.

Fourth, although defenders would be immediately vulnerable to artillery attack at the rate of many thousands of rounds per minute, so would attackers—and the latter would be exposed. The vulnerability of a soldier on foot or in a jeep or truck would be at least ten times as great as that of a soldier in a foxhole—a much worse handicap for the North Koreans than their roughly two-to-one advantages in artillery and soldiers could compensate for. Similar considerations apply to gunfire during close-in battle.

Fifth, allied military equipment is much more capable than that of the DPRK. South Korean Type 88 or K-1 tanks, for example, have detection and targeting sensors similar to those of the U.S. M1 Abrams. They would be firing at even more primitive mixes of Soviet-style tanks than Coalition forces confronted in the Persian Gulf in 1991 and 2003. North Korea owns T-62 tanks, which entered production in the early 1960s, and tanks of earlier vintages. These tanks and similar systems are, to put it gently, not very good. They had a mediocre track record twenty-five years ago in the Arab-Israeli wars, and they would do even worse against modern antitank weapons and modern tanks.

Sixth, allied reconnaissance is much better than that of North Korea. The all-weather, day-night character of modern reconnaissance also makes it much more effective than it was during the Korean War, when both North Korean and Chinese armies were able to evade detection for long periods in preparing major attacks. In addition to starting with a solid defensive line, therefore, South Korean and U.S. soldiers have the ability to anticipate and counterconcentrate against any concerted DPRK breakthrough effort in one place. Not only could they detect any large-scale massing of armored vehicles through various platforms, like overhead reconnaissance satellites, lower-tech but effective RC-7B planes, and joint surveillance target attack radar system (JSTARS) radar-imaging aircraft. They could also generally monitor the movement of approaching human beings through devices such as ground radar and infrared detection systems.

Seventh, assuming passable weather conditions, direct fire from aircraft would also put North Korean armor and troops at serious risk. U.S. and ROK aircraft would quickly establish air superiority and devote at least 500 planes and helicopters to the ground attack beginning early in the battle. Using Maverick, Hellfire, and TOW missiles and laser-guided as well as satellite-guided bombs, the allied forces could expect to destroy roughly one armored vehicle in every two to four shots, if recent combat data are a guide. If they flew at the Desert Storm overall rate of about one sortie per aircraft per day, they would stand a good chance of destroying several hundred North Korean armored vehicles in a day's fighting (out of a total of roughly 10,000 to start with). Coalition aircraft were very effective in such attacks, even during bad weather, in the war to overthrow Saddam Hussein and would be devastating in Korea as well.

As time went on, North Korean targets would become more dispersed, fewer in number, and more difficult to locate and attack—but U.S. air reinforcements would arrive rapidly, allowing more firepower to be devoted to the mission. (It might be possible that the sortie rate could, as in Desert Storm, be maintained at two flights per day in the early going, but in light of the threat of a chemical attack, which would slow operations, it is safer to assume a sortie rate of one flight per day.) Because North Korea lacks sophisticated runway-destroying submunitions and accurate missiles, it probably could not prevent this outcome by effectively attacking the allied aircrafts' runways from afar, though it might occasionally score a lucky hit.

If the weather were poor, infrared and laser-homing missiles might not be effective. Indeed, they might not work at all. But some aircraft guns would remain capable. So would satellite-guided bombs such as the joint direct attack munition that was so effective in Serbia in 1999, Afghanistan in 2001–2002, and Iraq in 2003. Also, an attacker probably could not count on conditions of very heavy fog and clouds enduring more than a day or two. Even in the event of bad weather, JSTARS aircraft with radar capabilities for detecting moving armor might be able to help helicopters, jets, and bombers get near enough to DPRK forces that they could cause considerable damage, just as they did in Operation Iraqi Freedom. Some aircraft could use their guns—albeit at greater risk of being shot down—even in heavy fog. They could also drop dumb bombs and area-effect weapons from higher altitudes against soft vehicles and troops.

THE CRUX OF THE CONFRONTATION

Eighth, despite their huge number, North Korean commando forces would have limited effectiveness against South Korean defensive lines. Deploying by a special means like airplane, submarine, or tunnel does not necessarily make a commando more effective than a regular soldier. To be successful, airborne assault generally requires air superiority and suppression of the enemy's artillery and air-defense systems—and North Korea would not be able to achieve any of those advantages against dug-in allied defenses. Tunnel assault could be more effective. Troops arriving via underground passageways would be unable, however, to penetrate deeply into ROK defenses, given the limited length of the tunnels (just a few kilometers). Also, they would become highly vulnerable to ROK/U.S. counterattack against the tunnel entrances with artillery or aircraft-delivered munitions—counterattacks that could probably be initiated within a few minutes of the beginning of the assault.

Small infiltrations of North Korean special forces over land and by submarine are probably feasible. But these approaches would limit troop numbers to hundreds or at most a few thousand in any surprise raid—a potent capability only against relatively undefended targets. Moreover, troops infiltrating in this way would not be very mobile and would generally require a number of hours or days to reach key targets—enormously complicating the task of achieving surprise. These special forces might be able to cause some serious headaches in Seoul, for South Korean civilians elsewhere, and perhaps, in some cases, for deployment of reinforcements (by blowing up key bridges and the like). But their ability to deploy in force against key South Korean defenses, or other major military assets like airfields, is quite limited.

Ninth, North Korea's forces continue to fall into increasingly worse shape, despite the regime's efforts to maintain military readiness. Its special forces still train hard, and on the whole it does circumvent many of its resource constraints, while also studying and adapting to modern American military tactics. It also has prestationed a good quantity of military supplies where they would be needed in wartime and has many civilian transportation assets available for logistics support in time of war. But these efforts cannot change the facts that its economy is in disrepair, its ability to modernize forces is limited, and its resources for conducting frequent maneuver exercises for the bulk of its armed forces are wanting.

CONCLUSION

The Korean peninsula is a good place to wage defensive warfare. Possible channels of attack are few and narrow, and the terrain is heavily prepared with explosives and obstacles. Also, the combination of South Korean armed forces and U.S. units in Japan and South Korea makes for a remarkable military capability. The allied defensive posture is the best in the post–Cold War world, bar none. Ground combat equipment such as advanced tanks; Cobra and Apache attack helicopters and F-16 fighters; TOW antitank weapons and multiple launch rocket systems with area-effect munitions; advanced all-weather, day-night reconnaissance systems; and well-trained, dedicated troops represent enormous power.

Allied forces, with South Korea providing most or all of the ground combat units in a sector targeted for an attempted breakthrough, could almost certainly hold off a North Korean surprise attack. They could do so even if bad weather greatly reduced the effectiveness of allied aircraft early in such a battle and if frozen rice fields, marshes, and rivers were usable by DPRK vehicles. Dug-in and well-armed allied forces profiting from excellent surveillance and targeting systems would exact a huge toll on advancing

North Korean troops; if the attack continued long enough for the weather to clear, the battle would become even more lopsided. North Korean use of chemical weapons would not change the situation markedly, because such an attack is expected and because it could also hamper the DPRK's offensive operations.

This chapter has focused on the initial defense of South Korea because, if it can be successfully carried out, there is little doubt about the outcome of a war in Korea thereafter. U.S. military reinforcements would provide overwhelming combat capability within two to three months. If Seoul could be held in the meantime, combined allied forces would surely prevail decisively in the ensuing counteroffensive.

Moreover, no arms control proposal for Korea would logically lead to a treaty-mandated cutback in U.S. forces worldwide. (That would happen only if the United States made a decision that a more stable Korean peninsula permitted a somewhat smaller defense budget.) This being the case, when evaluating the conventional arms control issue in succeeding chapters, the focus should be on the initial defensive, holding operation; if it can be successfully carried out, any needed counteroffensive would surely succeed as well.

North Korea's defensive posture is rather good as well, given Korean terrain and its large military and the proximity of Seoul to many of its forces. The DPRK could hold the ROK capital "hostage;" allied forces, even with precise weaponry and the possibility of preemptive attacks, would not be able to protect Seoul very well at first. The allies would surely win any war on the peninsula, even one they started preemptively, but such an option would be very bloody and thus should remain a very last resort. Even limited preemptive action against North Korea's nuclear facilities should be a near-last resort, given its potential for sparking a broader war.

It is to the conventional arms reduction issue, and to the broader agenda of our proposed grand bargain, that the book now turns. (Appendix 1 provides more military detail for those who wish it.) The next chapter describes the proposal in its various dimensions and suggests a strategy for promoting it. Chapter 4 evaluates the military implications and military desirability of the proposed conventional arms cutbacks. Chapter 5 suggests how such a plan, combined with economic assistance from Japan and other outside powers, might help the DPRK reform its economy. Finally, Chapter 6 explores the longer-term question of how the U.S.-Korea relationship and American strategic posture in the Asia-Pacific region might change over time, in the event that the Korean confrontation can finally be ended.

CHAPTER
3

THE GRAND BARGAIN

How should Washington, Seoul, Tokyo, Beijing, and other interested capitals deal with the crisis in Korea? A new approach is needed. The two prevailing schools of thought for how to handle North Korea have both largely failed at this point.

The "coercion" school, led by President Bush, assumes that North Korea can be brought to its knees as a result of tightening pressure and sanctions—or perhaps that it can even be made to collapse, allowing for a relatively nonviolent change of government. But the history of the last decade suggests that the easily angered North Korean leadership may instead simply dig in its heels and refuse to budge, escalating the crisis further through its nuclear weapons program in particular.

In addition, if sanctions are tightened, the DPRK may respond as it did to a worsening external economic environment in the 1990s—allowing its economy to decline and its people to starve rather than giving up power. In fact, North Korea's weakness may increase the odds it would sell nuclear materials abroad to raise cash—the ultimate nightmare scenario for the United States and its allies.

Moreover, this hard-nosed approach holds no appeal for South Korean President Roh Moo Hyun, as again became clear during President Roh's Washington summit with President Bush in May of 2003. President Roh thinks a policy of engagement can work; he also fears the consequences of a failed policy of coercion, most notably the increased risk of a devastating war on the peninsula. He may be willing to reduce aid to North Korea if nuclear weapons activities continue there but to date has shown little stomach for stronger measures. Other key countries in the region, notably Japan and China as well as Russia, tend to take positions similar to South Korea's. Japan has recently toughened up on its firms that have sent military technologies to North Korea in the past and has introduced more rigorous inspections of shipping to and from North Korea, but it is reluctant to go much further than that.

The traditional nuclear/missile engagement school has run into a dead end as well. Its crowning achievement was the 1994 Agreed Framework, an important and useful accord that did cap North Korea's nuclear program for eight and a half years. But it did not stop the program, as later revealed by discovery of the DPRK's uranium enrichment effort. It also appears to have contributed to a North Korean habit of extortion—developing destabilizing weapons and then bargaining to give them up for huge amounts of aid. At best, it did nothing to break North Korea of that habit.

Given the state of the DPRK economy, Pyongyang will likely continue to pursue such cash fixes as long as it can find new ways to demand them from the outside world. The final problem for the limited engagement school, with its focus on the nuclear and missile issues, is that its arguments fall flat with President Bush. Mr. Bush already rejected such an approach at the beginning of his term in office; he firmly believes Pyongyang is attempting to blackmail him and is unwilling to deal with North Korea on such terms.

We propose a different way here, drawing on both the hawkish coercion and the nuclear/missile engagement schools but going beyond either one. It would offer North Korea more incentives, but also more stringent terms, than either of the above two approaches. To quote former Congressman Stephen Solarz, who chaired the House Subcommittee on the Asia–Pacific region in the 1980s, it would move beyond carrots and sticks to offer "steaks and sledgehammers." The proposal would insist on the complete and verifiable denuclearization of North Korea, under IAEA and NPT auspices, though the elimination of whatever small nuclear capability North Korea may already have could occur over a course of years to improve the accord's negotiability. This proposal would also end the testing, production, and deployment of medium- and long-range missiles as well as the export of all ballistic missiles; ideally, though less critically (and less verifiably), it would also require North Korea to eliminate existing stockpiles of such missiles.

The accord's centerpiece would require deep reductions in conventional forces, styled at least loosely after the Conventional Forces in Europe (CFE) Treaty. These would involve cuts of about 50 percent, or perhaps even more, in heavy weaponry on the peninsula. Such a "Conventional Forces in Korea" (CFK) accord would require proportionate reductions in different geographic zones, though again in the interest of negotiability it would allow North Korea to keep a substantial quantity of arms near the DMZ, since Pyongyang undoubtedly views such weapons as important for deterrent capability.

The proposed accord would further insist on the permanent return of all Japanese kidnapping victims and their families to Japan, as well as the initiation of a human rights dialogue similar to the one China now conducts with the outside world (however begrudgingly). It would also require North Korea to sign and verifiably implement the biological weapons and chemical weapons conventions and formally forswear terrorism as well as hostile acts near its border with South Korea and on ROK territory. The DPRK would end its counterfeiting and drug trafficking activities. Diplomatic ties would also need to be established and maintained with South Korea, with family reunion visits accelerated. Some of these demands could be softened partially or implemented only over time, but the nuclear and conventional force elements of the proposal would have to be adopted.

In return, North Korea would be offered numerous incentives and reassurances. From the United States it would receive an explicit and public nonaggression pledge, and perhaps even an active security guarantee if such reassurance would increase its willingness to negotiate. The pledge would become permanent only once North Korea complied with its denuclearization obligations and other elements of the accord (and further agreed never to impede the delivery of food to its population should huge numbers of North Koreans again be at risk of starvation as they were in the mid- to late 1990s). But it would become effective on an interim basis as soon as the deal was concluded and remain in effect as long as North Korea continued to comply with the disarmament schedule it had agreed to.

North Korea would also gain diplomatic relations with the United States, removal from the U.S. list of state sponsors of terrorism, and a lifting of trade sanctions. Some of the last have been at least temporarily eased in recent years, but they remain onerous on the whole, as Table 3.1 shows. A peace treaty involving the two Koreas and the United States and China would be signed, though it might be most appropriate to delay this for a year or so until it was clear that all parties were taking their new obligations seriously. (To protect against the possibility that North Korea might dupe the United States, convincing it to sign a peace treaty and then ending its compliance with the grand bargain, Washington could state that its obligations under the peace treaty were conditional on full implementation of the rest of the agreement.)

TABLE 3.1 U.S. SANCTIONS ON NORTH KOREA
Application of Sanctions

Year	Related Laws	Sanctions
1950	Export Control Act	Bans many exports to North Korea
1950	Trading with the Enemy Act	Freezes North Korean assets in the United States; announces the Overseas Assets Control Regulation which virtually places a ban on trade and monetary transactions with North Korea
1951	Trade Agreement Extension Act	Prohibits US from giving North Korea most-favored-nation-status.
1962	Foreign Assistance Act	Bans grant of aid to North Korea
1975	Trade Act of 1974	Prohibition from giving Generalized System of Preferences benefits to North Korea
1975	Export Control Act	Applies comprehensive embargo on North Korea by the US Ex-Im Bank
1986	Act on Ex-Im Bank	Prohibits giving credits to North Korea by the US Ex-IM Bank
1988	Export Control Act	North Korea subjected to bans on trade, benefits of the Generalized Systems of

		Preferences, the sale of articles listed among the munitions control items, and aid and credits from the Ex-Im Bank due to US determination that North Korea supports terrorism; US instructions to vote against any international monetary institution's decision to grant aid to North Korea
1988	International Arms Trading Regulations (revised)	Bans sales of defense industry materials and services as well as imports and exports with North Korea
1992	Munitions Control Items	Confirms North Korea was involved in giving missile technology to Iran and Syria, the United States thus bans the export of articles listed among the munitions control items and government contracts for North Korea related to the manufacture of missiles, electronics, space aviation, and military aircraft

*Easing of Sanctions***

Year	Rationale	Relevant Sanctions Provisionally Lifted
1995	Agreed Framework	Allowed telecommunications between North Korea and the United States, use of credit cards for foreign travelers, opening of offices for journalists, use of US banks by North Korea for transactions not originating or terminating in the United States, import of magnesite for steelmaking in the United States, and some participation by U.S. firms in projects part of the Agreed Framework
2000	Moratorium on missile testing and the decision to implement the Perry process	Eased many sanctions that fall under the Trading with the Enemy Act, Export Administration Regulations, and the Defense Production Act, and allowed direct financial transactions between North Koreans and Americans as well as

> investment and use of North Korean facilities for shipment of goods. But retained prohibitions based on counterterrorism and nonproliferation concerns, as well as bans on weapons sales and most types of foreign assistance

* There have also been several sanctions placed on specific North Korean firms for trading or selling military equipment to foreign nations. Since 1990, ten North Korean firms have been sanctioned in 1992, 1996, 1998, 2000, 2001, and 2002. The United States eased some of the state sanctions in 1995 and 2000, though they remain in place.
** Sanctions were eased or suspended, not formally lifted.
Source: Based on Nicholas Eberstadt, *The End of North Korea* (Washington, D.C.: The AEI Press, 1999), p. 87; and Meghan O'Sullivan, *Shrewd Sanctions: Statecraft and State Sponsors of Terrorism* (Washington, D.C.: Brookings Institution Press, 2003), pp. 41-44, 296; and U.S. Department of State, press release from the Office of the Spokesman, January 20, 1995 and June 19, 2000. Press releases forwarded by Jeff Beller, U.S. Department of State, North Korea desk, May 14, 2003.

North Korea's energy requirements would be met, not with new nuclear reactors but with safer and faster conventional means of providing the power that would have been produced at Yongbyon. It would be promised technical aid, perhaps first and foremost from China, given that country's experience in developing entrepreneurial zones within a command economy. In addition to ongoing humanitarian assistance, it would begin to receive economic aid, principally from Japan and South Korea but also from the United States, at the level of roughly $2 billion a year (not counting humanitarian or emergency aid) for a decade.

By disbursing the aid year by year, outside countries would retain leverage over Pyongyang to ensure that it continued to cut conventional forces, undertake economic reforms, and otherwise comply with the demands of the road map. Pyongyang would retain leverage in that it could always cease its disarmament activities if outside aid were cut off. This leverage would be greatest in the accord's first five years, when disarmament activities would be concentrated, but would remain even thereafter, since Pyongyang could always build up weapons arsenals if other countries failed to meet their obligations.

External aid would be used to develop special economic and entrepreneurial zones, beginning with straightforward physical projects, such as infrastructure improvement. Over time, it would also be employed for other purposes, including assistance to North Korea's education, health care, and agricultural sectors as well as to national infrastructure outside the special economic zones. Most would not be provided in the form of cash.

Some of the elements of this proposal are straightforward and self-explanatory. A nonaggression pledge would not be difficult for the United States to make. It has suggested it would do so on previous occasions, and even with the Bush administration's emphasis on preemption, it certainly has no intent of attacking North Korea—particularly if the nuclear issue is addressed. It could reassure North Korea that it would not use weapons of mass destruction first in any war on the peninsula; it could also pledge not to use nuclear weapons first provided that Pyongyang pledged not to use chemical or biological weapons either.

Diplomatic relations, which the 1994 Agreed Framework promised to strive for, would not be a major concession by Washington either, if progress can be made toward resolving other security issues. The United States has diplomatic relations with many unsavory regimes, as North Korea would admittedly remain even during the implementation of this type of accord. The return of Japanese kidnapping victims does not threaten North Korea's security and should be a minor issue in the context of the broader deal suggested here, especially in light of the fact that North Korea allowed five victims to visit Japan last fall. While Pyongyang was undoubtedly displeased with the furor that its attempted act of magnanimity provoked in Japan, it caused that problem itself by failing to be transparent about the status of at least eight other kidnapping victims. Moreover, it has no core interests that are threatened by agreeing to the victims' return.

This chapter focuses on elements of the grand bargain that would likely be the most important and most challenging to pursue. These features characterize the nuclear, missile, conventional force, and economic reform issues. The last two are the most complex to assess and implement and the least frequently discussed in the policy debate to date, so chapters 4 and 5 turn to explaining our proposals on these subjects in greater detail. In addition to describing the main logic of our proposals for these four main substantive issues, this chapter also discusses the interests of the other main regional parties—especially South Korea, Japan, and China—and how they might be expected to view, and contribute to, the grand bargain we propose.

What about timing? On the nuclear front, fuel oil shipments would immediately resume, North Korea's plutonium activities would cease, and monitors would return to Yongbyon. (Indeed, these steps would be taken at the very beginning of negotiations.) Within months, or at most a year, the locations of the DPRK uranium enrichment program would be revealed and inspections would occur, plutonium would begin to be shipped out of North Korea, and a fast program to build North Korea new conventional power plants would begin. Completion of the nuclear deal would occur within several years, when whatever weapons the DPRK currently possesses would finally be presented for dismantlement.

On the conventional force reduction front, baseline weapons declarations would be made and initial inspections conducted (on both sides of the DMZ) within months. All reductions would be completed and excess weapons verifiably destroyed within three to five years. Similar schedules would apply to the elimination of chemical and biological weapons and ballistic missiles. Japanese kidnapping victims would all go home immediately; the first round of a human rights dialogue would begin within a year.

Economic reform efforts would begin in several dedicated economic zones within months, and aid would start to flow to those regions for infrastructural improvement and related activities quickly as well. Economic sanctions would be lifted immediately. (They could always be reimposed if the deal later fell apart.) Over time, reform efforts would spread to more of the country, and aid workers would begin to help North Korea's general medical and educational programs as well as to improve the national infrastructure. Diplomatic relations would be resumed immediately. A nonaggression pledge would be offered within a short time of the conclusion of the grand bargain as well, though, as noted, it could be made contingent on sustained North Korean compliance with the entire road map for stabilizing and transforming the peninsula. The formal signing of the peace accord might be delayed a year or so to first provide confidence that the overall deal was likely to stick.

ADDRESSING THE NUCLEAR ISSUE

Any resolution of the current crisis with North Korea must aim for the complete denuclearization of the DPRK. The danger of that country's selling, or possibly even using, nuclear materials is too great for other nations to tolerate its possession of fissile materials or actual weapons. The risk is heightened dramatically if the arsenal grows, allowing North Korea multiple degrees of freedom for trying to exploit its nuclear capabilities.

As a matter of principle, we consider the nuclear issue so serious that we agree with the gist of Secretary of Defense William Perry's stance in 1994, prior to the successful conclusion of the Agreed Framework. As Perry argued then, if all else had failed, a preemptive strike against Yongbyon might have had to be conducted. Such a strike would have run a significant risk of provoking an all-out war on the peninsula. That would have been extremely serious, likely leading to tens of thousands of ROK troop deaths, thousands of American losses, and even higher casualties among DPRK forces. Civilian populations might have suffered greater losses still. But that risk was no greater than the risk of allowing North Korea to develop, and possibly sell or even use, dozens of nuclear weapons.

However, the situation is even more complicated today. First, North Korea's underground uranium enrichment nuclear program will ultimately give it the ability to add a bomb or two a year to whatever existing arsenal it may already have, and U.S./ROK forces cannot preempt that program because they do not know where it is. Second, by the time this book is published, North Korea may have already added to its inventory of nuclear materials, perhaps doubling or tripling its inventory of reprocessed plutonium and building an arsenal of up to six or eight bombs before 2004. North Korea's initial trouble early in 2003 in restarting its reprocessing facilities cannot be expected to continue indefinitely. The resulting purified plutonium, once removed from the facility at Yongbyon, would also almost surely be undetectable and hence beyond the reach of any preemptive strike (short of all-out war and occupation of the DPRK—and even that option might fail to find a few grapefruit-sized masses of plutonium).

Third, the current ROK president has clearly stated his opposition to preemption against North Korea under any circumstances. Since South Korea would likely bear the greatest burden, and the highest risks of DPRK counterattack, in the event of any preemptive U.S. strike on Yongbyon, the political feasibility as well as the morality of a U.S. unilateral decision to preempt are open to serious challenge. Japan's view may be somewhat more hawkish than President Roh's, but only somewhat. Although Japanese animosity toward North Korea has increased dramatically in recent years, especially after confirmation of the abduction cases, Japan still prefers a peaceful solution to the North Korea crisis. It opposes military preemption or regime change through the use of force. Indeed, President Roh and Japanese Prime Minister Junichiro Koizumi declared publicly during their June 7, 2003, summit that the North Korean nuclear issue should be solved in a peaceful and diplomatic manner.

However, our conviction is that North Korea can be talked out of its current growing momentum toward developing a substantial nuclear arsenal. On this point we disagree with the suggestion of Director of Central Intelligence George Tenet (made in early 2003) that North Korea is now firmly wedded to its nuclear program and will try to convince the United States to tolerate it. If Tenet is proven right, it will quite possibly be because Washington makes a major mistake. There is no hard evidence—only an effort to "connect the dots"—to substantiate his claim.

We think North Korea's recent actions, however regrettable and however indefensible, follow a certain logic, an assessment that appears to be shared by several governments in Northeast Asia. If that logic is understood and properly addressed, through a policy of firmness and arms reductions with robust verification combined with incentives for better DPRK behavior, a successful resolution of the crisis can probably be reached. In any event, testing this hypothesis has relatively low costs and should serve to unite the United States with its regional security partners much more closely than is the case at present—making a coercive strategy feasible should it truly become necessary down the road.

Consider the recent diplomatic history. The Clinton administration, despite its significant accomplishments in slowing the DPRK nuclear program in 1994, may turn out to have inadvertently encouraged North Korea to view weapons programs as tools for gaining hard currency and diplomatic attention. That seemed to be how North Korea viewed its long-range missile program in the last couple of years of the Clinton presidency; it may explain the initiation of the uranium enrichment program in the late 1990s as well. (It is also possible that North Korea started the program in the hope that it could gain the energy, economic, and diplomatic benefits of the Agreed Framework as well as the security benefits of a nuclear arsenal.)

The Bush administration turned a cold shoulder not only to North Korea but even to South Korea and its pro-détente presidents Kim Dae Jung and Roh Moo Hyun. It also placed North Korea within its so-called axis of evil and talked about the necessity of more frequent use of military preemption. Under these circumstances, North Korea probably felt that pursuing a nuclear program more aggressively would improve its chances of gaining Washington's attention—or, if that failed, that it would at least provide some deterrence against a U.S. attack.

True, North Korea had already initiated its secret and illegal uranium enrichment program before Mr. Bush took office. It was trying to have its cake and eat it too—gain benefits from the 1994 Agreed Framework, in which its plutonium activities were capped, while hedging its bets and starting an underground nuclear program as well. It was a fundamentally unacceptable and unjustified decision and, we concede, one that casts some doubt upon the hypothesis that a grand bargain with the DPRK can really work. But North Korea has agreed to ambitious deals before; it has shown a clear interest in gaining the benefits of interaction with the outside world; and its recent actions can be explained partly by fear as opposed to pure aggressiveness. The weight of evidence suggests that, at a minimum, a more vigorous and sweeping negotiation should be attempted.

North Korea really did make important concessions in 1994. It gave up the potential to make dozens of bombs a year, thereafter starting a new program that might someday produce no more than one to two annually. It sacrificed a very large program and tried to develop a very small one in its place. This is not to defend North Korean behavior, only to emphasize that Pyongyang clearly valued the economic, diplomatic, and security benefits of the Agreed Framework much more than it valued pursuit of a large nuclear arsenal.

If our reading of North Korea is correct, it should be possible to avoid—or reverse—a rapidly deteriorating situation of the type that might raise the prospects of U.S. military preemption against the DPRK. This can probably be done without resort to very tough military or other measures such as U.N. sanctions prohibiting all countries from selling North Korea technologies usable in weapons programs, together with military enforcement of this ban. Through a combination of carrots and sticks—incentives and demands—it should be possible to convince Pyongyang to return to the more cooperative path it clearly seemed to be exploring in the 1999–2000 period. The preemptive threat should not be removed from the table, but neither should it be the preferred policy option for Washington or Seoul.

That said, the allies need to be tough in their nuclear demands on Pyongyang, and the rest of the grand bargain we propose cannot realistically move forward unless such demands are met. The nuclear aspects of a grand bargain with North Korea must do three things. First, as soon as negotiations begin, the DPRK must immediately freeze its nuclear reprocessing activities, reveal the locations of any plutonium that has recently been reprocessed, freeze research reactor operations, allow monitors back at Yongbyon, and cease further construction of its large reactors there.

Second, the direct obligations assumed by North Korea in regard to its Yongbyon nuclear facilities in the 1994 Agreed Framework must be upheld. North Korea must again agree to disable all capabilities at Yongbyon, allow the spent fuel there to be removed from the country, and also eventually account for the several kilograms of plutonium believed to have been reprocessed already in the early 1990s. It must do so in the knowledge that it will no longer be supplied the two light-water nuclear reactors provided for in the Agreed Framework. Those reactors could in theory produce materials for nuclear weapons—as evidenced by the U.S. concern about Iran's acquisition of similar technology at Bushehr.

Since North Korea's good faith in the nuclear area is open to greater doubt than it was a decade ago, it cannot any longer be trusted with such technology. Outside powers should still help North Korea with its energy needs and go beyond that to assist the DPRK with its electricity grid as well. Indeed, they should do so more quickly and at more generous levels than promised under the 1994 accord. But the energy must not be nuclear in origin.

Third, North Korea must allow the international community to verify that its current uranium enrichment program is ended and remains that way. This will require an on-site inspections process over an indefinite period of time. In particular, it would require North Korea to agree in advance to occasional "challenge" inspections, with little notice, at any sites where the international community has concerns about potential nuclear-related activities, as well as occasional interviews between international inspectors and DPRK weapons scientists. Several such inspections may be needed per year, and perhaps even more in the early phase of the accord. Although North Korea has resisted such inspections in the past, it has relented in situations where it felt the benefits worth the concession.

Some aspects of this plan require greater explanation.

The logic supporting the need to make this deal tough on North Korea is simple—it is North Korea that blatantly violated the Agreed Framework. Hence, in regard to the nuclear issue at least, it is North Korea that must now accept tougher demands on its future behavior, most notably tough inspections and no additional nuclear reactors. Whatever one's view on who was most responsible for the delays in implementing the Agreed Framework in the 1990s, these were delays, not a fundamental violation of its terms—that is, not until the DPRK initiated its uranium enrichment program in the late 1990s. The DPRK was slow to improve relations with South Korea, the United States delayed improvement of economic and diplomatic relations with the North, and both sides took steps that slowed the timetable for new reactor construction. But the basic logic of the energy-for-energy deal continued until the uranium enrichment program was developed and then discovered.

As noted, in regard to hidden nuclear programs, North Korea must fully acknowledge the existence of its uranium enrichment efforts, identify the sites involved in them, and allow inspectors to carry out verification of their dismantlement. Even though such enrichment efforts, if supervised by the IAEA, do not technically violate the NPT, they cannot be tolerated in the specific case of North Korea, given its history and recent provocations. After dismantlement is complete, North Korea must, as noted, also allow occasional challenge inspections, perhaps by the IAEA but with a strong U.S. role in helping select suspect sites, to ensure that it has not initiated any similar efforts.

There is no airtight way to do this with complete confidence that North Korea has not hidden another program. But nuclear programs, though possible to conceal from overhead satellites—as we learned in Iraq in the early 1990s and North Korea in the late

1990s—are hard to hide from inspectors. Even "basement bomb" programs require sophisticated equipment that is expensive and hard to move, such as complexes with hundreds of centrifuges, large magnets that form the core of devices known as calutrons, or large gaseous diffusion plants.

Inspectors in Iraq after Desert Storm were unable to disband Iraqi nuclear teams or find all the nuclear-relevant technologies there. But they did find Iraq's underground nuclear program to produce fissile materials, the most difficult part of making any nuclear weapon. Indeed, the discovery of the nuclear program was the main "smoking gun" they uncovered in all of their time in Iraq prior to Operation Iraqi Freedom in 2003.

In addition, normal national intelligence operations can provide additional checks on compliance. It was the ability of the United States to track North Korea's efforts to import equipment such as centrifuges that finally revealed the existence of the uranium program in 2002. Combining such national intelligence capabilities with inspections can be even more productive. When provided with good knowledge of how nuclear materials are produced and processed, free access to the inspected country's weapons scientists, data on any suspected nuclear sites, and data on suspicious technology imports, on-the-ground inspectors have a good track record.

If North Korea objected strenuously to being humbled by the presence of such inspectors, outside parties could consider several steps. U.S. bases in South Korea could also be inspected by North Koreans to verify the absence of nuclear devices, since the United States withdrew its nuclear weapons from the peninsula a decade ago. The United States certainly has considerable experience dealing with foreign inspectors on its military bases going back to the Cold War, and can handle the associated security considerations. Inspections in North Korea might also be carried out just by the United States and not by South Korea, if Pyongyang so preferred—or perhaps even in conjunction with Chinese or Russian experts. The inspections could be described as "cooperative threat reduction" efforts similar to those between the United States and Russia (despite the obvious differences) rather than as inspections motivated by suspicions of treaty violations, if desired.

Leaders in Washington and other key capitals can be flexible on the modalities of these arrangements, as long as the physical inspection processes are assured. Since the two Koreas and the United States envisioned such inspections as part of the Seoul-Pyongyang 1991 Joint Declaration on the Denuclearization of the Korean Peninsula (an accord that also committed the Koreas not to have facilities for reprocessing plutonium or enriching uranium), it should not be out of reach.

NORTH KOREA'S MISSILES

The United States, South Korea, and Japan should seek to stop North Korea's ballistic missile testing and production efforts, particularly for its medium- and long-range systems, as well as its missile exports. They need not be quite as absolutist in their demands on the missile issue as on the nuclear issue. For example, it would be tolerable that North Korea retain a stock of short-range missiles, if South Korea and Japan are willing to tolerate a certain number, and even a modest number of medium and longer-range variants. The allies should first try to talk North Korea into a complete ban on all types of ballistic missiles. But they should be willing to accept binding prohibitions on testing, production, and deployment of medium- and long-range missiles, as well as exports of all types of ballistic missiles. A few nuclear bombs in North Korean hands are a few too many, given the enormous devastation they could wreak. By contrast, a small stockpile of No Dong and Taepo Dong missiles poses only a limited threat to allied interests, especially in the context of a denuclearization accord. And a stockpile of short-range missiles poses less danger to ROK territory than does North Korean artillery. Therefore, some missile inventories can be tolerated.

North Korea produces reasonably good short-range missiles and has recently made progress on longer-range capabilities. For almost a decade, if not longer, it has had the capacity to produce about 100 SCUD-like missiles a year, with ranges of 300 to 500 kilometers, of which 500 or more have probably been sold abroad and another 500 deployed in its own arsenal. It tested the Nodong missile, with a range of 1,300 kilometers, in 1993 and may by now have deployed several dozen. It tested the Taepodong 1 three-stage rocket over Japan in 1998, though the test was only partially successful.

These weapons are of significant concern to the United States and its regional and global allies. The shorter-range types can, of course, reach the ROK. The Nodong can strike Japan, and the Taepodong missiles may soon be able to reach the United States. In addition, North Korea exports large numbers of these missiles to the Middle East and Persian Gulf regions, where they can be quite destabilizing. On balance, North Korea's missiles are a serious worry, even if not as much of a concern as nuclear weapons. They may be capable of carrying chemical, biological, and even nuclear weapons; the CIA assumes at a minimum that they can deliver chemical weapons. That said, it is not trivial to develop proper dispersing mechanisms for spreading chemical or biological agents at the proper altitude from a ballistic missile, nor is it easy to build a nuclear warhead small enough and tough enough to be delivered on a missile and to survive atmospheric reentry prior to detonating.

Since North Korea has tested its medium-range and long-range missiles only a couple of times and has never tested a nuclear weapon as far as we know, it is not obvious that it really is capable of delivering a nuclear weapon on a longer-range ballistic missile. The CIA now suspects that North Korea is trying to build nuclear bombs small enough to put on missiles, but is not sure. Indeed, North Korea's ability to disperse chemical agents with shorter-range missiles appears to be less than fully demonstrated. Given the fact that missile warheads can break up upon reentry, as was witnessed in Desert Storm, even this capability should probably not be taken for granted.

North Korea's missile capabilities became a major concern for the United States in the late 1990s. After North Korea tested the Taepo Dong 1 in 1998, sending it over Japan in a launching that was not entirely successful, the Clinton administration sought to clamp down on North Korean missile activities. It feared that that missile, and even more the Taepo Dong 2, still under development, would be potentially capable of reaching the United States. It relaxed some sanctions on North Korea as an inducement, and Pyongyang reciprocated with a flight test moratorium; it has not tested medium- or long-range ballistic missiles since.

In late 2000, the Clinton administration offered the possibility of a presidential visit and aid valued at up to a billion dollars—Pyongyang had first demanded cash—if North Korea would make the moratorium permanent, end missile exports, destroy existing medium- and long-range missile inventories, and cease future missile production. It is not clear just how close the deal really was to completion. There appear to have been major stumbling blocks over a number of issues, such as verification of any deal and whether North Korea would have to eliminate missiles it had already produced. In any case, there has been no movement on these negotiations since the Bush administration took office.

The Clinton administration's focus on North Korean missile capabilities was appropriate, even if its willingness to engage in a narrow deal compensating Pyongyang directly for restraint in this area was more questionable. The Clinton approach followed a certain logic, given the threat North Korean missiles posed to the United States and its allies regionally and globally. Moreover, it was an approach that Israel had also considered a decade earlier, when it contemplated offering a compensation package to Pyongyang to discourage it from selling missiles to the Middle East until talked out of the idea by the first Bush administration. But the Clinton approach still did smack of giving in to blackmail. And even if it had been concluded, it stood little chance of pushing North Korea to change its economy or its basic way of interacting with the outside world. The deal would have provided the DPRK a stopgap aid fix, not a plan for reform and recovery. This being the case, it might not have been long before Pyongyang sought to use some other weapon to demand additional payments to compensate for a faltering economy and a lack of alternative sources of revenue. But missiles should be part of any grand bargain.

The easiest missile deal now would be one that simply required North Korea not to test or deploy medium- and long-range missiles and not to sell any missiles, including shorter-range variants. Compliance with the former prohibitions would be easily verifiable; that with the latter would often be verifiable, meaning that if North Korea sought to violate them frequently, it would eventually be caught. A more ambitious proposal would require on-site inspections to verify that North Korea was also ending production of ballistic missiles. The most ambitious approach would require North Korea to destroy its existing missile stocks as well. This approach would also obviously require greater concessions from the DPRK. The allies need not insist on such a deal, however, or hold back aid in its absence. Even the more limited set of constraints on North Korea would address the allies' most important security interests.

CONVENTIONAL FORCE REDUCTIONS

Although the nuclear issue is the most acute security threat posed by North Korea, conventional force reductions are the true centerpiece of our proposal. It is conventional forces that have been at the heart of the half-century-long military standoff on the Korean peninsula. It is conventional forces that consume most DPRK military resources, thereby acting as an albatross weighing down the DPRK economy. It is conventional force reductions that, if properly carried out, can give hope to North Korea and give it the economic basis for no longer depending on bribes and blackmail to keep itself afloat.

These are lofty aspirations for a conventional arms reduction process. But how to make good on them? What type of conventional arms reduction plan could be significant enough in scope to free up large amounts of resources if adopted? How could it be made verifiable, so that the United States and the ROK would know they were not being tricked, and militarily stabilizing for all parties concerned? The allies would need to be sure that Pyongyang would not feel emboldened to attack by any force cutback package; Pyongyang in turn would need to be reassured that it was not being duped into letting down its guard and making itself vulnerable to preemptive attack. Given North Korea's limited knowledge of arms control and virtual lack of experience in the field, that will take some doing.

In broad strokes, we propose 50-percent cuts in heavy weaponry on the Korean peninsula, backed up by on-site verification procedures. This type of accord could be modeled after the

NATO–Warsaw Pact CFE Treaty. U.S. forces based in Korea would be counted against ROK holdings; U.S. forces elsewhere would not be. Forces near the DMZ would have to be cut back proportionately on both sides, just as the CFE Treaty imposed certain sublimits within certain geographic zones, though forces near the DMZ would not have to be drawn down to zero. Since North Korea's deterrent against any allied attack is largely its ability to hold Seoul hostage, it is not realistic to think that the DPRK would pull forces back from the DMZ entirely. As with the CFE Treaty, this treaty could be phased in over a period of about three years and then remain in force indefinitely.

The CFE Treaty held both alliance systems to the same quantitative limits on heavy weaponry. If North Korea found these terms too strict, however, the allies could be somewhat flexible. They would already have two major advantages that would not be constrained by a CFE-style approach: their advantages in weapons quality over North Korea and the huge U.S. military capability not based in Korea but available to the U.S.-ROK Combined Forces Command (CFC) if needed. So they could be somewhat flexible in the numerical ceilings they allowed North Korea. One approach would be for the allies to grant North Korea certain modest exemptions or loopholes in how its weapons were counted. Just as the Soviets were granted a certain allowance for internal security forces under the CFE Treaty, for example, North Korea might be permitted to exceed the common weapons ceilings by 10 percent or 20 percent on similar grounds.

Indeed, Washington and Seoul could go even further. They could propose a treaty by which heavy weaponry on the peninsula would be cut in half on both sides of the DMZ. North Korea would retain its significant quantitative advantages over the allies, but at lower levels of armament for both sides. We assess the major military implications of such cuts in conventional forces in

Chapter 4, showing how the United States and South Korea could be confident in their conventional deterrent under such an accord. They would still have enormous advantages in weapons quality, in military assets that are not counted within the CFE framework (such as advanced reconnaissance systems), and in U.S. reinforcement capability.

What about U.S. forces in particular? In theory, the allies might choose to meet their obligations under the "CFK treaty" by cutting ROK forces only, leaving the modestly sized U.S. capability in South Korea (including weapons in storage there) unaffected. But it would probably be wiser to make at least symbolic cuts in American weaponry as a sign of good faith. At the same time, Washington and Seoul must make clear that they categorically reject North Korea's traditional demand—that conventional weapons reductions be used as a vehicle for pushing U.S. forces off the peninsula.

A treaty modeled on the CFE Treaty would limit tanks, armored personnel carriers and fighting vehicles, large-bore artillery, combat jets, and helicopters. The CFE Treaty allowed relatively high levels for armored personnel carriers, holding artillery levels to the same ceiling applied to tank fleets. In Korea, the ceilings might be set somewhat differently, with a greater allowance for artillery given the DPRK's emphasis on this type of weapon. Seoul and Washington could accept such a provision as long as their aircraft were not unduly limited by the accord. But however the numbers are tweaked, the overall goal should be to reduce forces by about 50 percent—and even greater reductions need not be dismissed out of hand.

Treaties defined in these terms are difficult to negotiate. One must resolve a number of thorny issues, such as whether to count weapons-capable training aircraft as combat aircraft and where to define the cutoff between artillery and generally smaller mortars (the latter not being limited). It is also necessary to agree on how excess weapons will be destroyed and to work out verification provisions. Fortunately, the CFE experience provides considerable background for handling these and other matters. If North Korea wished, it could clearly seek guidance from Russia in how to draw from the CFE model without prejudice to its interests.

The CFE Treaty does not limit military manpower, and neither, presumably, would a CFK accord. In principle, if North Korea wished, it could keep all of its troops whose heavy equipment was destroyed, giving them rifles instead and turning them into infantry soldiers. This would be a violation of the spirit, though not the letter, of the accord we propose—less for its military significance than for its economic consequences. If North Korea kept the huge army it now fields, its prospects for economic recovery would diminish substantially. It is not practical to monitor or verify troop totals, so there is little to be done about this potential shortcoming of a CFK treaty, except to use economic analysis like that presented in Chapter 5 to try to convince Pyongyang that it would be hurting itself to keep a military of the current size. It may not be realistic to expect Pyongyang to cut military manpower by 50 percent, but at a minimum it should reduce it by 25 to 35 percent.

As noted, an accord like the CFE Treaty would also divide the peninsula into several zones and require roughly proportionate cuts in each area. North Korea would not be permitted to cut its forces in just the northern, eastern, and western sectors of the country and maintain its current strength near the DMZ. Cuts would have to be roughly proportionate in all major zones. One zone should encompass the western part of the DMZ, where DPRK forces posing the greatest threat to Seoul are located; perhaps a zone of roughly 50 kilometers on a side would make sense, though details could be left to negotiators.

Finally, this proposal would require on-site inspections, just as the CFE Treaty does. Each "alliance," that is, South Korea and the United States on one side and North Korea on the other (perhaps with China or Russia as official advisors and interlocutors to Pyongyang), would have to declare numbers and locations of all treaty-limited weaponry. Inspections would then confirm the initial declarations, verify destruction of weaponry, monitor weapons inventories at declared weapons sites each year thereafter, and look for illicit weaponry at "suspect sites" using challenge inspections. Using the CFE experience as a guide, but scaling down for the smaller number of parties and smaller (though denser) overall military forces involved here, dozens of inspections of each major type might be needed.

Would the North Korean military accept this kind of proposal? Of course, we do not yet know; the idea has not been tested. But there are reasons to think it might. First, this approach would hardly dismantle the North Korean armed forces. They would probably remain more than half a million strong even after 50-percent heavy force cuts and unfortunately would continue to demand well over 10 percent of the country's GDP. Second, this plan might even allow remaining DPRK forces to be maintained in somewhat better condition—a modest (though not major) downside to the proposal from the U.S./ROK point of view, as discussed more in Chapter 4, but a consolation for the DPRK.

Third, while this plan would require proportionate force cuts near the DMZ, it would not force North Korea to abandon all of its positions there and hence would not deprive the DPRK of its ability to threaten Seoul—perhaps the most important element of North Korea's military deterrent. Fourth, North Korea's military is involved in commercial activities itself and thus could benefit from any plan that held out promise for better North Korean commercial performance. On balance, there is no reason to abandon hope prematurely about Kim Jong Il's ability to win over his military to support this type of plan, should Kim decide he wants to pursue something like it himself.

ECONOMIC REFORM AND ECONOMIC AID FOR NORTH KOREA

Conventional force reductions are important for improving military stability on the Korean peninsula. But that motivation is not the most compelling for our proposed grand bargain. Rather, the greatest impetus comes from the fact that North Korea's economy is failing and needs a radical overhaul. Unless remedial action is taken, North Korea's recent pattern of extortionate behavior is likely to continue, for the simple reason that Pyongyang will have few alternative means of generating hard currency. Indeed, the problem could intensify; in the worst case, North Korea might be tempted to sell some of the nuclear materials it is now producing.

Moreover, conventional units are the primary military burden on North Korea's economy, accounting for perhaps 70 to 80 percent of the cost of the DPRK's armed forces. It is these capabilities—mechanized and infantry divisions, as well as air and naval forces—that account for the vast majority of North Korea's million-man military. Even though these enormous armed forces, the world's largest on a per capita basis, perform some civilian functions, they are for the most part a huge waste of resources. It is also the main, conventional forces that receive the output of most military-related industry.

For these reasons, economic reform and economic aid need to be part of the grand bargain. Current measures, such as humanitarian relief, are not enough. The DPRK has shown interest in economic reform itself, but it will need to be pushed to keep up and expand the effort.

In Chapter 5, we spell out in some detail how North Korean economic reform might work. But in broad terms, the main contours of the aid package should be as follows. First, this should be viewed as a development program, not a crash effort to bring North Korean living standards up to ROK levels. In other words, the model should be not Germany's absorption of East Germany but the U.S.-led effort to help Taiwan and South Korea develop decades ago (with suitable modifications, of course). Among its other implications, this philosophy points to an aggregate annual aid level of perhaps $2 billion (not counting aid for humanitarian purposes or energy projects or arms control activities), not tens of billions a year.

Second, most aid should not be provided in cash, given North Korea's proclivity to use it for the benefit of its leaders and its inability to devise sound development projects on its own. What assistance is provided in the form of money needs to be monitored to provide confidence that it is being well used, and needs to be directed to projects that Pyongyang and outside countries design together.

Third, while Japan may be willing to provide many of the needed resources, in part as a form of compensation for its colonization of the Korean peninsula in the first half of the twentieth century, other countries will need to play major roles. The United States will need to help, largely as a sign of sincerity. China will need to help, since it has at least the partial trust of the North Koreans and since it has experience creating special economic zones and gradual liberalization within the context of a command economy and a communist political system. South Korea will need to help, because official ROK aid will help motivate and facilitate private investment by South Koreans in the DPRK—and that may in the end be the most important engine of growth of all.

Finally, the aid programs need to continue for a decade or more. They can begin with infrastructure improvement in places like the Tumen River development zone, then be broadened both geographically and programatically. Ultimately, they should help North Koreans with education, health, and agriculture, though it may take time to gain Pyongyang's assent for some of these efforts.

UNITING THE GREAT POWERS BEHIND THE GRAND BARGAIN

The above discussion, particularly on economic reform and conventional force reductions, makes clear how critical the roles of regional players will be in attempting to realize our grand bargain. What are the key interests of Seoul, Beijing, and Tokyo, and under what circumstances would they be likely to support the kind of proposal we offer here?

The good news is that, while no Northeast Asian country has precisely the same order of security goals in Korea as the United States, their interests do not conflict. These facts suggest that it should be possible, through good diplomacy, to unify the United States, South Korea, Japan, and China behind a common strategy.

Washington's primary interests in Korea, in roughly the order listed, are to prevent nuclear proliferation, prevent war on the peninsula and in the region, maintain a strong U.S.-ROK alliance, stop international missile proliferation, and reduce the severity of the North Korean humanitarian crisis. It would also like to mitigate the oppressive nature of the DPRK government toward its own people.

Seoul's interests are similar, but the ranking is different—preventing nuclear proliferation ranks closer to last on the list than to first; preventing war and preventing a worsening humanitarian crisis are probably its top concerns. Tokyo's priorities may be more similar to Washington's, but of course it also is particularly concerned about the North Korean medium-range missile threat and the fate of the Japanese kidnapped by North Korea years ago. And finally, Beijing surely opposes nuclear proliferation on the peninsula as well, but it may worry most of all about North Korean collapse, with all of the associated humanitarian and refugee problems. It also would prefer not to see a military operation in Korea that brings U.S. forces anywhere near its borders or gives the United States a strategic pretext for keeping large numbers of military personnel in a reunified Korea.

In other words, the great powers should be able to reach a meeting of the minds. Their fundamental interests in Korea are not incompatible. Each would probably differ considerably from the others in the tactical implementation of any strategy toward North Korea. For example, should things get worse, they could disagree over whether to threaten the use of force and when if ever to use it. But such differences can be mitigated in severity, and perhaps even resolved, if the United States develops a grand bargain proposal and lobbies other regional powers to support it. Such a plan should have a very good chance of working and an even better chance to hold China, Japan, South Korea, and the United States together in how they approach the hermit kingdom in the coming months and years.

CHAPTER

4

TURNING SWORDS INTO PLOWS

How can the United States, Seoul, and their partners be confident that any arms cuts they make under an agreement with North Korea will do more good than harm? Were reductions to create holes in allied defenses, they could tempt North Korea to attack even if its own forces were also scaled back. It is essential that the allies know precisely which types of arms reductions would be stabilizing and which might be unequal or dangerous before embarking on negotiations.

Fortunately, as shown in this chapter, the allies have a good deal of flexibility. They can try to convince Pyongyang to accept an accord styled after the CFE Treaty, in which both alliances would be held to the same quantitative ceilings of heavy weaponry on the peninsula, but settle for less favorable terms if necessary. In fact, even a "CFK" treaty that imposed comparable percentage cuts in weapons holdings on both sides would be stabilizing. Allied forces would remain at least as strong relative to North Korea's, and they would have sufficient power in place to hold off an invasion even in the early going. The following analysis, largely military and technical in nature, explains why.

As noted earlier, an arms control concept modeled on the CFE Treaty would have some military benefits but even greater economic benefits. Because it would lead to a reduction in DPRK military expenditures, and because aid would accompany the arms cuts as part of our proposed grand bargain, resources would be freed for economic development projects. That could lead to a process of economic reform and recovery in North Korea as well as greater engagement between the DPRK and the outside world. Such a process would not guarantee peace, but it would probably tend to lower the chances of conflict on the peninsula. By giving Pyongyang a greater stake in sustained peaceful engagement, it should reduce the odds that North Korea would someday provoke yet another security crisis in order to bargain for resources from the outside world.

The main accord we analyze here would require cuts of 50 percent in all major types of heavy weaponry on both halves of the Korean peninsula. We find that such arms cuts would be militarily stabilizing and desirable. In fact, even greater reductions, as high as 65 to 75 percent, might well be considered, though we focus on 50-percent cuts, since they are already quite ambitious.

In addition, zonal limitations might be placed on the two sides' forces; for example, North Korea could be constrained not to deploy any greater percentage of its remaining forces south of

Pyongyang than the 65 to 70 percent it bases there today. In the interest of verifiability and practicality, the treaty would not cover military manpower, light arms, and antitank weapons. Nor would its scope extend to cruise missiles or land mines.

U.S. forces and equipment reserves on the Korean peninsula would be counted against South Korean allotments, but those beyond Korea (including U.S. forces in Japan) would not be, since they are also needed for other regions and purposes. The allies could decide how to apportion their holdings between U.S. and ROK weaponry. If they desired, U.S. forces on the peninsula could remain exactly at their current modest levels (even as they are relocated under the base realignment plan recently approved by Washington and Seoul). The treaty would be similar in style to the CFE Treaty, both in the types of weapons covered and in the on-site inspections that would be intrinsic to the accord. But the CFK Treaty's unequal ceilings of major equipment, which would allow North Korea to retain numerical advantages in several major categories of weaponry, would differ from the CFE Treaty's equal-ceiling approach.

Thus, this treaty would be more generous to North Korea than many would instinctively prefer. Our purpose in analyzing it, however, is not to recommend this treaty as the best one imaginable. Rather, we seek to show that even a treaty that is this generous to the North, allowing it to retain a quantitative edge in major weapons like artillery and tanks, would not harm the net military position of combined U.S.-ROK forces. Our goal is to demonstrate that Seoul and Washington have considerable flexibility as they consider the possible terms of a treaty that may help resolve a major crisis on the peninsula.

Our analysis proceeds from the judgment, explained in chapter 2, that North Korea does not now pose a major invasion threat against the ROK. It does retain a type of terrorist threat against

South Korea, and particularly nearby Seoul (the downtown of which is only 40 kilometers from the nearest point along the DMZ), in the form of missiles, long-range artillery, and special forces. These capabilities should give North Korea a strong assurance that, even if it cut its forces substantially, Seoul and Washington would not contemplate an offensive military thrust northward under any but the most extreme of circumstances. The DPRK could still quickly cause many thousands of casualties in Seoul, and tens of billions of dollars in property damage, with half the forces it possesses today. However, North Korea's forces today do not amount to a plausible invasion capability against South Korea.

Under this proposal for 50-percent cuts in heavy weaponry on the peninsula, North Korea would gain in two specific military ways. First, since its large infantry forces would not be constrained, their relative military significance would be increased somewhat as the role of heavy weaponry on the peninsula was reduced. Second, its remaining heavy forces might be able to recover at least some of the readiness they have lost in recent years in the face of North Korean economic collapse.

These mitigating factors, together with the ability to retain half of its forces currently deployed near the DMZ in their present positions, should help even the North Korean military see this type of accord as acceptable. Because the military is an important factor in DPRK politics and a key constituency for Kim Jong Il, its support is needed—even if North Korea would benefit principally in economic rather than military terms from the effects of such deep arms cuts.

The allies would gain even more than North Korea from this proposal. War on the peninsula would still be nearly unthinkable and hugely destructive to all sides—which is why North Korea would not lose its basic deterrent under this arms reduction plan.

But should war somehow occur, the allies' relative position would be improved at least somewhat by comparison with the status quo. The relative importance of U.S. airpower in Japan, to say nothing of reinforcements arriving from the United States, would increase considerably. South Korea would retain its most modern military systems, which typically compose one-third to one-half of its total holdings and are far better than any North Korean weapons.

The relative importance of allied defensive fortifications such as machine gun nests and antitank weapon positions below the DMZ would also grow as armored forces were reduced. Allied reconnaissance capabilities, communications systems, precision-guided munitions, and other asymmetric capabilities would be unchecked by the accord, further helping the United States and the ROK. The on-site inspection process would complicate any North Korean effort to surreptitiously concentrate its forces in one possible breakthrough sector prior to a surprise attack. Finally, the elimination of North Korea's chemical weapons capabilities (not directly part of this CFK accord but an element of the grand bargain as discussed in chapter 3) would further reduce the scale of the DPRK military threat.

IMPLICATIONS OF 50-PERCENT CUTS

Consider first how 50-percent cuts in tanks, large-bore artillery (with diameters larger than 100 millimeters), armored personnel carriers, and combat aircraft would affect the balance of heavy weapons on the Korean peninsula. One way to do this is to make a tally of each side's capabilities before and after the reductions, adjusting weapons inventories for the relative quality of equipment. That approach requires one to use some type of weighting mechanism to compare a given North Korean weapon to an allied version. This is an inherently difficult and somewhat imprecise process, but thankfully, methods that can be used to attempt it have been developed by defense research firms. For example, the TASCFORM system was created by the Analytical Sciences Corporation using a combination of detailed technical analysis and the judgment of retired military officers and other experts. That system is used below.

In rough numbers, our proposal would allow North Korea about 1,750 tanks, 1,500 armored personnel carriers (light tanks would count against this ceiling), 6,000 large-bore artillery tubes, and 400 combat aircraft. Combined South Korean and U.S. forces on the peninsula would retain about 1,300 tanks, 1,400 armored personnel carriers, and 2,600 pieces of large-bore artillery. They would also keep about 400 combat aircraft. To put it another way, North Korea would have to verifiably destroy about 9,000 pieces of heavy ground weaponry while South Korea and the United States together destroyed about 5,000 pieces; each side would cut up several hundred aircraft. Presumably, the oldest and most obsolescent weaponry would be the first to go. (Each side would choose how to comply with its own ceilings on weaponry.)

What would this do to net capability? Consider first the tank fleets on both sides. Of North Korea's 3,500 tanks, some 700 are indigenously produced versions of the Soviet T-62 design. Most of the remainder are old T-54/55 vintage Soviet designs. Using the TASCFORM scoring system, a new or well-maintained T-62 tank can be assessed at roughly 50 percent the overall effectiveness of a new M-1 and the T-54/55 at roughly 33 percent the capability of an M-1. So today's North Korean tank fleet, in aggregate, can be estimated by this measure to have the equivalent military potential of about 1,200 M-1 Abrams tanks (ignoring deterioration in North Korea's equipment, which this TASCFORM method does not account for). If obliged to make 50-percent reductions, the

North Koreans would presumably keep all of their T-62 tanks and as many of the others as possible. That would leave them a net equivalent value of about 650 M-1s—a 45-percent reduction in capability.

For allied forces, the net loss in capability as a result of the arms control proposal would be less in percentage terms. That is because U.S.-ROK top-tier equipment is so good—not only far better than North Korean equipment, but far better than older ROK equipment, which presumably would be eliminated under this type of arms control treaty. Specifically, South Korea's tank force is made up of about 1,000 K-1 tanks and another 1,300 primarily of M-47/48 vintage. The former share many of the components of the M-1 Abrams and are by conservative estimates at least 75 percent as good (particularly in the Korean context, where their lighter weight makes them more maneuverable).

The older ROK tanks, by contrast, score about 35 percent as well as an M-1. So today, allied tank forces have the equivalent capability of about 1,400 M-1s (including U.S. equipment). After the 50-percent reduction, they would retain a value of 1,000 M-1 equivalents—about a 30-percent diminution in net combat capability. The allied advantage over North Korea in tanks, by the TASCFORM measure, would grow from 10 percent to 50 percent.

Similar results can be found for other types of equipment. In the category of light tanks and armored personnel carriers, North Korea has roughly 3,000 fairly obsolete vehicles. Data on how many of each type it has are incomplete, but mandating a 50-percent cut would probably reduce the fleet's capabilities from a TASCFORM-equivalent of about 800 Bradley fighting vehicles to about 500. South Korea and the United States have about 2,100 top-flight weapons in this category and about 700 of lesser caliber, which would be the first to go under any 50-percent cut regimen. Their aggregate capabilities would probably decline from today's

1,900 Bradley equivalents to about 1,100—about the same percentage cut as for North Korea but preserving the allies' 2.2-to-1 advantage in overall capability.

Unclassified data about North Korean forces is not as readily available for artillery, so comparisons using the TASCFORM system are difficult to make. But North Korea would have to make very large cuts in its artillery force; this is the only major CFE/CFK weapons category in which it exceeds allied holdings by two to one. Moreover, South Korea and the United States could selectively preserve their most advanced artillery, such as long-range multiple launch rocket systems and systems colocated with counterartillery radar. (They could also continue to acquire more counterartillery radar and real-time data links between the radar and their own artillery batteries, such systems being unconstrained by CFK.) If the allies have any edge in artillery due to quality, it is not as great as those in the realms of tanks and APCs; most likely the two sides are roughly equal in overall capability. To the extent the data permit comparison, rough parity with regard to artillery would remain under the proposed treaty.

Finally, in the province of aircraft, North Korea's roughly 650 combat planes have the overall capacity of no more than 150 modern combat jets. (Recall as well that these numbers are in some ways too high because TASCFORM data does not factor in the actual state of repair of the equipment or the very poor level of training received by DPRK pilots.) The allies, with a total of some 800 combat jets and helicopters on the peninsula themselves, have the equivalent of about 350 of the most modern fighter jets, such as F-16C/Ds. After 50-percent cuts, North Korea's capabilities would decline to about 100 modern jet equivalents; the allies' would remain at more than 250, since they would probably be giving up primarily older ROK attack helicopters and F-5 jets. Their current 135 percent advantage would grow to 150 percent in this apples-to-apples comparison (admittedly not the best way to size up the importance of allied airpower, but a useful metric nonetheless).

So much for a static assessment of raw materiel. What about the capabilities of the remaining allied firepower when put in the geographic and warfighting contexts of the Korean peninsula? The clear issue of concern is the need to stave off an initial DPRK assault, since the eventual arrival of U.S. reinforcements—unconstrained by the proposed arms reduction treaty—would make any allied arms control concerns moot later in the war. (If they could hold initially, the arms control regimen would clearly help the allies, since overall U.S. capabilities exceed those of either of the Koreas by a considerable margin even today and would do so by an even greater margin under the proposed accord.)

First, would the amount of remaining allied heavy weaponry be adequate to cover the 250 kilometers or so of ROK perimeter along the DMZ? The answer is clearly yes. The Korean theater today is among the most militarized regions in human history, with a density of armored forces at least twice that of the intra-German border region during the Cold War. Today, the ROK force structure contains roughly one division for every 10 kilometers of the DMZ in the active-duty force and another division for every 10 kilometers of frontage in the reserves. By contrast, modern combat divisions are designed to communicate and operate as integrated units over at least 25 kilometers of a front. Even if allied forces applied the 50-percent cuts not only to their armored forces but also to their overall force structure and manpower, they would have enough strength just in active-duty units to maintain this standard force-to-space ratio.

This conclusion can be buttressed by a simple dynamic calculation, designed to answer two questions: Would remaining allied equipment be adequate to deliver the rate of fire needed to destroy advancing North Korean heavy weapons? Would it be able to stop advancing foot soldiers?

The answer to the first question is unambiguously yes; to the second it is almost certainly (but somewhat less definitively) also yes. As for heavy weapons, front-line allied forces today could probably generate at least four times the rate of firepower necessary to stop DPRK armored forces. Under the 50-percent cut regimen, they could be expected to retain at least twice as much firepower as needed (factoring in the effects of non-treaty-limited weapons such as antitank guns and TOW-2A antitank guided weapons as well as armor). And these results do not even include the effects of allied airpower, artillery, and mines or take into account simple mechanical breakdowns of North Korean armor. Thus, they are highly conservative from a U.S.-ROK perspective.

The detailed calculations behind this assessment will not be presented here, but the overall results are quite reassuring. To summarize the reasoning briefly, since North Korean forces would be traversing difficult terrain under fire, they would be doing very well to move forward at 5 kilometers per hour. Also, because of the constraints of space on the battlefield, a given North Korean division would occupy an area of perhaps 5 kilometers by 5 kilometers as it moved southward. If there were 1,000 armored vehicles in the division, only about 15 could therefore cross a given line per minute. This is a somewhat mechanistic way to model the North Korean advance, but captures the basic dynamic process and makes it possible to determine roughly how much firepower allied forces must be able to generate per unit of time.

Along that same 5-kilometer front, about 2 percent of total allied forces would probably be deployed in front lines. That means they would possess at least 20 tanks and 20 APCs, and a number of TOW positions. On average, each of these weapons or positions could fire three to five shots per minute, with a kill probability per shot of perhaps 0.25, meaning that each allied vehicle or TOW position would on average be capable of destroying about one DPRK armored vehicle per minute. This is a somewhat artificial calculation, given its assumptions of a constant rate of North Korean advance and a steady rate of allied fire, but it does indicate just how much weaponry allied forces would retain under the proposed framework.

The more complicated calculation concerns the allied effort to stop North Korean infantry soldiers from traversing the DMZ and regions below it on foot. Would the reductions in allied artillery that our proposed treaty regime requires make it more likely that North Koreans could survive long enough to reach and attack allied positions?

The answer appears to be perhaps, but not by very much. Across the notional 5-kilometer front discussed before, the allies might have deployed nearly 100 of their 6,000 mortars and 50 of their larger-bore longer-range artillery, assuming an even distribution of weaponry across the DMZ region. Each weapon could fire several times per minute and would typically have a lethal radius against humans of at least 10 meters. So these weapons could in theory barrage the entire front within their zone of responsibility at least once a minute and probably twice, delivering lethal fire at every point along that front and within a swath of land roughly 25 to 50 meters wide once a minute. Under current conditions, by contrast, they could inflict lethal fire once a minute within a swath 50 to 100 meters wide.

What does this mean? Since a soldier weighted down with equipment would have a hard time advancing much more than 100 meters a minute under fire, current conditions make his odds for survival seem extremely low. Under the proposed arms control regimen, they would improve somewhat. However, they would remain poor, given the sheer density of allied artillery firepower.

The allies would not actually deliver a barrage in this type of predictable cookie-cutter way. But the calculation nonetheless illustrates the fact that theoretical rates of artillery fire against North Korean soldiers would drop from the virtually unsurvivable to the merely horrific after 50-percent cuts in heavy large-bore tubes were made.

Machine gun nests and antipersonnel guns mounted on armored vehicles, to say nothing of aerial attacks and land mines, would also pose lethal risks to advancing North Korean foot soldiers. So the finding that allied artillery by itself might not be able to fully stop an advance of foot soldiers is of limited consequence.

One small drawback associated with a CFK accord is that a smaller North Korean army might maintain a slightly higher state of readiness. Available supplies, such as fuel, spare parts, and food for soldiers, could be divided up among a somewhat smaller group. However, this benefit would be quite modest in magnitude. As the Russian experience of late shows, moreover, downsizing armed forces during a period of general and rapid economic decline is not likely to be a prescription for improved military readiness. And, as noted, this feature of the arms regimen, while of modest importance, can be used to help convince the DPRK armed forces to support deep cuts. It should enhance the idea's basic negotiability.

CONCLUSION

Washington, Seoul, Tokyo, and Beijing should consider proposing a grand bargain with Pyongyang. A centerpiece of the plan should couple verifiable and sweeping conventional arms control with normalization of relations among the various parties, a lifting of U.S. sanctions, and economic development aid to North Korea that could reach the magnitude of $2 billion a year for about ten years. This type of plan would begin to demilitarize and stabilize the peninsula. Even more important, it would offer North Korea the realistic prospect of successful economic reform. That would give Pyongyang a major incentive to accept and comply with the grand bargain and reduce the odds that it will manufacture future security crises in order to bilk the international community out of much-needed resources.

Our analysis shows that a uniform 50-percent cut in holdings of major combat systems on both sides of the DMZ would be militarily desirable for South Korea and the United States. It would aid North Korea in a couple of modest ways, notably by increasing the relative importance of infantry and special forces (since manpower could not and would not be limited under this type of treaty). It would also help North Korea keep those units that were not retired under the treaty in a state of (somewhat) better readiness than they are today. But it would serve U.S.-ROK military interests even more. It would allow the allies to retain most of their best weaponry. It would increase the relative military importance of U.S. forces in Japan and of U.S. reinforcements from outside the region. Finally, it would also increase the relative importance of unconstrained military technologies in which the allies excel, such as advanced reconnaissance and communications systems and antitank weapons.

Although this chapter shows that an across-the-board 50 percent-cut regimen would be militarily acceptable to the United States and South Korea, it should probably not be their initial bargaining position. A more appropriate initial negotiating approach for the allies might propose common weapons ceilings for both sides—say, 1,500 tanks, 1,500 APCs/light tanks, 3,000 large-bore artillery tubes, and 500 to 750 combat aircraft. (Korea is less overmilitarized in terms of aircraft than of ground vehicles, so a higher ceiling may be appropriate here.) This proposal would follow the CFE precedent of insisting on parity in numbers of weapons and uphold the political principle that North Korea should not receive any special treatment vis-a-vis South Korea. Pragmatically speaking, it would also allow the allies to fall back to the 50-percent cut proposal in the course of negotiations. There is nothing wrong with having some flexibility in allied negotiating positions as long as the final deal denuclearizes North Korea and allows major progress on other key issues.

CHAPTER
5

FIXING A FAILED ECONOMY

North Korea is now well into its second decade of negative economic growth. After an early history of respectable command-economy performance, it began to lose momentum in the 1970s. The end of the Soviet Union, and the associated loss of aid as well as favorable trade terms, then exacerbated what was increasingly a failed experiment in North Korea's blend of communism with its own *juche* system of self-reliance. In the 1990s, problems of famine emerged, energy supplies became less dependable, and any remaining hope of economic recovery under the communist system dissipated. Economic deterioration slowed in the late

1990s, but that hardly amounted to a recovery. That is where things stand today.

North Korean leaders do not seem to know what to do about their predicament. They are obviously unwilling to step down, opening up the country's politics and economics in a Northeast Asian version of "shock therapy." They have tried numerous reforms—price liberalization, special economic zones, and limited business transactions with South Koreans—though with little to show for them to date. Even as they tentatively explore reform ideas, their instincts still push them in the direction of high military investment—out of inertia, or under the continued strong influence of the military in North Korean policymaking, or in the hope that they can sell arms, extort tribute, or even still find a way to defeat South Korea's armed forces and reunify the peninsula.

Looked at another way, there are probably intense political and bureaucratic struggles within North Korea, with some politicians favoring economic reforms and the military often opposing them. Kim Jong Il seems inclined to support reform, but only very cautiously and haltingly—in a way that to date has produced very poor results. Viewed in these terms, reform must build up internal momentum to continue, and reformers must convince skeptical military leaders as well as other hard-liners that change will not weaken the party's hold on power or harm its security position vis-a-vis the ROK and the United States.

North Korean leaders have clearly not yet been prepared to take the risks associated with China-style economic reforms on a large scale. It is unclear that such reforms would work in the DPRK, though they probably would if the regime's leaders would really give them a serious try, as shown by economists such as Marcus Noland at the Institute for International Economics (as discussed further below). Indeed, North Korea should be able to increase its GDP by more than 50 percent, and perhaps even double it, by reducing military spending, taking legal steps to make its country more appealing for outside investors, behaving less aggressively, and allowing more entrepreneurial activity.

There are no guarantees of success. But there are also few drawbacks to trying to push the North Koreans along the reform path—and providing the resources needed to have a serious prospect of success, to the extent that North Korea makes the reforms needed to give its economy a chance. Failure would leave us no worse off than we are today. Success would admittedly help a totalitarian regime stay in power. But the alternative of further economic collapse, misery, and starvation for the citizens of the DPRK, as well as the possibility that North Korea would sell nuclear weapons or take other extreme provocative actions if on the verge of collapse, is worse. Just as China has come a great distance from the days of Mao without a revolution or formal overthrow of communism, and just as Vietnam has allowed successful entrepreneurial activity within a communist system, North Korea may ultimately be able to do so as well.

THE RISE AND FALL OF THE NORTH KOREAN ECONOMY

North Korea began its history with a relatively strong economic inheritance and then got off to a strong start in its economic competition with South Korea. Over time, however, its economy became increasingly distorted, militarized, and dependent on trade with the Soviet Union. That set the stage for a gradual collapse after the end of the Cold War—a collapse that continues to unfold today.

Right after World War II, the new country of North Korea possessed three-fourths of the peninsula's mining production, at least 90 percent of its electricity generation capacity, and 80 percent of its heavy industry. The South, with a better climate, had been kept largely as an agricultural region during the period of Japanese colonization over the then still-unified peninsula. Building on its inheritance, North Korea nationalized major industries in the mid- to late 1940s and quickly succeeded in driving up its production substantially. These trends probably contributed to Kim Il Sung's confidence that he would win a war against the South, which he proceeded to unleash in 1950.

North Korea continued to outperform South Korea in the period immediately after the Korean War. But the seeds of the DPRK's eventual economic deterioration were soon sown. It collectivized agriculture in 1953. It provided most citizens with impressively long educations but wasted much of the time on indoctrination in communist thought. It increasingly invested in heavy industry, too much of it defense-related, while turning inward and autarkic. The *juche* concept of self-reliance was first articulated by Kim Il Sung in 1955. It resulted in North Korea's having very low levels of foreign trade and kept it from joining the communist community's Council for Mutual Economic Assistance (COMECON).

By the late 1960s, North Korea was also devoting 15 to 20 percent of its GDP to the military, in comparison to ROK levels that were generally closer to 5 percent. DPRK economic growth gradually slowed. Although still respectable through the mid-1970s, it began to lag behind South Korea's growth rate as ROK income levels reached those of the DPRK. Pyongyang attempted to boost its economic output with a change in philosophy in the early 1970s, borrowing capital on international markets and purchasing whole factories from abroad. But oil price shocks and global recession thwarted that strategy too.

Things went from bad to worse in the succeeding years. North Korea came to depend more and more on economic relations with the Soviet bloc, importing arms and exporting minerals, textiles, steel, and other goods. It also increased its own arms exports, largely to Iran. But this economic strategy was setting the DPRK up for a major fall once the Soviet Union dissolved in 1991. At that time, in addition to losing most of its markets, North Korea also lost access to subsidized oil from the Soviet Union. North Korea was fortunate that China was willing to provide coal and oil on favorable terms thereafter, once Beijing realized that the alternative was to see an intensification in the flow of North Korean economic refugees into the PRC. But even so, by the end of the decade, North Korean energy resources were only about 50 percent of what they had been in 1990.

For thirteen consecutive years (through 2003), North Korea suffered a continuous period of economic decline. Its GDP and per capita income levels have been cut roughly in half over that period. And starvation became a serious problem in the mid- to late 1990s. Alternating periods of drought and flooding exacerbated agricultural problems, as did soil deterioration caused by decades of unsustainable practices. The resulting famine, though partially alleviated by food aid from abroad, killed hundreds of thousands of people, at a minimum.

ATTEMPTS AT REFORM

For the better part of twenty years, North Korea has shown an interest in finding a "third way," like China's under Deng Xiaoping and successive leaders, between pure communism and capitalism. But unlike China, it has not demonstrated a serious commitment to this economic strategy and has not achieved much success to date.

As things have gotten worse, North Korea has grown even more dependent on its habits of extortion, drug trafficking, counterfeiting, whatever arms exports it can still find markets for, and cash remittances from overseas North Koreans. It has maintained some foreign trade, to the annual tune of roughly $1.5 billion to $1.75 billion in imports and $700 million to $1 billion in exports in recent years—but those numbers are down by roughly half from 1980s levels.

About 50 percent of all North Korean imports come from China, with Japan and South Korea next on the list. Exports go principally to Japan, South Korea, and China. North Korea also still receives aid from China, the ROK, Japan, the United States, and the European Union. This is provided mostly in the form of food and energy and averages up to $1 billion annually. (Some of these data are dated, given the difficulty of making estimates for a secretive country such as North Korea, but the main external players remain the same, and the dollar figures have probably changed only modestly in the last couple of years.)

Given its spotty track record to date and the traditional communist rhetoric still used by its leadership, North Korea's true dedication to pursuing economic reform can be doubted. DPRK leaders undoubtedly fear that liberalizing the economy would lead inescapably to political liberalization—and thus their own loss of power. Still, even as they probably harbor that fear, Kim Jong Il and associates do seem to be trying to find alternatives to *juche* and pure communism.

Kim Jong Il has visited China at least three times since May 2000, traveling to economic centers in Beijing, Shanghai, and Shenzhen and receiving briefings from Chinese economists. He has undoubtedly also had briefings from Chinese political experts about how to reform the economy without losing hold of the country—something that the PRC's Communist Party has managed to do over the past quarter century. Functionaries in the Korean Workers Party have met with their Chinese counterparts to explore reform ideas at the working level.

Hard-liners in North Korea are probably not sold on reform, and even proponents of change undoubtedly worry about its potential to snowball into a broader political movement that would challenge their hold on power. But real interest in new economic ideas surely exists. The challenge for U.S., ROK, Japanese, and Chinese leaders is to try to give North Koreans incentives and encouragement to try the reform path more seriously. Hoping for economic and political collapse, the visceral preference of some Bush administration hardliners, is understandable at one level given the horrors of the North Korean regime. But it is more likely to lead to further suffering for the North Korean people and further export of dangerous weapons (perhaps including nuclear materials) by North Korea than to rapid regime change.

North Korean reforms to date have been of three main types. First, special economic zones have been created, particularly a region in the country's extreme northeast around the Tumen River, as well as the Sinuiju Special Administrative Region, the Geumgang Mountain Special Tourism Zone, and the Gaeseong Industrial Zone. Foreign investment has been encouraged in these zones and elsewhere. Second, arrangements have been reached with South Korea to allow tourists to visit the North, with expensive surcharges demanded by Pyongyang for the privilege. Third, prices have been liberalized, wages increased, and some limited level of private agriculture tolerated. Most recently, "farmers' markets" have been allowed to sell more goods.

In addition, North Korea has lobbied for a lifting of U.S. trade sanctions and removal from the U.S. list of state sponsors of terrorism. It has also attempted rapprochement with Japan. Though generally unsuccessful to date, these efforts have probably been motivated in part by the expectation that such steps could lead to the foreign private investment as well as the international financial institutional support that the DPRK so desperately needs.

North Korea's special economic zone in the Rajin-Sonbong area, also known as the Tumen River delta, was initiated in the early 1990s. It is a region of more than 700 square kilometers, geographically isolated from much of the rest of the country (undoubtedly a deliberate choice by Pyongyang). Despite its extreme location, it benefits from relatively good natural port potential. In this region, North Korea grants more favorable terms to foreign investors than China and Vietnam granted in their similar zones, at least on paper. Foreign firms can own all the capital invested in a given project, repatriate profits, access the region without visas, enjoy guarantees against nationalization of their assets, and be granted 50-year leases on land.

However, North Korea has not succeeded in attracting much capital to the region. By the end of the 1990s, no more than $34 million had been invested, and progress appears not to have accelerated since then. The zone's appeal is limited by poor infrastructure, great distances from Pyongyang and other cities, and high wage rates. Clearly, unresolved geopolitical tensions also put a damper on the enthusiasm of many companies to invest there. The region's greatest potential may be as a transshipment point for commerce in the region rather than as a major manufacturing hub, in any event. But whatever its prospects, recent times have seen a decline in South Korean ventures in the North and continued frustrations on the part of would-be foreign investors with political and economic conditions in the region and the country as a whole.

As for tourism, North Korea has succeeded in convincing South Koreans to pay substantial fees of several hundred dollars a person for the opportunity to visit certain important sites. However, much of the cash appears to have wound up in the hands of the regime for its own uses and not devoted to nationwide development efforts. This is a major problem with cash transfers to North Korea, be they from aid or business deals or weapons buyouts. We return to this issue below.

Finally, North Korea liberalized prices and raised wages in 2002 in much of the country. Unfortunately, given the DPRK's distorted industrial production base, poor trade balance, and limited natural resources, liberalization did not quickly produce positive results. Indeed, severe inflation has become a problem of late, and some industries are reportedly not able to pay workers the higher wages that had been promised.

PROSPECTS FOR RECOVERY AND REFORM TODAY

Against this backdrop, what can be concluded about the chances for successful North Korean reform, should the regime really be willing to make a go at a serious plan?

First, the North Korean workforce would seem to have the potential to make this type of plan work. Certainly its South Korean counterpart has demonstrated that Korean culture, with its emphases on hard work and group effort, is capable of remarkable things. In addition, North Korea's population is reasonably well educated, even if it has been fed far too heavy a dose of propaganda in schools for far too long and cut off from the ways of the outside world as well. There would certainly be a necessary transition period, but on balance North Korea's human raw materials are impressive.

Second, China's experience provides a very important model for North Korea, as DPRK leaders have apparently recognized on their occasional trips to China's economic zones over the years. The fact that the PRC could take an economy that Mao had largely destroyed and, without losing power, turn it into one of the fastest growing in the world must hold enormous appeal for the DPRK. Vietnam's experiences are encouraging as well.

There are, to be sure, reasons why reform could be harder in North Korea than in China (or even Vietnam). China's reforms began only after Mao had departed the scene, whereas Kim still rules the DPRK. China was able to accomplish many of its reforms by making agriculture more efficient, taking workers off the land and putting them into industrial activity. North Korea already has a large fraction of its workers in industry, however, and a relatively modest fraction in agriculture, so it would have to work harder.

Specifically, it would have to find ways to take workers from unproductive industry and from the military to devote to more productive nonagricultural enterprises. This is one of the chief reasons we focus so intently in this book on downsizing North Korea's armed forces: The DPRK will need its youngest, strongest workers for more important tasks in the years ahead. Finally, China is not a perfect model. It still faces major economic problems—weak state-owned industries, a fragile financial system, excessive production of unneeded and unwanted goods that falsely inflates GDP growth figures, and huge income disparities from region to region. That said, North Korea would do very well to have China's problems.

The most thorough public study of North Korea's economy, while sober on the likelihood that North Korean leaders will strongly support reform, is very positive on economic grounds about what reform could accomplish. In his book *Avoiding the Apocalypse,* Marcus Noland shows that North Korean real GDP might be expected to grow anywhere from 60 to almost 100 percent under various assumptions about reform (see Figure 5.1). As he puts it, "There are solutions to North Korea's economic problems. . . . The real issue is whether reform would be compatible with the continued existence of the Kim Jong Il regime. . . ." On the latter point, Noland is agnostic, as are we. But that is no argu-

FIGURE 5.1 POSSIBLE NORTH KOREAN REFORM PATHS

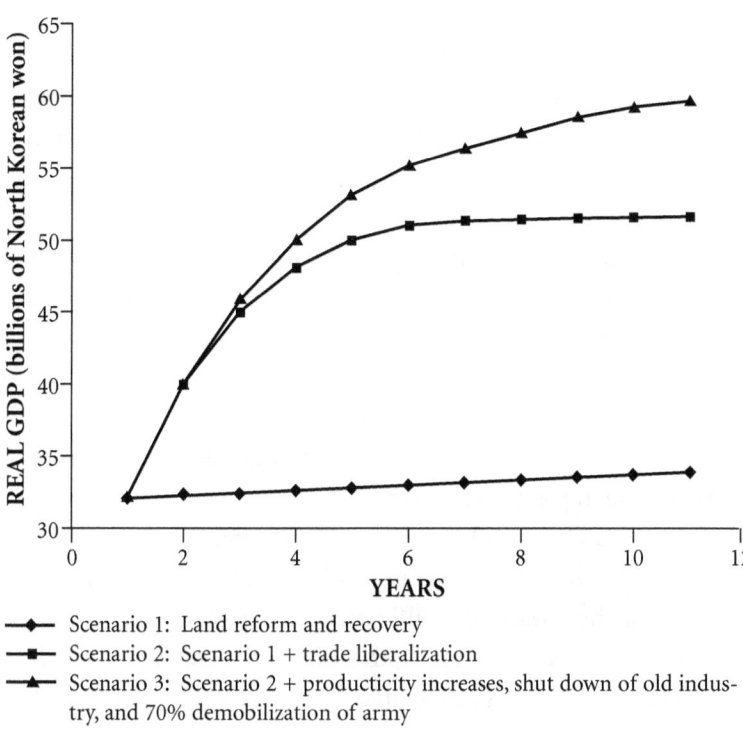

- Scenario 1: Land reform and recovery
- Scenario 2: Scenario 1 + trade liberalization
- Scenario 3: Scenario 2 + producticity increases, shut down of old industry, and 70% demobilization of army

Source: Based on Marcus Noland, *Avoiding the Apocalypse: The Future of the Two Koreas* (Washington D.C.: Institute for International Economics, 2000), p. 93

ment against proposing the idea of reform and a grand bargain to Pyongyang and trying to negotiate an acceptable arrangement.

Other economic studies reach similar conclusions. The combination of reforms, aid, trade liberalization, and private investment offers considerable promise to the DPRK, even within a system of autocratic governance—if its leaders are seriously prepared to embark on such a course. Certainly many scholars and officials in Northeast Asia have concluded that North Korea has little choice but to try such reforms; one can only hope leaders in Pyongyang get the message and act upon it.

THE ROLE OF EXTERNAL AID IN REFORM

Given this context—a North Korean regime apparently interested in economic reform but also extremely unsure of how to make it work while also maintaining political control—how can outside powers play a constructive role?

The first point to make is that there are clearly no guarantees for success here. But the potential negative aspects of trying seem few. The requisite resource levels are extremely modest in comparison with the security implications for the United States and the region of the likely alternatives—a collapsing North Korea, a North Korea willing to sell fissile materials abroad, or war on the peninsula. If the effort at reform succeeds, it will gradually change the nature of North Korean society, making life better for North Korean citizens while forcing DPRK leaders to modify at least some of their ways. If it ultimately fails, we will be no worse off than we would have been otherwise, especially since the North Korean nuclear program would have been capped in the interim period in any event. (The United States and its partners cannot seriously be expected to support such an economic reform plan unless North Korea ceases its nuclear activities first, as discussed in Chapter 3.)

In addition, aid would not be provided in a lump sum. It would be disbursed over time. There would be a strong presumption that it would be continued from year to year, even in the event of setbacks in the North Korean economic reform process. But outside countries would retain an unspoken leverage over Pyongyang to influence it to continue its compliance with the grand bargain and gradually expand economic reforms. International financial institutions such as the World Bank could play a useful role here, not only by providing some of the needed resources but by monitoring North Korean efforts to make proper use of them.

In the first couple of years, the aid program would focus on improvements to infrastructure, largely in special economic zones. Implementation of such projects should be relatively straightforward, assuming all parties desire it. However, broadening the aid effort to the national level will require North Korea to accept a greater international presence on its territory and to accept more changes to its nationwide educational, agricultural, public works, and health care sectors.

The DPRK's fears can be mitigated to some extent by asking China to provide most of the on-the-ground development experts (though funding would of course come in large measure from Japan, South Korea, and the United States). In addition, successful efforts in the special economic zones may by then have increased North Korea's confidence in the desirability of the package deal. Still, this will admittedly be a difficult path for North Korea to take and will require serious diplomatic work in the implementation phase even after the basic bargain is struck.

But on balance, there are reasons for optimism. There are analogous models for development programs that offer promise in this context, such as the previous experiences of China and Vietnam. A combination of China-style economic reforms with substantial external assistance for infrastructure development and programs in areas such as agriculture, health, and education would build on ideas that have worked in the past, albeit not in these exact circumstances.

Above and beyond humanitarian relief and energy and arms control assistance, North Korea will probably need an average of $2 billion a year for a decade to embark on the path of economic recovery. In per capita terms, this amount of money is commensurate with the amounts of aid given to other countries that became development success stories in the past, such as Taiwan and the ROK—roughly $50 to $75 per capita per year. There are models for providing even more funding; for example, in the Marshall Plan, annual per capita funding was generally over $100, and in recent aid programs in the Balkans and in the Palestinian territories it has reached or exceeded $200. But the Marshall Plan was designed largely to rebuild infrastructure that had already once existed, in societies that knew how to make productive use of large-scale investments, and the Balkan and Palestinian programs have been somewhat wasteful and not always impressive in their effectiveness.

Thus, the $2-billion-per-year level (expressed in constant 2003 dollars) seems about right, provided that it is sustained at least a decade and accompanied by proper technical advice. As a matter of practice, as noted, funding would focus first on large-scale infrastructure in certain economic development zones, following the Chinese model—also a model that North Korean leaders have shown some interest in to date. It could then gradually spread out over the country to develop the national infrastructure and provide educational, health, and agricultural services to most North Korean citizens.

These amounts of aid are far less than the tens of billions of dollars a year Germany spent in quickly bringing East Germany up to western economic levels after their reunification. But Germany's basic strategy was to elevate East German living standards immediately through direct transfers to individuals. This model is simply too expensive. Even in Germany, it failed to alleviate high unemployment in the former communist economy. It does not seem a particularly appropriate model for Korea—especially because in the Korean context, the two countries would remain separate and populations would not relocate. To put it differently, in Korea, the aid effort would amount not to a welfare program but to a development strategy. The goal would not be to artificially inflate incomes in North Korea; it would be to build infrastructure, improve the education and health of the workforce, and thus to begin to attract private capital. Even in the best case, only over a good deal of time would North Korean living standards approach those of the South.

There is good reason to think that Japan might provide much of the needed external assistance as a form of compensation for its colonial occupation of Korea in the first half of the twentieth century. Japan provided a total of $500 million in funds to the ROK in the 1960s; adjusting that number upward to account for inflation and economic growth would lead to figures in the range of $5 billion to $10 billion.

Although Japan would likely provide much of the aid under this proposal, other outside assistance would be critical. As an expression of its good faith and its commitment to improving relations, the United States would have to go beyond its current humanitarian aid, also lifting all trade sanctions and providing additional funds for development of North Korea's infrastructure as well as other aid initiatives. Its annual aid to North Korea for development purposes might then reach $300 million a year, roughly speaking. Adding in humanitarian and fuel supplies at the level of recent years would bring the total to about $500 million annually. Such an aid level would remain well below the assistance provided to Israel and Egypt, of course. But it would be roughly comparable to the next tier of top recipients of U.S. assistance—Jordan (slated to receive $460 million in the 2004 budget request), Afghanistan ($550 million), Pakistan ($395 million), and Colombia ($575 million). The United States, one of the least generous aid providers among the major industrial economies in terms of percentage of national wealth, can certainly afford this expansion in aid to North Korea.

South Korea and China would clearly be critical players as well. They have each been providing greater aid to North Korea than has the United States of late. South Korea, which has largely recovered from the 1997 financial crisis, would presumably be in a position to provide much more assistance under this type of radical overhaul in North-South relations. But its private sector would be the real growth engine, investing in North Korea on a major scale over time. Aid would serve largely to lay the economic groundwork for this private investment. China's role would be critical for helping DPRK leaders learn how to create a mixed economy that will retain command features in some areas but enterprise zones in others and that will gradually carry out price liberalization nationwide.

CONCLUSION

The prospects for this aid effort are, as noted, unclear. But if North Korea wants to make it work, the idea has a very good chance of gradually succeeding. That is particularly true if expectations are reasonable—North Korea need not become another South Korea, or even another China, anytime soon. Vietnam might be a better near-term standard. As first priorities, North Korea simply needs to fix its economy enough to take care of the basic survival needs of its people, get out of its habit of trying to use dangerous weapons programs to extort hard currency, and stop counterfeiting and drug running. More broadly, it must accept a vision for constructive engagement with the international community. By convincing Pyongyang to do so, the United States and its partners can use aid to achieve much better national security.

Moreover, there are benefits to making this type of effort that go beyond its immediate prospects for economic success. By uniting the major powers of Northeast Asia into pursuit of a single vision for the Korean peninsula, it will provide a common road map to guide the interactions of Washington, Seoul, Tokyo, and Beijing. These four capitals have had a difficult time uniting around any Korea policy, and their confusion and open dissension hurt the prospects for collaboration. They also make it exceedingly difficult to coordinate policy in the event that things go badly wrong and more dire measures need to be considered.

A combination of conventional force reductions and major economic reform initiatives strikes many observers as too much to add to the North Korea agenda. But a more limited form of engagement, despite some earlier successes, has since largely failed. Focusing on North Korea's nuclear program and missile programs also holds little appeal for President Bush, who feels he is being blackmailed by Pyongyang's words and deeds in these areas. Moreover, without a broader reform effort, North Korea will remain a broken economy and its leaders will almost surely continue to resort to extortion in the future, given their stark lack of alternatives for gaining hard currency. President Bush's initial instincts to add tough demands on conventional forces to the negotiating agenda with North Korea were correct; paradoxically, so are President Roh's instincts about needing to offer Pyongyang more incentives and more encouragement. It is now time to get serious about deciding how to combine these seemingly disparate goals into a proposal for a grand bargain with North Korea.

CHAPTER
6
A NEW ALLIANCE

No book like this, which has spelled out a detailed road map and vision for improving relations with the DPRK, would be complete without offering a vision for the long-term relationship between the United States and the Republic of Korea. Whether the ROK remains a country of its current size, joins in a confederation of some type with a reforming and demilitarizing North Korea, or absorbs the DPRK, the question is important.

It is very important for Koreans, clearly, since the ROK alliance with the United States is that country's only formal security relationship and has a great bearing on the ROK's role in the region. It is only slightly less important for the United States, since it will say much about the nature of the U.S. security role in Northeast Asia after the intra-Korean confrontation is defused, which it will be someday, one way or another.

Our principal argument is that the U.S.-ROK alliance will make sense even in the aftermath of an acute North Korean threat. That alliance need not include large numbers of American forces on Korean soil, but it would be strongest and most useful to both parties if it included at least some. It could consist of roughly 10,000 to 30,000 troops—enough to include militarily significant units but with considerable flexibility as to their exact size and disposition. The forces, like the U.S.-ROK security alliance more broadly, would be oriented toward a broad range of security tasks, including nontraditional missions such as counterterrorism and peace operations.

Defense against a hypothetical large-scale Chinese attack would not be seen as a pressing mission for such a forward posture. But defenses against more limited Chinese attacks (for example, over disputed resources located where "exclusive" economic zones overlap) might be, even if no conflict with the PRC were

TABLE 6.1 NUMBER OF US TROOPS BASED IN FOREIGN COUNTRIES(As of September 30, 2002)

Country and Region	Number
Europe	
Belgium	1,458
Bosnia and Herzegovina	3,082
Germany	68,701
Iceland	1,665
Italy	12,466
Serbia (includes Kosovo)	2,804

Spain	2,621
Turkey	1,587
United Kingdom	10,258
Afloat	5,003
Other Europe	2,903
__Total Europe (not including former Soviet Union)	112,548
__Total former Soviet Union	129
East Asia and Pacific	
Japan	41,848
Korea, Republic of	37,743
Afloat	16,090
Other East Asia and Pacific	704
__Total East Asia and Pacific	96,385
North Africa, Near East, South Asia	
Bahrain	1,560
Other North Africa, Near East, South Asia	3,260
__Total North Africa, Near East, South Asia	4,820
Total Sub-Saharan Africa	263
Total Western Hemisphere	1,913
Undistributed	14,426
__Total Foreign Countries	230,484

Source: Department of Defense, Washington Headquarters Services, Directorate for Information Operations and Reports, *Active Duty Military Personnel Strengths by Regional Area and by Country (309a)*, September 30, 2003, (http://web1.whs.osd.mil/mmid/m05/hst0902.pdf [May 21, 2003]).

Note: Only countries with more than 1,000 troops listed individually. Other troops in that region are accounted for in the "other" row.

The total break down according to service is: Army, 104,140; Air Force, 53,340; Navy, 40,491; Marine Corps, 32,513.

TABLE 6.2 NUMBER OF U.S. TROOPS IN THE ASIA PACIFIC REGION (as of September 30, 2002)

Area of Deployment	Total	Air Force	Army	Marine Corps	Navy
U.S. Territories					
Alaska	15,906	9,136	6,630	41	99
Hawaii	34,608	4,289	15,985	5,680	8,654
Guam	3,149	1,433	34	91	1,591
East Asia and Pacific					
Japan	41,848	13,099	1,856	19,217	7,676
Korea, Republic of	37,743	8,719	28,527	155	342
Afloat	16,090	0	0	2,288	13,802

Source: Department of Defense, Washington Headquarters Services, Directorate for Information Operations and Reports, *Active Duty Military Personnel Strengths by Regional Area and by Country (309a)*, September 30, 2003, (http://web1.whs.osd.mil/mmid/m05/hst0902.pdf [May 21, 2003]).

Note: There are less than 1,000 troops dispersed in other countries throughout the region.

The total size of the Pacific Fleet, including in U.S. waters, is 140,400. International Institute for Strategic Studies (IISS), *The Military Balance: 2002/2003* (London: Oxford University Press, 2002), p. 25.

expected, as an insurance policy. The U.S. presence would ideally consist of fewer Army forces than are based in South Korea today but more Marines and Navy sailors.

Clearly, the idea of a long-term U.S.-ROK alliance makes sense only if the South Korean people support it. Given the strategic implications and diplomatic sensitivity of any such alliance, and its potential impact on Korean-Chinese relations in particular, it would be inappropriate for Americans to assume that Koreans will favor such a formal security partnership in the future.

Were American officials to insist on it too strongly, moreover, they could hurt their own case. If the United States were seen as wanting a continued alliance too much, Beijing might see the idea as an attempt at encirclement of China, and many Koreans might agree with that assessment. Koreans could also have a nationalistic reaction, feeling that they were being asked to again act as the junior partner in a security alliance that no longer truly served their interests. We make a case for a continuation of the alliance in this chapter, and believe that American and Korean officials should make the case as well. But if the Korean people wind up firmly against the idea, it would be better to end the alliance—or change it to something very different—than to try to strongarm the ROK into retaining it.

Assuming, however, that the governments in Seoul and Washington do favor keeping the alliance even after reunification or radical demilitarization of the peninsula, they should start laying the political and diplomatic groundwork—with their own legislatures and publics on the one hand and other countries in Northeast Asia on the other.

The views of China should be solicited and considered, but only up to a point: If they see continued stationing of American forces in Korea to be in their fundamental interest, Korea and the United States should stand firm. They should explain why they think it would serve China's interests too, possibly helping to serve as a foundation for a broader regional collective security arrangement that could eventually include the PRC if circumstances warranted it. But they should also be prepared to sustain the U.S. presence unapologetically, regardless of the reception the idea engendered in Beijing.

The stakes involved in this issue are very high. South Korea, a relatively small country geographically, is nevertheless the third largest economy in Asia. Perhaps even more important, it is the only focal point in Northeast Asia where all large regional countries have a keen interest in the prevailing local balance of power.

The two specific questions addressed in this chapter are as follows: What would be the overarching purposes of the U.S.-ROK alliance, and the associated American military presence on the peninsula, after an end to the ROK-DPRK conflict? In addition, what specific types and numbers of U.S. forces would best serve those purposes?

PURPOSES OF U.S. FORCES IN KOREA AFTER REUNIFICATION

A U.S. military presence on a reunified Korean peninsula could, as an insurance policy, help deter any untoward Chinese actions against Korea and damp tensions in the Japan-Korea relationship. More concretely, it would provide a regional hub for military activities against other threats, such as pirates, terrorists, and possible instability in the waterways of Southeast Asia.

In each case, stationing U.S. forces in Korea would produce a much more credible form of security commitment than simply retaining a formal alliance agreement between the two countries. Only the presence of U.S. forces would guarantee that Americans would be immediately involved in any conflict an outside country might wage against the Republic of Korea; only such a presence would demonstrate beyond a reasonable doubt the seriousness and military readiness of the alliance.

Seoul would retain the right to veto U.S. use of bases on its territory for operations that did not serve ROK objectives. Many European allies have done so over the years—in cases such as the 1973 Mideast war (when U.S. aircraft were not allowed to land anywhere except Portugal to refuel) and the 1986 bombing of Libya (when France denied the United States aerial overflight rights). Saudi Arabia and Turkey have also been restrictive about which types of military operations could be conducted from their territories, most notably in regard to combat operations over Iraq. Washington does not always appreciate such allied resistance, of course. But for countries worried about being linked too closely to American action abroad, it provides a useful form of checks and balances—and foreign policy independence.

As for the first above issue, a major overland Chinese threat to Korea appears quite improbable. To the extent it causes other countries in the region concern in the future, China seems less likely to put direct military pressure on Korea—a longstanding independent country with a clear ethnic, linguistic, and cultural identity that makes it a poor candidate for invasion—than to use force to gain resources or territory it considers its own. Taiwan and the South China Sea are the most notable examples of where China might use force, though disputes over overlapping economic zones at sea could also arise with Korea and Japan.

In other words, to the extent it may pose a threat to its neighbors, China seems more likely to act as an irredentist power seeking to back up claims to specific localized regions, most of them at sea, than to pursue empire or regional hegemony. This conclusion is reinforced by the fact that China has resolved a number of territorial disputes with neighbors and demilitarized several borders in recent years.

However, international relations being what they are, it is not implausible that someday China could appear seriously threatening to Korea's core interests. Having U.S. forces in Korea would give future Chinese leaders who might contemplate making any such threats further reason for pause. It is not so much that a small U.S. presence in Korea, together with ROK forces, could confidently stop any hypothetical Chinese military action. But they could perhaps slow it. In addition, the presence of U.S. forces would immediately implicate the United States in any such conflict, with the associated near certainty that American military reinforcements would subsequently be deployed. That fact could strengthen deterrence.

Knowing in advance that this dynamic might operate, Korean leaders would probably be less inclined to develop a nuclear arsenal as a hedge against Chinese pressure. If a continued U.S. presence in Korea reduced the prospects of nuclear proliferation in the region, that in itself would be a very important accomplishment.

A U.S. force presence in Korea would also be beneficial for Japanese–South Korean relations. First, it could reassure the Koreans, who would not have to wonder if they were a second-class ally of the United States in the event of a major dispute with Japan over disputed territories or maritime resources. Second, the Japanese government might also prefer this arrangement. With U.S. military facilities also in Korea, Japan would avoid becoming singularized as the only country in the region hosting U.S. forces, and Tokyo would probably find it easier to sustain the support of the Japanese people for the security alliance.

Both Japan and Korea are small, mountainous, and heavily populated countries where land, airspace, ports, and other requirements for military bases and operations are at a premium. Also, although both countries recognize the importance of having a deterrent in place against instability in the region, both are also appropriately sensitive to the need to cultivate good relations with their neighbors and avoid creating the perception that they are trying to contain China or any other specific country. Under these circumstances, asking either country to provide the United States with military bases without the other's also doing so seems imprudent.

Also, keeping forces in the two countries would help Washington retain influence with both Korea and Japan, similarly to how the United States has ensured its influence with even more quarrelsome neighbors, such as Greece and Turkey or Israel and Egypt, by forging close military relations with both sides. In this way, the United States could also help facilitate tightening of a trilateral network of military officers and officials—complementing other steps to introduce confidence-building measures and expand military-to-military exchanges in the region.

So much for possible threats. More positively, keeping U.S. forces in Korea actually could enrich the Asia-Pacific community and help it achieve further stability in the future. To begin with, strong ties among countries with much different cultures and histories help bind the globe together. The strong trans-Pacific alliances the United States maintains with Japan and Korea refute those who anticipate a dangerous clash of civilizations.

The U.S.-Japan and U.S.-Korea security relationships are the principal intercultural and interethnic security unions in the world today. If they are increasingly integrated, moreover, they can help create a stronger security network in the region, beginning with better ties between Seoul and Tokyo. Having U.S. forces in both Japan and the ROK should facilitate this relationship by ensuring strong American influence with both Northeast Asian countries.

Second, and more concretely, strong security structures appear to be very good mechanisms for keeping the peace. As history shows, they are much better than a system of numerous independent states operating in an anarchical international environment. They are also better than paper treaties and last-minute public commitments of security assistance in the event of major crisis or conflict, like those issued unsuccessfully in Europe before the world wars.

A number of Koreans share this view, seeing value in the U.S.-ROK alliance well beyond its immediate benefits for stability on the peninsula. Some condition their support on Chinese acquiescence to the idea, or at least a major effort by Seoul and Washington to gain such acquiescence; others support it unconditionally. It is too soon to know how the Korean public will feel if and when the Korean confrontation is over and the traditional main purpose of the formal security partnership is thus eliminated. But many Korean scholars and officials are already on record in support of a continuation of the alliance.

All countries in the Asia-Pacific region appear genuinely to desire a stable regional setting. If any specific disagreements lead to armed conflict, as many do acknowledge is a possibility, countries in the region would like to limit those disputes to localized areas and defuse them as quickly as possible. Therefore, the stabilizing benefit of a strong regional security architecture should offer a certain reassurance throughout the region.

Some have argued against a long-term U.S.-Korea alliance on the grounds that, among other consequences, it could cause problems in the U.S.-China relationship by making China feel that the alliance was directed against it. But alliance enlargement has worked reasonably well in Europe, and if done well in Asia, it might succeed there too. Some People's Liberation Army military officers have suggested that if a future U.S. military presence in a reunified Korea were kept distant from Chinese borders and clearly not oriented toward China, the PRC might be able to tolerate it. Such a positive result might be particularly likely if U.S.-China relations were good at the time of the change.

Keeping the bilateral alliances intact would hold even more appeal if the United States and its current alliance partners envisioned a formal security community that could eventually include countries like China should those countries be inclined to participate—and should their security behavior prove sufficiently cooperative. Leaders in Seoul, Tokyo, and Washington should tell Beijing that they do not rule out an alliance with China once it satisfies conditions similar to those demanded of new NATO members—civilian control of the military, agreement not to settle disputes with neighbors by force, and democratic and economic reforms.

To prove their seriousness, and to address other kinds of security threats besides the prospect of traditional war, the United States, Japan, and Korea could increase collaboration on certain security tasks among themselves. They could also do so in conjunction with neutral states in the region such as Russia and China (as well as several Southeast Asian countries, some of them U.S. allies and some not). These types of efforts could cover everything from training for peacekeeping and humanitarian relief to search-and-rescue exercises to counterpiracy and counterdrug operations to joint preparations for counterterrorist operations.

Some such activity is already under way, in fact. The United States has conducted peacekeeping exercises with Russia and search-and-rescue exercises with Chinese participation; Japan has conducted search-and-rescue exercises with Russia and joined with South Korea to deliver humanitarian assistance. But much, much more needs to be done.

Some would agree with the need for multilateralism but argue for looser and more inclusive structures, perhaps patterned after the Organization for Security and Cooperation in Europe (OSCE), as well as a dissolution of formal alliances in the region. But hinging everything on relatively weak institutions, confidence-building measures, and security dialogues also seems unwise. Such measures and dialogues, though very worthwhile, are better for preserving a widely endorsed status quo than for solving fundamental disputes between countries. They do not reflect a solemn commitment by countries to defend each other's security the way that formal alliances do. Since some fairly fundamental issues still remain to be addressed in the Asia-Pacific region and the status quo is not universally accepted, much more than confidence-building measures and dialogues will continue to be needed to assure stability.

Because the U.S.-Japan and U.S.-Korea alliances have considerable credibility at this point in history, it makes sense to keep them, as most countries in the Asia-Pacific region recognize. Alliances between various Asian powers are by no means impossible, but they do not appear imminent given the still fragile relations between great Asian powers such as Japan, China, and Korea.

Throwing away what works now in the hope that something new can be built from scratch seems imprudent. That approach underrates the value of working military alliances, which help ensure high and uniform standards in military equipment and training. It is hard enough for one country to achieve good military readiness—witness the difficulties of the U.S. military after Vietnam, most memorably exemplified in the failed hostage rescue mission in Iran. Getting coalitions to a high state of joint readiness is remarkably difficult and cannot be done at the last minute through some improvised process; strong working alliances are needed.

A country like China that might tend to be worried about a continuation of the U.S.-ROK alliance, just as it has been concerned recently about revisions to the U.S.-Japan Defense Cooperation Guidelines, should feel reassured by one other point. As noted, U.S. allies would retain the right to tell Washington no in any specific crisis. The fact that U.S. forces would have peacetime access to bases on an ally's territory does not generally imply that they would have carte blanche to use those facilities in a crisis or war.

This argument is not to imply that Americans are generally trigger-happy and in need of frequent restraint from allies. Countries in the region should remember the American public's general aversion to combat casualties and its preference to avoid excessive foreign entanglements. Even with its new emphasis on preemption, the Bush administration has made efforts to argue that it will potentially apply only to a modest number of cases—

generally those involving terrorists and states sponsoring or aiding terrorists or pursuing weapons of mass destruction.

In addition, Korean and American views on the use of force share much in common after several decades of close collaboration. Therefore, China should not expect that Korea actually would say no if the United States wished to use forces based on the peninsula—and Americans should not worry too much that its ally would prove undependable. But a natural system of checks and balances would operate nonetheless, providing at least some reassurance to all interested parties in the region.

OPTIONS FOR U.S. FORCES IN A REUNIFIED KOREA

To review briefly, at present, the United States bases about 38,000 troops in Korea. About 28,000 are Army soldiers, primarily from the Second Infantry Division. They are part of the so-called Eighth U.S. Army and boast modern equipment including Abrams tanks, Bradley fighting vehicles, Patriot air and missile defense systems, multiple launch rocket system artillery, and Apache helicopters.

These Army forces are currently based primarily near the DMZ, at Camp Red Cloud and other facilities, though under a recently approved U.S.-ROK plan many are to be gradually moved southward in coming years. This planned change reflects the improved defensive capabilities of the ROK military. It is also motivated by the desirability of placing American forces in a better position from which to organize and begin a counteroffensive in the event of future conflict on the peninsula. Other elements of the plan would move the large U.S. military headquarters in downtown Seoul out of that crowded city and return the valuable real estate to use by the ROK.

Most of the 10,000 remaining South Korea–based U.S. troops are Air Force personnel, making up the Seventh Air Force, which flies roughly 90 combat aircraft (mostly F-16 multipurpose jets). The fighters are distributed between Osan, just to the south of Seoul, and Kunsan in the southern half of South Korea on the western coast. Some 3,000 American civilians and 10,000 Koreans also work for the U.S. armed forces in Korea. Additional supplies for U.S. forces, such as more tanks, are also stored there.

What U.S. units should be deployed in Korea after reunification? Three options are discussed below. To the extent that China was seen as a major potential overland threat to Korea, a U.S. force posture not unlike the current one—though perhaps even larger—might be retained. If such a Chinese overland threat were considered less worrisome than broader security challenges in the region's maritime zones, as we argue is the case, the U.S. Army would be less important than the Air Force and Navy.

Or, as a third option, a balanced approach might be taken—less Army-centric than the current U.S. force posture but including significant ground force elements nonetheless. That approach would combine the missions of the second option mentioned above, for which Air Force and Navy assets would be key, with peacekeeping, antiterrorist strikes, maintenance of missile defense capabilities, and other possible missions that also place a premium on the Army and/or the Marine Corps. Each of these ideas is developed at greater length below.

Option I: Focus on the Territorial Defense of Korea

Consider the daunting scenario of an overland attack by China. Korea and the United States could mount a forward defense at the

A New Alliance

Yalu River (assuming that Korean reunification had occurred by then). Perhaps more likely, however, would be an initial strategy to consolidate defenses around Seoul and other major cities (the large majority of which will surely remain in the southern half of the peninsula for many years after reunification). That would allow protracted air attacks, not unlike those in the Iraq wars, against Chinese forces' logistics lines.

Given the degree of the assumed threat, it would make sense to keep a U.S. troop presence at least as large as today's. By retaining all U.S. ground forces in Korea or even building them up, the United States and Korea would be sending a message that they remained vigilant to a possible attack against Korean territory. Symbolically, the United States would also be communicating to China that it considered its involvement in any future ground war on the peninsula every bit as inevitable as is the case today vis-a-vis the North Korean threat.

Militarily speaking, keeping the better part of a U.S. division and the Eighth Army still in Korea would also provide the basis for rapid and substantial reinforcement in the event of conflict, just as is the case today. Specifically, combining two full brigades with troops flying from the United States to man pre-positioned Army equipment stocks, together with the Twenty-fifth Infantry Division in Hawaii and Marine Corps equipment stationed on boats in Guam, the United States might be able to deploy nearly a Desert Shield equivalent of ground power to Korea within two weeks. It could have four to five divisions there within a month. (Desert Shield was the initial deployment, roughly 200,000 strong, to protect Saudi Arabia from any Iraqi attack in the fall of 1990.) Given the capabilities of Korean forces, that much rapid reinforcement might not be critically important. But the fact that the United States had the wherewithal to deliver it would reinforce deterrence by adding a second major pillar to a prompt alliance defense capability.

Before adopting this kind of option, Washington and Seoul would want to approach Beijing. Ideally, they would resolve whatever security problems made this option seem necessary in the first place. A U.S. force posture explicitly designed to deal with a possible Chinese attack would reflect—and likely serve to perpetuate as well—a most unfortunate great-power security relationship in Northeast Asia. It should be avoided if at all possible.

Even if it could not be avoided, the United States and the ROK would want to explore mutual reassurance measures with China, and perhaps arms control measures as well, to mitigate the dangers associated with these kinds of deployments and security postures. Force deployments could be limited near the border, for example, and hotlines could be set up to allow prompt resolution of any military tensions that might arise where the forces came closest to each other. But it is to be hoped that the kind of circumstances that would argue for adopting this option will not come to pass.

Option II: Focus on Maritime Interests

The rationale for worrying about such a major Chinese overland threat seems unpersuasive in the end, at least given recent trends in China-ROK and China-U.S. relations. Any major-power conflicts in the future East Asian setting seem more likely to involve limited stakes and probably competing claims to islands or seabed resources rather than cross-border aggression. For these reasons, the United States might serve Korea's and its own immediate interests better with mobile and deployable forces rather than with large Army units. A combination of Navy and Air Force units would be best suited to operations around sea lanes, small islands, oil rigs, and the like.

These types of units would also be most appropriate for addressing threats like piracy, which remains a problem in the region. Indeed, collaboratively addressing the piracy threat and preparing counterterrorist capabilities as well could provide a meaningful multilateral security mission for a wide range of Asia-Pacific countries. It could provide a first concrete step toward what might, in principle, eventually become a formalized regional security community that even involved the PRC. Taking this step could help prove to China the sincerity of the U.S., Japanese, and Korean position that their bilateral alliances might someday be broadened to a more inclusive regional security architecture.

Navy and Air Force projection forces would be best positioned in southern Korea. Using bases south of Seoul, and therefore far from the Yalu River, would have the added benefit of antagonizing China less than bases further north might.

China still might not like this option much better than Option I. Specifically, its leaders may agree that maritime disputes are the most likely type to erupt in the region, and that any steps taken to strengthen U.S. capabilities for handling them may therefore work against its interests. That does not mean that Seoul and Washington need to grant Beijing a veto over the future of their security relationship. The interests of the United States and its allies in the region—protection of borders, free trade, equitable exploitation of maritime resources—are legitimate and nonaggressive, and China should not have a veto over how they choose to defend them. That said, there is no particular reason to expect a fundamental clash of interests between Northeast Asian powers on these or other matters.

If U.S. forces in Korea were seen primarily for their relevance to Southeast Asian security, U.S. Navy units might take on greater desirability than U.S. Air Force units. It is true that aerial refueling can allow most land-based fighters and surveillance aircraft to operate at indefinite distances from home base. But a practical limit on difficult combat operations is generally one or at most two refuelings. Given pilot fatigue and other factors, it is generally impractical to conduct missions lasting more than several hours for small planes or roughly half a day for larger ones.

Air Force combat jets operating out of Korea would therefore be of limited use in places like the southern reaches of the South China Sea. However, enough potential danger zones are within tactical flying distance of southern South Korea—largely areas where maritime resources are disputed and areas where pirates, other criminals, or terrorists could operate—that a mix of Air Force and Navy assets seems most appropriate given the logic of this option.

Option III: Focus on Maritime Interests As Well As Collective Security

Finally, to the extent that U.S. forces in Korea were to be used for the above missions as well as in a gradually growing multilateral security community in the Asia-Pacific region, a wide range of forces would make sense. For example, unless basing were available in a place like Australia, some of the Marines now on Okinawa might be moved to Korea. They could conduct routine patrols and other special missions from there.

They could also train with Korean, Japanese, and perhaps someday also Russian and Chinese forces for peacekeeping and counterterrorist missions. Army forces might play a role in such joint training too; they have the advantage of sharing doctrine and basic operational concepts with other countries' militaries, which are generally dominated by ground forces. Moreover, the Army has gained considerable experience in counterterrorist operations in Afghanistan and elsewhere, so having a role in such efforts would be natural.

Since the Marines would be deploying by sea for their patrols, it would be best, though not essential, that they be based in southern Korea. Army forces, by contrast, might set up training grounds wherever space best permitted—though some basic access to ports and airfields would be needed, and close proximity to the Chinese border should probably be avoided. If Korea reunifies, such Army facilities might even be located slightly north of the current DMZ, where the economic stimulus of a military base might be most needed. The U.S. ground forces would not need to be particularly large or heavy; they might involve one of the new medium-weight Stryker brigades, or even a traditional light force.

CONCLUSION

Although short on military detail, the above options lay out the basic strategic issues confronting Korean and U.S. leaders as they contemplate life after the DPRK threat. That is something that they should begin to consider soon, and start talking about publicly once they reach agreement on the appropriate enduring roles and missions for U.S. forces.

This plan would not be ready for adoption even if the grand bargain we propose were accepted by all sides; it requires not just progress on arms control and economic reform but a true end to the intra-Korean conflict. But once the grand bargain begins to be put into effect, it could develop an increasing momentum, so it is important to be thinking in these terms even today. It is also important to debate what kind of long-term U.S. military presence in Korea might be desirable before arms control treaties that might constrain that presence are negotiated. Secretary of Defense Donald H. Rumsfeld seems to agree at least with this point, given his recent interest in rethinking the United States' global force posture and Korea basing options in particular.

The plausible range of U.S. forces in a peaceful or a reunified Korea could be wide. It could usefully involve as few as 10,000 to 15,000 troops. That would be enough for a major air or naval base and a small ground-force contingent usable for multilateral peacekeeping training and special operations like counterterrorism. But a more appealing number might be in the range of 20,000 to 30,000, given the wide range (and difficulty) of likely security tasks in the region.

Given the operational and fiscal benefits associated with basing forces in the region where they would most likely be used, such a deployment would actually save the American taxpayer money. That would be true even if South Korea did not expand its modest host-nation support payments by one dollar. Cost arguments should simply not play a major role in this debate.

If the resulting U.S. military presence in a reunified Korea consisted of 20,000 to 30,000 troops focused on a broad range of security tasks, the following force posture might make sense. One of the two brigades of the U.S. Army's Second Infantry Division now in Korea could return to the United States or be disbanded. The other could remain in Korea somewhere near its current location, perhaps even on territory now part of the DPRK (in the event of confederation or reunification), though not too close to China. Headquarters structures and pre-positioned military supplies now associated with the Eighth Army could be returned to the United States, on the presumption that major U.S. ground-combat reinforcements to the peninsula would not be needed. These changes in the Army would reduce U.S. uniformed strength in Korea by some 15,000 individuals.

U.S. airpower in Korea could remain at roughly the current strength. Alternatively, it might be scaled back slightly, with forces at Kunsan retained and those located further north at the Osan base reduced.

But more U.S. forces might be added in Korea: either some of the Marines now on Okinawa or a naval unit that might even include an aircraft carrier battle group. It would probably be preferable that bases be found in the Philippines, Australia, or elsewhere in Southeast Asia for such capabilities, in order to diversify the U.S. presence in the region and to station some assets near the volatile South China Sea area.

However, the United States may not be able to find a Southeast Asian host for such bases, so Korea may wind up being the best available place to put them. Adding some of the Okinawa Marines or an aircraft carrier battle group to the southern part of Korea would restore some of the numbers lost by reducing the Army presence on the peninsula and keep total U.S. forces in Korea nearer to the 30,000 level.

This balanced approach would combine elements of deterrence and reassurance—strengthening the will and capabilities of the United States and its close allies to resist the most likely types of aggression in the region while also collaborating with a wide array of countries on missions like counterterrorism, counterpiracy, and peacekeeping training.

Like the grand bargain we propose in this book, with its equal emphases on toughness and inducements toward North Korea, it takes the best of what both liberals and realists have to offer. It builds pragmatically toward a more inclusive multilateral security structure for the Asia-Pacific region while retaining proven bilateral arrangements in the meantime—just as the grand bargain would retain strong deterrence and place serious demands on North Korea while also offering hope, and assistance, for working toward a transformed relationship.

APPENDIX 1
MODELING AN ATTEMPTED NORTH KOREAN BREAKTHROUGH

The qualitative arguments advanced in Chapter 2 against the plausibility of a North Korean breakthrough, though powerful, are not quite conclusive. Most notably, they fail to integrate different factors and weapons into a single analytic framework or to examine the dynamics of actual battle. Structured quantitative and dynamic simulations of military scenarios can provide independent assessments of the state of the balance. (These methods are also used in Chapter 4.)

How to do this? The discipline of military science does not tell us how to reduce warfare to mathematical equations; there is no widely accepted methodology for doing so. Detailed Pentagon dynamic models of war, in addition to being classified, are often so complex and opaque that they obscure key assumptions built into them. Sometimes they rely on data characterizing various weapons and other defense systems that are not well known, particularly if the technologies have not been realistically tested. There are also reports from the chairman of the Joint Chiefs of Staff, the congressionally mandated National Defense Panel, and key former Pentagon civilian officials that existing models have major weaknesses—such as underestimation of the role of airpower. This conclusion is reinforced by the fact that the Pentagon was apparently less accurate in its predictions of 1991 U.S. Gulf War casualties than were most independent analysts using much simpler methodologies. The Pentagon's problems may persist.

Appendix 1

Two specific types of simpler dynamic simulations, the Kugler-Posen "attrition-FEBA expansion model" and the Epstein "adaptive dynamic model," appeared in the 1980s. They work best for modeling traditional tank warfare—not necessarily what would unfold in Korea. Yet any attempted North Korean invasion would require the DPRK to penetrate prepared defensive positions, so there are some analogies. A thorough analysis by Nick Beldecos and Eric Heginbotham using these two models predicted stalemate north of Seoul even under conservative assumptions about allied capabilities and performance. Since their work, the situation has improved further for the allies.

It would also be reassuring to reach these conclusions through yet another method. For example, consider the likely fate of North Korean armored vehicles and infantry soldiers as they moved southward into allied defenses in one attack sector of roughly 15 kilometers width in the western part of the peninsula. The below analysis is for today's balance; Chapter 4 considers the situation after 50 percent cuts.

The first question in such an analysis is, to what extent could North Korea build up forces in a major attack corridor without detection by allied intelligence prior to launching its breakthrough attempt? Once the buildup was detected, allied commanders would probably begin to counterconcentrate against it, so the maximum advantage for North Korea would accrue from a reinforcement operation that could be done secretly. Western overhead reconnaissance assets generally allow fairly accurate estimates of an adversary's strength to be made. In the 1991 Gulf War, for example, Coalition intelligence estimates of Iraqi equipment and manpower at certain points in the war were inaccurate by up to 25 percent or so, but not more than that. Still, it is best to err on the side of conservatism for the purposes of any such calculation, and assume that North Korea might be able to clandestinely establish a force concentration up to 50 percent greater than normal along part of the DMZ. Rather than base only 20 percent of its total firepower along a given axis, for example, it might instead have 30 percent there. A secret North Korean buildup of that magnitude would make for a total force in the attack sector of perhaps 1,000 tanks, 1,000 armored personnel carriers, a total of 3,000 pieces of large-bore artillery, and 500 recoilless rifles. Some 300,000 soldiers might man this equipment and also constitute infantry units with a total of 2,000 mortars, air-defense systems, antitank weapons, and automatic rifles.

Assuming no prior warning of this concentration of North Korean power, allied forces would presumably continue to deploy roughly 20 percent of their own ground equipment in the same corridor, distributed among three defensive lines and mechanized backup forces. The front line of defenses in the sector at issue would then include roughly 100 tanks, of which 50 might be the modern Type 88 or K-1, 150 armored personnel carriers, 400 artillery pieces, 500 mortars, about 10 antitank guns, recoilless rifles, air defenses, antitank weapons such as TOW-2As, and roughly 50,000 troops. Again as much manpower and equipment would back up these frontline forces in the second and third defensive "Hollingsworth lines" combined. Mechanized ROK units and the U.S. Second Infantry Division could move up the corridor once the intensity of the breakthrough attempt was recognized, and airpower could be concentrated there too, but these forces are not assumed to take part in the initial engagement modeled below.

The typical forward North Korean unit would need to traverse roughly 5 to 20 kilometers of terrain to reach the first line of allied defenses. Most movement by DPRK tanks and other armored vehicles would need to take place off roads (possible only in midwinter conditions in most areas). That is because highway bridges

Appendix 1

would be destroyed, artillery barrages would be targeted heavily on roads, explosive charges would be detonated to provoke rock slides in places where roads are bordered by cliffs, and carpet bombing would be conducted from aircraft onto roads. Under such off-road circumstances, North Korean vehicles would not be able to move very fast. Given that the fastest advances in history against poor defenses have only been about 20 kilometers per day, they would be unlikely to average more than five kilometers per hour as they neared allied positions. That is a dangerously slow pace for armored vehicles in hostile territory, operating without any real air cover and against dug-in defenders. Against targets moving at 10 kilometers per hour at 2,000 meters distance, for example, U.S. M60A3 tank rounds would expect kill probabilities of at least 0.2 per shot. That would increase to 0.5 per round if the incoming vehicles slowed, for example, to 2 kilometers per hour in places (or if they slowed somewhat less but were at closer range). In the Gulf War, U.S. tanks (primarily M1A1s) may have averaged kill probabilities as high as 0.8 per round, according to U.S. Army data. South Korean Type 88 tanks are of similar or better calibre than M60A3s and perhaps as good as M1A1s. The other principal South Korean tank, the M48, is not as good, although in its modern "A5" configuration it possesses the same gun as the M60A3. All of those tanks can perform well in poor weather conditions, even if their optical ranges are reduced. Modern TOW missiles are also quite effective; even older varieties would do well against the DPRK armored force.

Individual North Korean division-size formations would generally need to be spread out over a depth of at least 5 kilometers and a comparable width. The North Korean force considered here would be the equivalent of at least three armored divisions (and an additional equivalent number of infantry divisions). So even if this force spread itself across the full 15-kilometer attack corridor, it would remain at least 5 kilometers deep. Looked at another way, it would be "an hour" deep—at the assumed pace of 5 kilometers per hour, it would take sixty minutes to cross over a given line from start to finish. If each allied tank round or antitank weapon had a kill probability of just 0.25 against DPRK tanks, a very conservative estimate given the record of modern systems in the Gulf War, allied forces could sustain several times the rate of fire needed to take three shots at each North Korean armored vehicle, reducing its survival probability to less than 50 percent. And this calculation does not even count other weaponry, such as TOW-2A missiles, heavy machine guns, airpower, or mechanized reinforcements.

The above discussion shows why a traditional armored attack by North Korea would be so straightforward to defeat. But what if its armor were reserved as an exploitation force only, and the initial North Korean attack consisted of massive artillery barrages followed by a huge infantry assault? In fact, much of the above analysis and modeling would still be relevant, but it still is of interest to try to gauge the dynamics of such an extensive preparatory artillery bombardment nonetheless.

First, consider just how vulnerable DPRK soldiers on foot or in jeeps or trucks would be against allied artillery. As noted, South Korea would have about 2,000 mortars and artillery pieces in the front lines of the sector at issue. The lethal radii of mortars and artillery are at least 10 to 20 meters against exposed humans (though just 1 to 3 meters against dug-in positions or armored vehicles like those the allies would benefit from). The sheer density of artillery fire that those 2,000 tubes could produce is staggering. Across the 15-kilometer front, they could essentially maintain a continuous line of lethal fire just to their north. Although they would probably not operate this way, they could theoretically barrage a roughly 100-meter-wide swatch of land across the entire

Appendix 1

front once per sixty seconds. This calculation does not even include the additional effects of allied machine guns and other automatic weapons, which could be almost as deadly themselves. For their part, South Korean troops would generally not be vulnerable to such small-arms fire unless their bunkers were directly approached and penetrated. But North Korean troops would be highly vulnerable, day or night, to automatic weapons in the final 200 to 300 meters of their assaults of a given defensive line.

So to stand any chance of success, North Korea would have to first cause massive losses in allied defensive lines with preparatory artillery bombardments. The above calculation suggests, in fact, that it would have to cause allied losses in excess of 50 percent to give its own soldiers a remote chance of surviving transit through perhaps the most dangerous swath of land in the world. It is very unlikely that it could do so. In this dueling, North Korean tubes would be vulnerable to allied fire guided by counterartillery radar of a type the DPRK does not possess. Instead, it must rely on forward spotters—special forces who would quietly approach South Korean lines and estimate the position of artillery based on sight and sound. Unclassified data permitting precise calculations are unfortunately not available, but allied artillery could easily be three to five times more accurate and at least five times more lethal (even allowing for the hardness of many North Korean artillery shelters) than the more numerous DPRK tubes. Achieving a five-to-one or greater advantage in the artillery duel would more than compensate for the allies' numerical artillery disadvantage in the attempted breakthrough sector. The tables could turn even more in the allies' favor if they were able to jam radio transmissions between forward-deployed North Korean spotters and the artillery batteries those spotters were attempting to direct. Also, if the weather cleared at all, North Korean artillery and shelters could be attacked with high effectiveness by an allied air force that already knows most of their locations and could use laser-guided bombs against them. (Attacks using JDAMs could occur even in bad weather.)

CHEMICAL WEAPONS

North Korea's only real hope of overcoming this overwhelming array of handicaps is probably to employ weapons of mass destruction. Fortunately, when superimposed on a conventional balance tilted heavily to the allies' advantage, even such extreme measures are highly unlikely to swing the basic course of battle in the DPRK's favor.

The primary concern is chemical weapons. Any nuclear weapons the DPRK may have are unlikely to be of great benefit on the battlefield. If they exist, they are probably too big to be deliverable by missile, and too few in number to risk being carried in airplanes or armored vehicles where they could well be destroyed before reaching South Korean targets. A surprise North Korean nuclear strike that got through allied defenses might nevertheless be able to create a hole of perhaps one to two kilometers radius in South Korean defensive lines. But that would open up DPRK forces to the prospect of rapid U.S. nuclear retaliation, quite likely in the same sector where they had attacked South Korean defenses—probably denying North Korea the opportunity to exploit the gap that had been created. North Korean biological weapons would probably be too difficult to employ in a militarily effective manner that did not also threaten DPRK troops, and would in any case be of limited benefit in the early days of a surprise attack.

The chief effect of DPRK chemical attacks against fixed infrastructure such as ports and airfields would be to slow operations, necessitating that allied forces wear chemical gear and routinely

Appendix 1

decontaminate that gear as well as other equipment. For airpower, the tempo of operations might be cut in half by enemy use of chemical weapons (or even the threat of use). But a robust pace of aerial attack could continue nonetheless. Also, airbases in Japan would be out of range of almost all of North Korean missiles now deployed—and more Japanese airfields could now be available to the United States in light of the revised 1997 U.S.-Japan Defense Cooperation Guidelines. Any aircraft carriers on station in the region could also be operated out of range of missile attack (though that might not even be necessary, because North Korea would probably not be able to find and target them during hostilities). Transport ships coming from the United States with reinforcements and supplies could be slowed down by chemical weapons used against major South Korean ports. But the flow of supplies would not be stopped. Smaller vessels could use other ports that had not been contaminated. Also, the United States has several dozen ships with self-contained cranes and an increasing number with roll-on roll-off capabilities that minimize the need for shore equipment. They would make it possible to unload supplies even in ports where fixed shore equipment had been contaminated and not yet rendered usable.

Furthermore, each type of DPRK chemical attack would be difficult to execute properly. Planes conducting aerial attacks—the more effective way to deliver chemical munitions for maximum effect—would run a high risk of being shot down. Submarines with special forces aboard might be able to literally hand-carry chemical warheads into ports—but that would require penetrating militarily sensitive areas and approaching an unloading area undetected, hardly a trivial undertaking. Developing missile systems to disperse chemical or biological agents is technically challenging. Moreover, in the next few years, improvements in U.S. theater missile defense capabilities may reduce the odds that

DPRK missile warheads could reach fixed, well-defended sites. And even if future defenses achieve only modest reliability, present North Korean missiles have average miss distances or "circular errors probable" of about one kilometer—large enough that many ports or airfields might escape the lethal range of chemical warheads anyway.

In addition to attacks against major fixed assets, North Korea could conduct an artillery barrage with those weapons capable of reaching allied troops from their current positions. By using 100 tons of chemical agent, it could, under low-wind conditions, contaminate more than 200 square kilometers of territory—enough to blanket allied forces in the attempted breakthrough sector. Such an attack would probably use nonpersistent or "high-volatility" chemical agents. Use of persistent chemicals might cause very serious troubles to allied forces, who probably do not have adequate protection and decontamination equipment against such attacks. But it would also prevent North Koreans, who likely lack sufficient numbers of good protective suits and would have trouble covering several kilometers of land on foot while wearing them anyway, from exploiting any holes they created in a timely fashion.

Chemical attacks using nonpersistent or "high-volatility" agents would still be very dangerous. But they would generally require only that allied units use gas masks (not suits), and then only for a relatively short time. In addition, although wearing gas masks is always difficult, it is far less taxing when one is manning a fixed defensive position than when on the assault. In that regard, North Korean military leaders could face a difficult choice if attempting to profit from their gas attack promptly—either force their own troops to breathe heavily through gas masks while attacking, or delay the attack (and still leave them vulnerable to gas that might persist longer than expected and be carried in unexpected directions by the wind). South Korea could lose

Appendix 1

some troops in the very early stages of a chemical attack, if they were surprised. But most troops keep their masks nearby at all times. This assessment is reinforced by reference to other wars in which chemical weapons were generally not a dominant cause of casualties. For example, in the Iran-Iraq War they were responsible for less than 5 percent of all casualties. Even in World War I battles involving chemical weapons, when protective equipment was rudimentary, poison gas caused no more than one-third of all casualties and less than 10 percent of all deaths. And when used most lethally in the form of relatively persistent mustard gas, it was often unhelpful for offensive operations because it contaminated large areas of land for an extended period. Given that allied forces have several times the firepower needed to halt a North Korean attack, as demonstrated above, a degradation of several percent in their strength should not change the basic course of battle.

APPENDIX 2
AGREED FRAMEWORK BETWEEN THE UNITED STATES OF AMERICA AND THE DEMOCRATIC PEOPLE'S REPUBLIC OF KOREA

Geneva, October 21, 1994

Delegations of the governments of the United States of America (U.S.) and the Democratic People's Republic of Korea (DPRK) held talks in Geneva from September 23 to October 21, 1994, to negotiate an overall resolution of the nuclear issue on the Korean Peninsula.

Both sides reaffirmed the importance of attaining the objectives contained in the August 12, 1994 Agreed Statement between the U.S. and the DPRK and upholding the principles of the June 11, 1993 Joint Statement of the U.S. and the DPRK to achieve peace and security on a nuclear-free Korean peninsula. The U.S. and the DPRK decided to take the following actions for the resolution of the nuclear issue:

I. Both sides will cooperate to replace the DPRK's graphite-moderated reactors and related facilities with light-water reactor (LWR) power plants.

1) In accordance with the October 20, 1994 letter of assurance from the U.S. President, the U.S. will undertake to

make arrangements for the provision to the DPRK of a LWR project with a total generating capacity of approximately 2,000 MW(e) by a target date of 2003.

- The U.S. will organize under its leadership an international consortium to finance and supply the LWR project to be provided to the DPRK. The U.S., representing the international consortium, will serve as the principal point of contact with the DPRK for the LWR project.

- The U.S., representing the consortium, will make best efforts to secure the conclusion of a supply contract with the DPRK within six months of the date of this Document for the provision of the LWR project. Contract talks will begin as soon as possible after the date of this Document.

- As necessary, the U.S. and the DPRK will conclude a bilateral agreement for cooperation in the field of peaceful uses of nuclear energy.

2) In accordance with the October 20, 1994 letter of assurance from the U.S. President, the U.S., representing the consortium, will make arrangements to offset the energy foregone due to the freeze of the DPRK's graphite-moderated reactors and related facilities, pending completion of the first LWR unit.

- Alternative energy will be provided in the form of heavy oil for heating and electricity production.

- Deliveries of heavy oil will begin within three months of the date of this Document and will reach a rate of 500,000 tons annually, in accordance with an agreed schedule of deliveries.

Appendix 2

3) Upon receipt of U.S. assurances for the provision of LWR's and for arrangements for interim energy alternatives, the DPRK will freeze its graphite-moderated reactors and related facilities and will eventually dismantle these reactors and related facilities.

- The freeze on the DPRK's graphite-moderated reactors and related facilities will be fully implemented within one month of the date of this Document. During this one-month period, and throughout the freeze, the International Atomic Energy Agency (IAEA) will be allowed to monitor this freeze, and the DPRK will provide full cooperation to the IAEA for this purpose.

- Dismantlement of the DPRK's graphite-moderated reactors and related facilities will be completed when the LWR project is completed.

- The U.S. and the DPRK will cooperate in finding a method to store safely the spent fuel from the 5 MW(e) experimental reactor during the construction of the LWR project, and to dispose of the fuel in a safe manner that does not involve reprocessing in the DPRK.

4) As soon as possible after the date of this document U.S. and DPRK experts will hold two sets of experts talks.

- At one set of talks, experts will discuss issues related to alternative energy and the replacement of the graphite-moderated reactor program with the LWR project.

- At the other set of talks, experts will discuss specific arrangements for spent fuel storage and ultimate disposition.

Appendix 2

II. The two sides will move toward full normalization of political and economic relations.

  1) Within three months of the date of this Document, both sides will reduce barriers to trade and investment, including restrictions on telecommunications services and financial transactions.

  2) Each side will open a liaison office in the other's capital following resolution of consular and other technical issues through expert level discussions.

  3) As progress is made on issues of concern to each side, the U.S. and the DPRK will upgrade bilateral relations to the Ambassadorial level.

III. Both sides will work together for peace and security on a nuclear-free Korean peninsula.

  1) The U.S. will provide formal assurances to the DPRK, against the threat or use of nuclear weapons by the U.S.

  2) The DPRK will consistently take steps to implement the North-South Joint Declaration on the Denuclearization of the Korean Peninsula.

  3) The DPRK will engage in North-South dialogue, as this Agreed Framework will help create an atmosphere that promotes such dialogue.

IV. Both sides will work together to strengthen the international nuclear non proliferation regime.

  1) The DPRK will remain a party to the Treaty on the Non-Proliferation of Nuclear Weapons (NPT) and will allow implementation of its safeguards agreement under the Treaty.

Appendix 2

2) Upon conclusion of the supply contract for the provision of the LWR project, ad hoc and routine inspections will resume under the DPRK's safeguards agreement with the IAEA with respect to the facilities not subject to the freeze. Pending conclusion of the supply contract, inspections required by the IAEA for the continuity of safeguards will continue at the facilities not subject to the freeze.

3) When a significant portion of the LWR project is completed, but before delivery of key nuclear components, the DPRK will come into full compliance with its safeguards agreement with the IAEA (INFCIRC/403), including taking all steps that may be deemed necessary by the IAEA, following consultations with the Agency with regard to verifying the accuracy and completeness of the DPRK's initial report on all nuclear material in the DPRK.

Robert L. Gallucci
Head of Delegation of the United States of America, Ambassador at Large of the United States of America

Kang Sok Ju
Head of the Delegation of the Democratic People's Republic of Korea, First Vice-Minister of Foreign Affairs of the Democratic People's Republic of Korea

APPENDIX 3
EXCERPTS FROM THE NATIONAL SECURITY STRATEGY OF THE UNITED STATES OF AMERICA
September 2002

Preface by the President

The great struggles of the twentieth century between liberty and totalitarianism ended with a decisive victory for the forces of freedom—and a single sustainable model for national success: freedom, democracy, and free enterprise. In the twenty-first century, only nations that share a commitment to protecting basic human rights and guaranteeing political and economic freedom will be able to unleash the potential of their people and assure their future prosperity. People everywhere want to be able to speak freely; choose who will govern them; worship as they please; educate their children—male and female; own property; and enjoy the benefits of their labor. These values of freedom are right and true for every person, in every society—and the duty of protecting these values against their enemies is the common calling of freedom-loving people across the globe and across the ages.

Today, the United States enjoys a position of unparalleled military strength and great economic and political influence. In keeping with our heritage and principles, we do not use our strength to press for unilateral advantage. We seek instead to create a balance of power that favors human freedom: conditions in which all nations and all societies can choose for themselves the rewards and challenges of political and economic liberty. In a world that is safe, people will be able to make their own lives better. We will defend the peace by fighting terrorists and tyrants. We will preserve the peace by building good relations among the great powers. We will extend the peace by encouraging free and open societies on every continent.

Defending our Nation against its enemies is the first and fundamental commitment of the Federal Government. Today, that task has changed dramatically. Enemies in the past needed great armies and great industrial capabilities to endanger America. Now, shadowy networks of individuals can bring great chaos and suffering to our shores for less than it costs to purchase a single tank. Terrorists are organized to penetrate open societies and to turn the power of modern technologies against us.

To defeat this threat we must make use of every tool in our arsenal—military power, better homeland defenses, law enforcement, intelligence, and vigorous efforts to cut off terrorist financing. The war against terrorists of global reach is a global enterprise of uncertain duration. America will help nations that need our assistance in combating terror. And America will hold to account nations that are compromised by terror, including those who harbor terrorists— because the allies of terror are the enemies of civilization. The United States and countries cooperating with us must not allow the terrorists to develop new home bases. Together, we will seek to deny them sanctuary at every turn.

The gravest danger our Nation faces lies at the crossroads of radicalism and technology. Our enemies have openly declared that they are seeking weapons of mass destruction, and evidence indicates that they are doing so with determination. The United States will not allow these efforts to succeed. We will build defenses against ballistic missiles and other means of delivery. We will cooperate with other nations to deny, contain, and curtail our enemies' efforts to acquire dangerous technologies. And, as a matter of common sense and self-defense, America will act against such emerging threats before they are fully formed. We cannot defend America and our friends by hoping for the best. So we must be prepared to defeat our enemies' plans, using the best intelligence and proceeding with deliberation. History will judge harshly those who saw this coming danger but failed to act. In the new world we have entered, the only path to peace and security is the path of action.

As we defend the peace, we will also take advantage of an historic opportunity to preserve the peace. Today, the international community has the best chance since the rise of the nation-state in the seventeenth century to build a world where great powers compete in peace instead of continually prepare for war. Today, the world's great powers find ourselves on the same side— united by common dangers of terrorist violence and chaos. The United States will build on these common interests to promote global security. We are also increasingly united by common values. Russia is in the midst of a hopeful transition, reaching for its democratic future and a partner in the war on terror. Chinese leaders are discovering that economic freedom is the only source of national wealth. In time, they will find that social and political freedom is the only source of national greatness. America will encourage the advancement of democracy and economic openness in both nations, because these are the best foundations for domestic stability and international order. We will strongly resist aggression from other great powers—even as we welcome their peaceful pursuit of prosperity, trade, and cultural advancement.

Finally, the United States will use this moment of opportunity to extend the benefits of freedom across the globe. We will actively work to bring the hope of democracy, development, free markets, and free trade to every corner of the world. The events of September

Appendix 3

11, 2001, taught us that weak states, like Afghanistan, can pose as great a danger to our national interests as strong states. Poverty does not make poor people into terrorists and murderers. Yet poverty, weak institutions, and corruption can make weak states vulnerable to terrorist networks and drug cartels within their borders.

The United States will stand beside any nation determined to build a better future by seeking the rewards of liberty for its people. Free trade and free markets have proven their ability to lift whole societies out of poverty—so the United States will work with individual nations, entire regions, and the entire global trading community to build a world that trades in freedom and therefore grows in prosperity. The United States will deliver greater development assistance through the New Millennium Challenge Account to nations that govern justly, invest in their people, and encourage economic freedom. We will also continue to lead the world in efforts to reduce the terrible toll of HIV/AIDS and other infectious diseases.

In building a balance of power that favors freedom, the United States is guided by the conviction that all nations have important responsibilities. Nations that enjoy freedom must actively fight terror. Nations that depend on international stability must help prevent the spread of weapons of mass destruction. Nations that seek international aid must govern themselves wisely, so that aid is well spent. For freedom to thrive, accountability must be expected and required.

We are also guided by the conviction that no nation can build a safer, better world alone. Alliances and multilateral institutions can multiply the strength of freedom-loving nations. The United States is committed to lasting institutions like the United Nations, the World Trade Organization, the Organization of American States, and NATO as well as other long-standing alliances. Coalitions of the willing can augment these permanent institutions. In all cases, international obligations are to be taken seriously. They are not to be undertaken symbolically to rally support for an ideal without furthering its attainment.

Freedom is the non-negotiable demand of human dignity; the birthright of every person—in every civilization. Throughout history, freedom has been threatened by war and terror; it has been challenged by the clashing wills of powerful states and the evil designs of tyrants; and it has been tested by widespread poverty and disease. Today, humanity holds in its hands the opportunity to further freedom's triumph over all these foes. The United States welcomes our responsibility to lead in this great mission.

George W. Bush
THE WHITE HOUSE, September 17, 2002

I. Overview of America's International Strategy

"Our Nation's cause has always been larger than our Nation's defense. We fight, as we always fight, for a just peace—a peace that favors liberty. We will defend the peace against the threats from terrorists and tyrants. We will preserve the peace by building good relations among the great powers. And we will extend the peace by encouraging free and open societies on every continent."

President Bush
West Point, New York
June 1, 2002

The United States possesses unprecedented—and unequaled—strength and influence in the world. Sustained by faith in the principles of liberty, and the value of a free society, this position comes with unparalleled responsibilities, obligations, and opportunity.

Appendix 3

The great strength of this nation must be used to promote a balance of power that favors freedom.

For most of the twentieth century, the world was divided by a great struggle over ideas: destructive totalitarian visions versus freedom and equality.

That great struggle is over. The militant visions of class, nation, and race which promised utopia and delivered misery have been defeated and discredited. America is now threatened less by conquering states than we are by failing ones. We are menaced less by fleets and armies than by catastrophic technologies in the hands of the embittered few. We must defeat these threats to our Nation, allies, and friends.

This is also a time of opportunity for America. We will work to translate this moment of influence into decades of peace, prosperity, and liberty. The U.S. national security strategy will be based on a distinctly American internationalism that reflects the union of our values and our national interests. The aim of this strategy is to help make the world not just safer but better. Our goals on the path to progress are clear: political and economic freedom, peaceful relations with other states, and respect for human dignity.

And this path is not America's alone. It is open to all. To achieve these goals, the United States will:

- champion aspirations for human dignity;
- strengthen alliances to defeat global terrorism and work to prevent attacks against us and our friends;
- work with others to defuse regional conflicts;
- prevent our enemies from threatening us, our allies, and our friends, with weapons of mass destruction;
- ignite a new era of global economic growth through free markets and free trade;

- expand the circle of development by opening societies and building the infrastructure of democracy;
- develop agendas for cooperative action with other main centers of global power; and
- transform America's national security institutions to meet the challenges and opportunities of the twenty-first century.

III. Strengthen Alliances to Defeat Global Terrorism and Work to Prevent Attacks Against Us and Our Friends

"Just three days removed from these events, Americans do not yet have the distance of history. But our responsibility to history is already clear: to answer these attacks and rid the world of evil. War has been waged against us by stealth and deceit and murder. This nation is peaceful, but fierce when stirred to anger. The conflict was begun on the timing and terms of others. It will end in a way, and at an hour, of our choosing."

President Bush
Washington, D.C. (The National Cathedral)
September 14, 2001

The United States of America is fighting a war against terrorists of global reach. The enemy is not a single political regime or person or religion or ideology. The enemy is terrorism—premeditated, politically motivated violence perpetrated against innocents.

In many regions, legitimate grievances prevent the emergence of a lasting peace. Such grievances deserve to be, and must be, addressed within a political process. But no cause justifies ter-

Appendix 3

ror. The United States will make no concessions to terrorist demands and strike no deals with them. We make no distinction between terrorists and those who knowingly harbor or provide aid to them.

The struggle against global terrorism is different from any other war in our history. It will be fought on many fronts against a particularly elusive enemy over an extended period of time. Progress will come through the persistent accumulation of successes—some seen, some unseen.

Today our enemies have seen the results of what civilized nations can, and will, do against regimes that harbor, support, and use terrorism to achieve their political goals. Afghanistan has been liberated; coalition forces continue to hunt down the Taliban and al-Qaida. But it is not only this battlefield on which we will engage terrorists. Thousands of trained terrorists remain at large with cells in North America, South America, Europe, Africa, the Middle East, and across Asia.

Our priority will be first to disrupt and destroy terrorist organizations of global reach and attack their leadership; command, control, and communications; material support; and finances. This will have a disabling effect upon the terrorists' ability to plan and operate.

We will continue to encourage our regional partners to take up a coordinated effort that isolates the terrorists. Once the regional campaign localizes the threat to a particular state, we will help ensure the state has the military, law enforcement, political, and financial tools necessary to finish the task.

The United States will continue to work with our allies to disrupt the financing of terrorism. We will identify and block the sources of funding for terrorism, freeze the assets of terrorists and those who support them, deny terrorists access to the international financial system, protect legitimate charities from being abused

Appendix 3

by terrorists, and prevent the movement of terrorists' assets through alternative financial networks.

However, this campaign need not be sequential to be effective, the cumulative effect across all regions will help achieve the results we seek. We will disrupt and destroy terrorist organizations by:

- direct and continuous action using all the elements of national and international power. Our immediate focus will be those terrorist organizations of global reach and any terrorist or state sponsor of terrorism which attempts to gain or use weapons of mass destruction (WMD) or their precursors;

- defending the United States, the American people, and our interests at home and abroad by identifying and destroying the threat before it reaches our borders. While the United States will constantly strive to enlist the support of the international community, we will not hesitate to act alone, if necessary, to exercise our right of self defense by acting preemptively against such terrorists, to prevent them from doing harm against our people and our country; and

- denying further sponsorship, support, and sanctuary to terrorists by convincing or compelling states to accept their sovereign responsibilities. We will also wage a war of ideas to win the battle against international terrorism. This includes:

- using the full influence of the United States, and working closely with allies and friends, to make clear that all acts of terrorism are illegitimate so that terrorism will be viewed in the same light as slavery, piracy, or genocide: behavior that no respectable government can condone or support and all must oppose;

- supporting moderate and modern government, especially in the Muslim world, to ensure that the conditions and ideologies that promote terrorism do not find fertile ground in any nation;

- diminishing the underlying conditions that spawn terrorism by enlisting the international community to focus its efforts and resources on areas most at risk; and

- using effective public diplomacy to promote the free flow of information and ideas to kindle the hopes and aspirations of freedom of those in societies ruled by the sponsors of global terrorism.

While we recognize that our best defense is a good offense, we are also strengthening America's homeland security to protect against and deter attack. This Administration has proposed the largest government reorganization since the Truman Administration created the National Security Council and the Department of Defense. Centered on a new Department of Homeland Security and including a new unified military command and a fundamental reordering of the FBI, our comprehensive plan to secure the homeland encompasses every level of government and the cooperation of the public and the private sector.

This strategy will turn adversity into opportunity. For example, emergency management systems will be better able to cope not just with terrorism but with all hazards. Our medical system will be strengthened to manage not just bioterror, but all infectious diseases and mass-casualty dangers. Our border controls will not just stop terrorists, but improve the efficient movement of legitimate traffic.

While our focus is protecting America, we know that to defeat terrorism in today's globalized world we need support from our

Appendix 3

allies and friends. Wherever possible, the United States will rely on regional organizations and state powers to meet their obligations to fight terrorism. Where governments find the fight against terrorism beyond their capacities, we will match their willpower and their resources with whatever help we and our allies can provide.

As we pursue the terrorists in Afghanistan, we will continue to work with international organizations such as the United Nations, as well as non-governmental organizations, and other countries to provide the humanitarian, political, economic, and security assistance necessary to rebuild Afghanistan so that it will never again abuse its people, threaten its neighbors, and provide a haven for terrorists.

In the war against global terrorism, we will never forget that we are ultimately fighting for our democratic values and way of life. Freedom and fear are at war, and there will be no quick or easy end to this conflict. In leading the campaign against terrorism, we are forging new, productive international relationships and redefining existing ones in ways that meet the challenges of the twenty-first century.

REFERENCES

CHAPTER 1

p. 24: *"In some ways, it resembles. . . ."* See U.S. Department of State, *Country Reports on Human Rights Practices, 2001* (March 2002), available at www.state.gov/g/drl/rls/hrrpt/2001/eap/8330pf.htm; Kang Chol-Hwan and Pierre Rigoulot, *Aquariums of Pyongyang: Ten Years in the North Korean Gulag* (New York: Basic Books; 2001).

p. 24: *"This is not just the view. . . ."* Cited in David E. Sanger, "Bush Takes No-Budge Stand in Talks with North Korea," *New York Times*, April 17, 2003, A11.

p. 25: *"But he has presided. . . ."* For one good summary, see Peter Carlson, "Sins of the Son," *Washington Post*, May 11, 2003, D1.

p. 26: *"In addition, while Kim Jong Il's extravagant tastes. . . ."* Kongdan Oh and Ralph C. Hassig, *North Korea Through the Looking Glass* (Washington, D.C.: Brookings; 2000: 81–104).

p. 26: *"It also exports arms. . . ."* Bureau of Verification and Compliance, U.S. Department of State, *World Military Expenditures and Arms Transfers, 1998* (Washington, D.C.: Government Printing Office; 2000: 43, 45); International Institute for Strategic Studies, *The Military Balance 2002/2003* (Oxford, England: Oxford University Press; 2002: 332–336).

p. 27: *"North Korea's current economic growth rate. . . ."* Central Intelligence Agency, *World Factbook 2002* (December 2002), available at www.cia.gov/publications/factbook/geos/kn.html.

p. 27: *"What began half a century ago. . . ."* See Oh and Hassig, *North Korea Through the Looking Glass*, 9–11; on the concept of sovereignty as responsibility, see Francis M. Deng, ed., *Sovereignty as Responsibility* (Washington, D.C.: Brookings; 1996).

p. 28: *"Kim does not have the oil wealth. . . ."* Don Oberdorfer, *The Two Koreas: A Contemporary History* (Reading, Mass.: Addison-Wesley; 1997: 156, 160, 202); Stephen T. Hosmer and Thomas W. Wolfe, *Soviet Policy and Practice Toward Third World Conflicts* (Lexington, Mass.: Lexington Books; 1983: 72, 77); Arms Control and Disarmament Agency, *World Military Expenditures and Arms Transfers, 1990* (Washington, D.C.: Government Printing Office; 1991: 132).

p. 28: *"That could possibly mean a conventional invasion. . . ."* Victor D. Cha, "Hawk Engagement and Preventive Defense on the Korean Peninsula," *International Security* 27 (Summer 2002): 46–67.

p. 29: *"But it has also done things...."* North Korea also has a very deeply ingrained sense of national pride and protection of sovereign rights, and its negotiators tend to be easily offended or put in a noncooperative mood. See Scott Snyder, *Negotiating on the Edge: North Korean Negotiating Behavior* (Washington, D.C.: U.S. Institute of Peace; 1999: 143–158).

p. 29: *"Free economic zones...."* On Deng's economic reforms in China, see Harry Harding, *China's Second Revolution* (Washington, D.C.: Brookings Institution; 1987: 90–95).

p. 30: *"At home, it lifted price controls...."* Susan Shirk, "A New North Korea?" *Washington Post*, October 22, 2002, 27.

p. 30: *"It then allowed five...."* James T. Laney and Jason T. Shaplen, "How to Deal with North Korea," *Foreign Affairs* 82 (March/April 2003): 16–17.

p. 30: *"That may have had more to do...."* Bureau of Verification and Compliance, U.S. Department of State, *World Military Expenditures and Arms Transfers, 1998* (Washington, D.C.: Government Printing Office; 2000: 142).

p. 30: *"Although technically still included...."* U.S. Department of State, *Patterns of Global Terrorism, 2001* (May 2002), p. 68; Paul Pillar, *Terrorism and U.S. Foreign Policy* (Washington, D.C.: Brookings Institution; 2001: 161, 170); U.S. Department of State, "Overview of State-Sponsored Terrorism," *Patterns of Global Terrorism 2000* (Washington, D.C.: 2001: 4), available at www.state.gov/s/ct.../index.cfm?docid=2441&CFNo Cache=TRUE&printfriendly=tru.

p. 30: *"The last time it kidnapped...."* "A Monstrous Admission," *Columbus (Ohio) Dispatch*, October 1, 2002, 10A.

p. 31: *"That number stands in stark contrast...."* On when North Korea's uranium enrichment program began, see Sanger, "Bush Takes No-Budge Stand...." A11.

p. 31: *"Given the security benefit...."* Korean Peninsula Energy Development Organization (KEDO), *Annual Report* (New York: KEDO; December 2001: 14), available at www.kedo.org.

p. 31: *"It also violates a 1991 accord...."* In the 1994 accord, North Korea committed itself to remaining a party of the NPT; see Leon V. Sigal, *Disarming Strangers: Nuclear Diplomacy with North Korea* (Princeton, N.J.: Princeton University Press; 1998: 264); on the 1991 accord, see Oberdorfer, *The Two Koreas*, 260–265.

p. 32: *"Under such circumstances...."* For an argument that countries with such a combination of characteristics should be designated threats to international peace by the United Nations, see Anne-Marie Slaughter, "A Chance to Reshape the U.N.," *Washington Post*, April 13, 2003, B7.

p. 32: *"After Assistant Secretary Kelly confronted...."* David E. Sanger, "U.S. Not Certain If North Korea Has the Bomb," *New York Times*, October 17, 2002, 1.

p. 32: *"Then, on January 9...."* Laney and Shaplen, "How to Deal with North Korea," 18; CNN, "Oil shipments to N. Korea Frozen," November 14, 2002, available at cnn.usnews.printthis.clickability.com/pt/cpt?action=cpt&expire=-1&urlID=4617588.

p. 32: *"In early February of 2003...."* David E. Sanger and Eric Schmitt, "Satellites Said to See Activity at North Korean Nuclear Site," *New York Times*, January 31, 2003, 1; Doug Struck, "Reactor Restarted, North Korea Says," *Washington Post*, February 6, 2003, 31; David E. Sanger, "Reactor Started in North Korea, U.S. Concludes," *New York Times*, February 27, 2003.

p. 33: *"While China and Russia...."* Colum Lynch and Doug Struck, "China Blocks U.N. Statement Condemning N. Korea," *Washington Post*, April 9, 2003, 16.

p. 33: *"In mid-February...."* John Pomfret, "China Urges N. Korea Dialogue," *Washington Post*, April 4, 2003, A16.

p. 33: *"Similarly, Russia stated...."* Michael Wines, "Warning to North Korea on Nuclear Arms," *New York Times*, April 12, 2003, A5.

p. 33: *"Some Bush administration insiders...."* David E. Sanger, "Viewing the War as a Lesson to the World," *New York Times*, April 6, 2003, B1; Thom Shanker, "Lessons from Iraq Include How to Scare North Korean Leader," *New York Times*, May 12, 2003.

p. 34: *"Indeed, North Korea stated...."* Howard W. French, "North Korea Says Its Arms Will Deter U.S. Attack," *New York Times*, April 7, 2003.

p. 34: *"In early April, its withdrawal...."* Barbara Slavin, "North Korea Pulls Out of Non-Nuclear Treaty," *USA Today*, April 10, 2003, 10.

p. 34: *"Even as Pyongyang prepared...."* Glenn Kessler and Walter Pincus, "N. Korea Stymied on Plutonium Work," *Washington Post*, March 20, 2003, 24.

p. 34: *"North Korea hinted as well...."* Bill Gertz, "North Korea May Export Nukes," *Washington Times*, May 7, 2003, 1; David E. Sanger, "U.S. Suspects North Korea Moved Ahead on Weapons," *New York Times*, May 8, 2003; David E. Sanger with Howard W. French, "North Korea Prompts U.S. to Investigate Nuclear Boast," *New York Times*, May 1, 2003, A18.

p. 34: *"(That would be a daunting task....)"* Michael Levi, "North Korea's Loose Nukes," *The New Republic*, May 26, 2003; David E. Sanger, "Bush Shifts Focus to Nuclear Sales by North Korea," *New York Times*, May 5, 2003, 1; James Brooke, "North Korea Suspends Its Passenger Ferry Link with Japan," *New York Times*, June 9, 2003.

REFERENCES

p. 34: *"To justify the action. . . ."* See Associated Press, "N. Korea Annuls Nuclear Pact," *Washington Post*, May 13, 2003, A13; and President George W. Bush, "National Strategy to Combat Weapons of Mass Destruction," December 2002, 3. Specifically, the document reads, "The United States will continue to make clear that it reserves the right to respond with overwhelming force—including through resort to all of our options—to the use of WMD against the United States, our forces abroad, and friends and allies. In addition to our conventional and nuclear response and defense capabilities, our overall deterrent posture against WMD threats is reinforced by effective intelligence, surveillance, interdiction, and domestic law enforcement capabilities."

p. 35: *"In a March 2003 statement. . . ."* Doug Struck, "'With Circumspection,' U.S. Planes to Resume Spy Flights Off N. Korea," *Washington Post*, March 13, 2003, A1.

p. 35: *"(North Korea might need. . . .)"* See Michael R. Gordon with Felicity Barringer, "North Korea Wants Arms and More Aid from U.S., Chief of C.I.A. Suggests," *New York Times*, Februrary 13, 2003, A17; Sigal, *Disarming Strangers* 21–22; David Albright, "North Korea's Current and Future Plutonium and Nuclear Weapon Stocks," *ISIS Issue Brief*, January 15, 2003, available at www.isis-online.org.

p. 35: *"In mid-February of 2003. . . ."* James Brooke, "U.S. Plan for Penalties Draws a Threat from North Korea," *New York Times*, February 18, 2003.

p. 35: *"If so, the attempt. . . ."* Bill Gertz, "North Korea Tested a Cruise Missile," *Washington Times*, February 27, 2003, 4; and Eric Schmitt, "North Korean Fliers Said to Have Sought Hostages," *New York Times*, March 8, 2003, A1.

p. 35: *"On March 2. . . ."* Bill Gertz, "Revealed: N. Korea Fired Laser at U.S. Troops," *Washington Times*, May 13, 2003, A1.

p. 36: *"Assistant Secretary Kelly also suggested. . . ."* Dana Milbank, "U.S. Open to Informal Talks with North Korea," *Washington Post*, December 30, 2002, 1; James Brooke, "South Korea Criticizes U.S. Plan for Exerting Pressure on North," *New York Times*, December 31, 2002, 1; Glenn Kessler, "Security Assurances Weighed for N. Korea," *Washington Post*, January 9, 2003, 1; and Barbara Demick, Paul Richter, and John Daniszewski, "U.S. Hints at Aid if N. Korea Abandons Arms," *Los Angeles Times*, January 13, 2003, 1.

p. 36: *"In his state of the union speech. . . ."* Maura Reynolds, "Bush Assails N. Korean Leader," *Los Angeles Times*, January 3, 2003, 1; David E. Sanger, "Bush Says Shift by North Korea Could Bring Aid," *New York Times*, January 15, 2003, 1; Sang-hun Choe, "N. Korea Lashes Out After Bush Speech," *Philadelphia Inquirer*, January 30, 2003; Bob Woodward, *Bush at War* (New York: Simon and Schuster; 2002: 340); Howard Fineman, "I Sniff Some Politics," *Newsweek*, May 27, 2002, 37.

References

p. 36: *"In early March of 2003...."* Mark Matthews and David L. Greene, "Bush Says Force Now An Option on North Korea," *Baltimore Sun*, March 4, 2003; and Howard W. French, "South Korea's President-Elect Rejects Use of Force Against North Korea," *New York Times*, January 17, 2003.

p. 37: *"Their difference of opinion...."* See Joseph Curl, "North Korea Gets Stern Warning," *Washington Times*, May 15, 2003, 1; Joseph Curl, "U.S. Keeps Preemption Doctrine 'Open,'" *Washington Times*, May 13, 2003, 1; Dana Milbank and Karen DeYoung, "President Sees 'Progress' on N. Korea," *Washington Post*, May 15, 2003, 2.

p. 37: *"Shortly after taking office...."* Steven Mufson, "Bush Casts a Shadow on Korea Missile Talks; Lack of 'Transparency' in North Cited," *Washington Post*, March 8, 2001, A1.

p. 37: *"By April 2002...."* See Hearing of the Subcommittee on Foreign Operations, Export Financing and Related Programs of the U.S. Senate Committee on Appropriations, April 24, 2002.

p. 37: *"Although still willing...."* David E. Sanger, "U.S. Sees Quick Start of North Korea Nuclear Site," *New York Times*, March 1, 2003, A1.

p. 37: *"For example, in the spring of 2003...."* Others have advocated a very hard line against North Korea as well. See James A. Baker, "No More Caving on North Korea," *Washington Post*, October 23, 2002, 27; Nicholas Eberstadt, *The End of North Korea* (Washington, D.C.: American Enterprise Institute; 1999); Henry Sokolski, "Let's Not Do It Again," *National Review Online*, October 24, 2002, available at www.nationalreview.com/comment; Joshua Muravchik, "Facing Up to North Korea," *Commentary* (March 2003), 33–38; Victor Cha, "Isolation, Not Engagement," *New York Times*, December 29, 2002, D9.

p. 37: *"Beijing would almost certainly not accept...."* See David E. Sanger, "Nuclear Standoff: Administration Divided Over North Korea," *New York Times*, April 20, 2003, A15.

p. 38: *"President Bush did not adopt this policy...."* Glenn Kessler, "N. Korea Policy to Mix Diplomacy and Pressure," *Washington Post*, May 7, 2003, 1.

p. 39: *"The above events, as well as suspicions...."* Oberdorfer, *The Two Koreas*, 365–368, 387–393; Robert S. Litwak, *Rogue States and U.S. Foreign Policy* (Washington, D.C.: Woodrow Wilson Center; 2000: 231).

p. 39: *"North Korea also claimed...."* Robert S. Norris, Hans M. Kristensen, and Joshua Handler, "NRDC Nuclear Notebook: North Korea's Nuclear Program, 2003," *Bulletin of the Atomic Scientists* (March/April 2003), 74–75.

p. 40: *"According to Vice Admiral Lowell Jacoby...."* Statement for the Record of Vice Admiral Lowell E. Jacoby, Director, Defense Intelligence Agency, "Global Threat Testimony," Senate Select Committee on Intelligence, February 11, 2003, 4.

p. 40: *"The United States must...."* Speech by William J. Perry at the Brookings Institution, "Crisis on the Korean Peninsula: Implications for U.S. Policy in Northeast Asia," Washington, D.C., January 24, 2003, available at www.brookings.edu.

p. 40: *"Finally, North Korean nuclear weapons...."* Testimony of Ashton B. Carter before the Senate Committee on Foreign Relations, "Three Crises with North Korea," February 4, 2003.

p. 40: *"At the same time...."* Oberdorer, *The Two Koreas*, 124–138.

p. 41: *"President Roh has recently taken steps...."* Associated Press, "S. Korea to Send Non-Combatants to Gulf," *Washington Post*, April 3, 2003, A31.

p. 42: *"The fundamental difference...."* See also Balbina Y. Hwang, "The Myth of Anti-Americanism in South Korea," *U.S.-Korea Tomorrow* 6 (January 2003), 4–9.

p. 42: *"For example, just a few years ago...."* Oberdorfer, *The Two Koreas*, 391–392.

p. 43: *"Visions or road maps...."* Richard N. Haass and Meghan L. O'Sullivan, "Terms of Engagement: Alternatives to Punitive Policies," *Survival* 42 (Summer 2000), 120–121.

p. 43: *"Such a tactical approach...."* See the forthcoming Brookings Institution book by Robert Gallucci, Dan Poneman, and Joel Wit. Even some of the key elements of the Agreed Framework, such as providing North Korea with fuel oil, were not clearly conceptualized until late in the negotiation process.

p. 43: *"As a result, it had a hard time...."* Sigal, *Disarming Strangers*, 52–65.

p. 44: *"If it made strategic sense...."* Sigal, *Disarming Strangers*, 66–67.

p. 44: *"For example, in a 1999 government review...."* Dr. William J. Perry, Ambassador Wendy Sherman, and coauthors of the North Korea policy review team, "Review of United States Policy Toward North Korea: Findings and Recommendations," Washington, D.C., October 12, 1999, available at www.state.gov/www/regions/eap; Sigal, *Disarming Strangers*, 250–254.

p. 45: *"This approach would amount to...."* This approach was also endorsed shortly after Mr. Bush became president by a large group of former Reagan, Bush, and Clinton administration officials and other experts. See Morton I. Abramowitz, James T. Laney, Robert A. Manning, and coauthors from Independent Task Force, *Testing North Korea: The Next Stage in U.S. and ROK Policy* (New York: Council on Foreign Relations; 2001). For more recent arguments along similar lines, see Brent Scowcroft and Daniel Poneman, "Korea Can't Wait," *Washington Post*, February 16, 2003; Samuel R. Berger and Robert L. Gallucci, "Two Crises, No Back Burner,"

References

Washington Post, December 31, 2002, 17; William S. Cohen, "Huffing and Puffing Won't Do," *Washington Post*, January 7, 2003, 17; Testimony of Ashton B. Carter before the Senate Committee on Foreign Relations, "Alternatives to Letting North Korea Go Nuclear," March 6, 2003; Sonni Efron, "Experts Call for N. Korea Dialogue," *Los Angeles Times*, March 7, 2003 (citing testimonies by Robert Einhorn as well); Letter from the Independent Task Force on Korea to the Administration, Council on Foreign Relations, November 26, 2002, available at ww.cfr.org/publication_print.php?id=5304&content=; Selig S. Harrison and other members of the Task Force on U.S. Korea Policy, "Turning Point in Korea: New Dangers and New Opportunities for the United States," Center for International Policy and the University of Chicago Center for East Asian Studies, February 2003.

p. 45: *"It also received...."* Howard W. French, "Former Leader Is Caught Up in South Korean Maelstrom," *New York Times*, April 6, 2003, A12.

p. 45: *"In addition to its other advantages...."* See Reuters, "S. Korea Urges U.S. Initiative for North," *Washington Post*, March 29, 2003, A12.

p. 46: *"Such a plan would begin...."* For a similar idea, see Robert J. Einhorn, "Advice to the New President Roh Moo Hyun," *U.S.-Korea Tomorrow*, 6 (April 2003), 8–9.

p. 46: *"Given North Korea's worries...."* See Doug Struck, "Citing Iraq, N. Korea Signals Hard Line on Weapons Issues," *Washington Post*, March 30, 2003, 30; and James Brooke, "North Korea Watches War and Wonders What's Next," *New York Times*, March 31, 2003.

p. 47: *"By providing more carrots...."* Gary Samore, "The Korean Nuclear Crisis," *Survival* 45, (Spring 2003), 19–22.

p. 47: *"That said, in our judgment...."* Such a strike would not, of course, likely destroy either the DPRK uranium enrichment program or the possible stock of one to two bombs North Korea may already have; nor would it destroy any additional plutonium moved from Yongbyon prior to the attack. But it could destroy DPRK nuclear reactors at the site, entomb the associated plutonium, and destroy the reprocessing facility—all with limited risk of radioactive fallout, according to former Secretary of Defense William Perry and former Assistant Secretary Ashton Carter. See Ashton B. Carter and William J. Perry, "Back to the Brink," *Washington Post*, October 20, 2002, B1.

p. 47: *"However, in our view...."* For another view emphasizing the potential of diplomacy, see Michael Armacost, Daniel I. Okimoto, and Gi-Wook Shin, "Addressing the North Korea Nuclear Challenge," Policy Paper, Asia/Pacific Research Center, Institute for International Studies, Stanford University, April 15, 2003.

References

p. 47: *"True, North Korean hard-liners. . . ."* See Philip W. Yun, "The Devil We Know in N. Korea May Be Better than the Ones We Don't," *Los Angeles Times*, May 7, 2003.

p. 48: *"If a proposed package deal. . . ."* See Oh and Hassig, *North Korea Through the Looking Glass*, 114–124.

p. 48: *"It might prefer to have. . . ."* For a similar argument, see Joseph S. Nye, "Bush Faces a Tougher Test in N. Korea," *Boston Globe*, May 7, 2003, 23.

p. 48: *"Secretary of Defense Rumsfeld recently argued. . . ."* Bill Sammon, "N. Korea 'Solution' a Market Economy," *Washington Times*, May 14, 2003, 1.

p. 50: *"Accordingly, a recent Center for Strategic and International Studies (CSIS) report. . . ."* CSIS Working Group, "Conventional Arms Control on the Korean Peninsula," Center for Strategic and International Studies, Washington, D.C., August 2002, available at www.csis.org. See also Alan D. Romberg and Michael D. Swaine, "The North Korea Nuclear Crisis: A Strategy for Negotiation," *Arms Control Today* 33 (May 2003), 4–7.

p. 51: *"The Perry report also took aim. . . ."* Perry, Sherman, and coauthors, "Review of United States Policy Toward North Korea," 7–8.

p. 52: *"Those talks went slowly. . . ."* Snyder, *Negotiating on the Edge*, 58–60, 143–153; Sigal, *Disarming Strangers*, 52–65, 78.

p. 52: *"Indeed, North Korea has itself. . . ."* David E. Sanger, "North Korea Says It Seeks to Develop Nuclear Arms," *New York Times*, June 10, 2003.

p. 53: *"Likewise, North Korea would not. . . ."* For one argument by a knowledgeable former official that going for too much too fast could overload the system, see Testimony by Robert J. Einhorn before the Senate Foreign Relations Committee, "Negotiations with North Korea," March 6, 2003, available at www.csis.org.

p. 53: *"These four countries need to be united. . . ."* See Snyder, *Negotiating on the Edge*, 149–150.

p. 54: *"A recent article. . . ."* Laney and Shaplen, "Peace in Korea," 27–28; Abramowitz, Laney, Manning, and coauthors, *Testing North Korea*, 40–41.

p. 54: *"So does a recent paper. . . ."* Kim Dong Shin, *The ROK-U.S. Alliance: Where Is It Headed?* Strategic Forum Paper No. 197 (Washington, D.C.: National Defense University, April 2003).

p. 54: *"(A more recent Council on Foreign Relations task force. . . ."* See Morton I. Abramowitz and James T. Laney, co-chairs, and Eric Heginbotham, Project Director, *Meeting the North Korean Nuclear Challenge* (New York: Council on Foreign Relations, 2003).

"A 1991–1992 accord. . . ." For a fascinating discussion of the late 1980s and early 1990s, a period during which the end of the Cold War dramatically

influenced the Korean peninsula, tending to further strengthen South Korea's position, see Oberdorfer, *The Two Koreas*, 186–280.

p. 54: *"But such a proposal...."* CSIS Working Group, "Conventional Arms Control on the Korean Peninsula," 13–17.

CHAPTER 2

p. 57: *"Conventional forces are the crux...."* Some of this chapter is an updated version of an earlier analysis, Michael O'Hanlon, "Stopping a North Korean Invasion: Why Defending South Korea Is Easier than the Pentagon Thinks," *International Security* 22 (Spring 1998), 135–170.

p. 59: *"And even if the attack failed...."* Reportedly, Pentagon models estimate about 50,000 U.S. and 500,000 South Korean military casualties during the first three months of war. See Don Oberdorfer, "A Minute to Midnight," *Newsweek*, October 20, 1997, 18.

p. 59: *"U.S. forces needed for the defense...."* Secretary of Defense Les Aspin, *Report on the Bottom-Up Review* (Washington, D.C.: U.S. Department of Defense, October 1993, 13–22); Secretary of Defense William S. Cohen, *Report of the Quadrennial Defense Review* (Washington, D.C.: U.S. Department of Defense, May 1997, 12–13, 24–26, 30).

p. 61: *"First, so many North Korean weapons...."* North Korea, as discussed elsewhere in this chapter, has about 500 artillery tubes within range of Seoul. Each could fire one or more rounds a minute at the South Korean capital over an extended period of time. Unless their locations were virtually all known in advance, permitting preemptive attack against these sites, U.S. and ROK forces would be able to destroy them only after observing the trajectories of shells launched by these artillery tubes and then firing weapons at them. Even in a best case for coalition forces, a typical North Korean weapon would be able to fire several shots before being destroyed.

p. 62: *"Winning decisively in Korea...."* See "Lessons from the Iraq War: Strategy and Planning," *Strategic Comments*, 9 (May 2003).

p. 62: *"Similar conclusions follow...."* Such ideas have reportedly been investigated in regard to Korea (and Pyongyang surely has figured that out); see Thom Shanker, "Lessons from Iraq Include How to Scare North Korean Leader," *New York Times*, May 12, 2003.

p. 63: *"For North Korea, in fact...."* On the comparison with Europe, see, for example, Fran Lussier, *U.S. Ground Forces and the Conventional Balance in Europe* (Washington, D.C.: U.S. Congressional Budget Office; June 1988: 7–28, 91–99). About one-fourth of the total NATO and Warsaw Pact forces were either deployed in the Germany-Poland-Czechoslovakia area or immediately deployable to that zone using pre-positioned stocks. That made for a total of roughly 2.5 million troops and 60,000 armored vehicles in a zone with a front three times the length of the Korean DMZ—similar numbers, per kilometer of front, to what prevails near the DMZ. But forces in the Germanys, Poland, and Czechoslovakia were based as far as 200 to 300 kilometers from the intra-German border, whereas most of those in the Koreas are within roughly 100 kilometers of the front. See also James C. Wendt, "U.S. Conventional Arms Control for Korea: A Proposed Approach," RAND Note (Santa Monica, Calif.: RAND Corporation; 1993: 14); Don Oberdorfer, *The Two Koreas: A Contemporary History* (Reading, Mass.: Addison-Wesley; 1997: 313); Defense Intelligence Agency, *North Korea: The Foundations for Military Strength, Update 1995* (Washington, D.C.: U.S. Defense Intelligence Agency; 1996: 13.)

p. 63: *"Another three to four attack corridors. . . ."* Nick Beldecos and Eric Heginbotham, "The Conventional Military Balance in Korea," Breakthroughs (Spring 1995), p. 3; and Yong-Sup Han, "Designing and Evaluating Conventional Arms Control Measures: The Case of the Korean Peninsula," Ph.D. dissertation, RAND Corporation 1993, pp. 31, 155.

p. 65: *"It then might try. . . ."* Defense White Paper 2000 (Seoul: Ministry of National Defense, Republic of Korea; 2000: 47–49); Kongdan Oh and Ralph C. Hassig, *North Korea Through the Looking Glass* (Washington, D.C.: Brookings; 2000: 110–111).

p. 65: *"Its forces are generally not postured. . . ."* Homer T. Hodge, "North Korea's Military Strategy," Parameters (Spring 2003), 68–81.

p. 66: *"That would translate to. . . ."* International Institute for Strategic Studies (IISS), *The Military Balance 2002/2003* (Oxford: Oxford University Press; 2002: 299); Marcus Noland, *Avoiding the Apocalypse: The Future of the Two Koreas* (Washington, D.C.: Institute for International Economics; 2000: 271, 314); Kongdan Oh and Ralph C. Hassig, *North Korea Through the Looking Glass* (Washington, D.C.: Brookings Institution; 2000: 42); Bureau of Verification and Compliance, U.S. Department of State, *World Military Expenditures and Arms Transfers, 1998* (Washington, D.C.: Government Printing Office; 2000: 90).

p. 66: *"It also has 4,000 underground facilities. . . ."* International Institute for Strategic Studies, *The Military Balance 2002/2003* (Oxford: Oxford University Press; 2002: 153–154; Ministry of National Defense, ROK, *Defense White Paper 2000*, 58; Department of Defense, "2000 Report to Congress: Military Situation on the Korean Peninsula," September 12, 2000, 4–7, available at www.defenselink.mil/news/Sep2000/korea 09122000.html.

p. 67: *"The various small naval vessels. . . ."* International Institute for Strategic Studies, *The Military Balance 2002/2003*, 153–154; Department of Defense, "2000 Report to Congress," 5; also see Ministry of National Defense, ROK, *Defense White Paper 2000*, 52.

References

p. 68: *"North Korean airpower. . . ."* On the Cold War "WEI/WUV" system, see, for example, William P. Mako, *U.S. Ground Forces and the Defense of Central Europe* (Washington, D.C.: Brookings Institution; 1983; 114–125); War Gaming Directorate, U.S. Army Concepts Analysis Agency, "Weapon Effectiveness Indices/Weighted Unit Values III" (Bethesda, Md.: U.S. Army Concepts Analysis Agency; 1978: Q-49–Q-62, Q-72–Q-76, R-14-R-16; for published details on TASCFORM databases, see Michael O'Hanlon, *The Art of War in the Age of Peace: U.S. Military Posture for the Post-Cold War World* (Westport, Conn.: Praeger; 1992: 64–67); Michael O'Hanlon, *Defense Planning for the Late 1990s: Beyond the Desert Storm Framework* (Washington, D.C.: Brookings Institution; 1995: 43).

p. 68: *"For example, although the U.S. Office of Naval Intelligence. . . ."* Statement of Lieutenant General Patrick M. Hughes, Director, U.S. Defense Intelligence Agency, before the Senate Select Committee on Intelligence, "Global Threats and Challenges to the United States and Its Interests Abroad," February 5, 1997, 11; Office of Naval Intelligence, *Worldwide Submarine Proliferation in the Coming Decade* (Washington, D.C.: U.S. Department of Defense; May 1995: 14).

p. 69: *"(South Korea spent an average. . . ."* International Institute for Strategic Studies, *The Military Balance 2002/2003*, 299.

p. 69: *"Indeed, Seoul now actually. . . ."* Statement of General Thomas A. Schwartz, Commander in Chief, United Nations Command/Combined Forces Command, and Commander, United States Forces Korea, before the Senate Armed Services Committee, March 5, 2002, available at defenselink.mil.

p. 69: *"Moreover, while it does cover. . . ."* Department of Defense, "2000 Report to Congress," September 12, 2000, 14; Statement of General Thomas A. Schwartz, March 5, 2002, 19.

p. 70: *"Factoring in attack helicopters. . . ."* O'Hanlon, *Defense Planning for the Late 1990s*, 43.

p. 70: *"Trevor Dupuy's assessment. . . ."* Trevor N. Dupuy, *Attrition: Forecasting Battle Casualties and Equipment Losses in Modern War* (Fairfax, Va.: HERO Books; 1990: 105–110, 148).

p. 70: *"Indeed, the Pentagon's official assessment. . . ."* Department of Defense, "2000 Report to Congress: Military Situation on the Korean Peninsula," September 12, 2000, 8, available at www.defenselink.mil/news/Sep2000/ korea09122000.html.

p. 70: *"According to the United States. . . ."* Statement of General Thomas A. Schwartz, March 5, 2002, 17.

p. 71: *"Associated troop numbers. . . ."* Under the 1993 BUR, the United States planned to deploy roughly 4–5 Army divisions plus the very extensive support equipment for about 2 large Army corps, 4–5 Marine brigades (making for a grand total of roughly 6 ground-combat divisions between the Army and the Marines), 4–5 aircraft carrier battle groups and associated wings of aircraft, 10 Air Force fighter wings (a Navy or Air Force tactical combat wing typically includes 72 operational aircraft), 100 Air Force bombers, and probably also missile defenses, special forces, and reserve forces. It would not have deployed Army National Guard combat units in significant numbers; plans for attack submarines, frigates, and a few other major assets were unclear. Les Aspin, *Report on the Bottom-Up Review* (Washington, D.C.: Department of Defense; 1993: 19).

The 1997 Quadrennial Defense Review was less precise about force requirements but essentially reasserted the BUR's results. Specifically, it stated, "The results of this analysis demonstrated that a force of the size and structure close to the current force was necessary to meet the requirement set out in the strategy of being able to win two, nearly simultaneous, major theater wars in concert with regional allies. While slightly smaller forces were capable of prevailing without a significant increase in risk in the base case of the analysis, a larger force was judged necessary to conduct these operations with acceptable risk when either enemy chemical weapons were used or shorter warning times were played." See William S. Cohen, *Report of the Quadrennial Defense Review* (Washington, D.C.: Department of Defense; 1997: 24). The 2001 review adopted a somewhat less demanding overall two-war planning benchmark, arguing that only one war at a time need involve all-out overthrow and occupation efforts. But it kept the same force structure, if anything implying an even slightly larger force for a war in which an enemy government would be overthrown and occupation of its territory carried out—as would likely be the case in Korea. See Donald H. Rumsfeld, *Quadrennial Defense Review Report* (Washington, D.C.: Department of Defense; 2001). On Operations Plan 5027, the war plan for Korea, see Oberdorfer, *The Two Koreas*, 325.

p. 71: *"Indeed, some reports suggest. . . ."* Ministry of National Defense, ROK, *Defense White Paper 2000*, 82.

p. 71: *"A modest additional ground force element. . . ."* Daniel Cooney, "U.S. Planes in S. Korea Will Remain as Deterrent," *Washington Post*, April 2, 2003, A13.

p. 71: *"Airfields available for U.S. combat aircraft. . . ."* Frances Lussier, *An Analysis of U.S. Army Helicopter Programs* (Washington, D.C.: U.S. Congressional Budget Office; 1995: 71–75); IISS, *The Military Balance 2002/2003*, 24; Michael O'Hanlon, "Restructuring U.S. Forces and Bases in Japan," in Mike M. Mochizuki, ed., *Toward a True Alliance: Restructuring U.S.-Japan Security Relations* (Washington, D.C.: Brookings Institution; 1997: 157); and Department of Defense, "2000 Report to Congress," 3.

REFERENCES

p. 71: "They are now expected. . . ." See for example, Vernon Loeb, "New Bases Reflect Shift in Military," *Washington Post,* June 9, 2003, 1.

p. 72: *"For that reason, Secretary of Defense William Perry. . . ."* Oberdorfer, *The Two Koreas* , 324–325.

p. 72: *"As a practical matter. . . ."* Rachel Schmidt, *Moving U.S. Forces: Options for Strategic Mobility* (Washington, D.C.: U.S. Congressional Budget Office; 1997: 29, 33–44, 79–95); Aspin, *Report on the Bottom-Up Review,* 20; Fran Lussier, *An Analysis of the Army's Force Structure* (Washington, D.C.: U.S. Congressional Budget Office; April 1997: 9); O'Hanlon, *Defense Planning for the Late 1990s,* 55–65; IISS, *The Military Balance 2002/2003,* 18–24.

p. 72: *"The former capability. . . ."* O'Hanlon, *Defense Planning for the Late 1990s,* 43; O'Hanlon, *The Art of War in the Age of Peace,* 66–67.

p. 73: *"The allies still conduct. . . ."* For more, see www.globalsecurity.org/military/ops/ex-usfk.htm.

p. 74: *"Attacks against Seoul. . . ."* See Oberdorfer, *The Two Koreas,* 313–324.

p. 75: *"Among them are that. . . ."* Joshua M. Epstein, "Dynamic Analysis and the Conventional Balance in Europe," *International Security* 12 (Spring 1988), 156; Robert L. Helmbold, "A Compilation of Data on Rates of Advance in Land Combat Operations," Research Paper CAA-RP-90-04 (Bethesda, Md.: U.S. Army Concepts Analysis Agency; February 1990: A-278–A-294, A-318–A-322); Barry R. Posen, "Measuring the European Conventional Balance: Coping with Complexity in Threat Assessment," in Steven E. Miller, ed., *Conventional Forces and American Defense Policy* (Princeton, N.J.: Princeton University Press; 1986: 114); Frances Lussier, *U.S. Ground Forces and the Conventional Balance in Europe* (Washington, D.C.: Congressional Budget Office; 1988: 86); Joshua M. Epstein, *Strategy and Force Planning: The Case of the Persian Gulf* (Washington, D.C.: Brookings Institution; 1987: 112–113); Eliot A. Cohen and John Gooch, *Military Misfortunes: The Anatomy of Failure in War* (New York: Free Press; 1990: 165–195); and Rod Paschall, *Korea: Witness to War* (New York: Berkley Publishing Group; 1995: 21, 167).

p. 75: *"Modern ground forces. . . ."* Stephen D. Biddle, David Gray, Stuart Kaufman, Dennis DeRiggi, and D. Sean Barnett, *Defense at Low Force Levels: The Effect of Force to Space Ratios on Conventional Combat Dynamics,* IDA Paper P-2380 (Alexandria, Va.: Institute for Defense Analyses; 1991: 7–41); William P. Mako, *U.S. Ground Forces and the Defense of Central Europe* (Washington, D.C.: Brookings Institution; 1983: 36–37); Robert McQuie, "Historical Characteristics of Combat for Wargames (Benchmarks)," CAA-RP-87-2 (Bethesda, Md.: U.S. Army, Concepts Analysis Agency; 1988); Joshua M. Epstein, *Conventional Force Reductions: A Dynamic Assessment* (Washington, D.C.: Brookings Institution; 1990: 58).

References

p. 76: *"But allied forces. . . ."* Under some circumstances, U.S. mines in Korea would be less helpful than they are frequently advertised to be by their proponents. They are estimated to number roughly 1 million (see Dana Priest, "56 in Senate to Press for Law Banning Use of Land Mines by U.S.," *Washington Post*, June 12, 1997, 12). But many would not be "installed" in the frozen ground in time to oppose a short-warning attack. See also Defense Intelligence Agency, *North Korea*, 58–59; Epstein, *Conventional Force Reductions*, 70; Engineer Studies Group, Department of the Army, *Measuring Obstacle Effectiveness: A Fresh Perspective*, vol. 1 (Fort Belvoir, Va.: 1975: 20); U.S. Army, *Ranger Handbook* (Fort Benning, Ga.: U.S. Army Infantry School; 1992: 6-1–6-12).

p. 76: *"Similar considerations apply. . . ."* On the effectiveness of artillery against exposed versus dug-in forces, see James F. Dunnigan, *How to Make War*, 3d ed. (New York: William Morrow; 1993: 125). Comparisons with the Iran-Iraq War are also telling here; in that conflict, most artillery-caused casualties were exposed soldiers attempting to effect an advance, and most successful infiltrations of minefields were the result of careful probing attacks rather than mass assaults. Both of these results involving armies of roughly comparable technology and training to North Korea's bode poorly for the latter's ability to carry out a successful massive surprise attack. See Anthony H. Cordesman and Abraham R. Wagner, *Lessons of Modern War, Volume 2: The Iran-Iraq War* (Boulder, Colo.: Westview Press; 1990: 433, 445, 447).

p. 77: *"They could also generally monitor. . . ."* See, for example, James L. Stokesbury, *A Short History of the Korean War* (New York: William Morrow; 1988: 102, 120); Jonathan Shimshoni, "Technology, Military Advantage, and World War I: A Case for Military Entrepreneurship," *International Security* 15 (Winter 1990/91), 205–207; Jane's Information Group, *Jane's Weapon Systems 1988–1989* (Alexandria, Va.: Jane's Information Group: 1988: 284–285, 399–406); David A. Fulghum, "Army Spy Aircraft Watch North Korea," *Aviation Week and Space Technology*, November 24, 1997, 58–59.

p. 79: *"Also, they would become highly vulnerable. . . ."* Headquarters, Depart-ment of the Army, *FM 100-5: Operations* (Washington, D.C.: Department of Defense; 1993: 8–4, 59); Nick Beldecos and Eric Heginbotham, "The Conventional Military Balance in Korea," *Breakthroughs* (Spring 1995), 5; Tony Capaccio, "If War Comes with North Korea, 'Buffaloes' Would Crush Caves," *Defense Week*, April 15, 1996, 7.

p. 80: *"But these efforts cannot change the facts. . . ."* Department of Defense, "2000 Report to Congress," 5-7; Statement of General Thomas A. Schwartz, 7–10.

CHAPTER 3

p. 84: *"He may be willing to reduce aid. . . ."* See Willis Witter, "Public Toughens Stance toward North," *Washington Times*, May 22, 2003, 17.

p. 84: *"Other key countries in the region. . . ."* See Doug Struck, "Bush's N. Korea Efforts Stymied," *Washington Post*, June 1, 2003, A22; Associated Press, "China, Russia Urge Nuclear-Free Korea," *Washington Post*, May 28, 2003.

p. 84: *"Japan has recently toughened up. . . ."* James Brooke, "North Korea Suspends Its Passenger Ferry Link with Japan," *New York Times*, June 9, 2003; Sachiko Sakamaki and Doug Struck, "Japan Cracks Down on Firms Tied to N. Korea," *Washington Post*, May 22, 2003, A23.

p. 90: *"It has suggested it would do so. . . ."* For a critique of the Bush administration's preemption concept but also an argument that it will not likely be applied widely, see Michael E. O'Hanlon, Susan E. Rice, and James B. Steinberg, "The New National Security Strategy and Preemption," Brookings Institution Policy Brief no. 113 (December 2002).

p. 93: *"But that risk was no greater. . . ."* Ashton B. Carter and William J. Perry, "Back to the Brink," *Washington Post*, October 20, 2002, B1. Reportedly, in 1994 U.S. planners estimated 52,000 U.S. military casualties (killed and wounded, probably corresponding to about 10,000 deaths) and about half a million ROK military casualties in the first three months of war. See Don Oberdorfer, *The Two Koreas: A Contemporary History* (Reading, Mass.: Addison-Wesley; 1997: 315).

p. 93: *"Second, North Korea's initial trouble. . . ."* On its initial setbacks, see Glenn Kessler and Walter Pincus, "N. Korea Stymied on Plutonium Work," *Washington Post*, March 20, 2003, 24.

p. 93: *"Since South Korea would likely bear the greatest burden. . . ."* See also Gary Samore, "North Korea, Again," *Survival* 45 (Spring 2003), 7–24.

p. 94: *"There is no hard evidence. . . ."* Michael R. Gordon with Felicity Barringer, "North Korea Wants Arms and More Aid From U.S., Chief of C.I.A. Suggests," *New York Times*, February 13, 2003.

p. 96: *"This can probably be done. . . ."* Testimony by Robert J. Einhorn before the Senate Foreign Relations Committee, "Negotiations with North Korea," March 6, 2003, available at www.csis.org.

p. 96: *"The preemptive threat should not be removed. . . ."* For a similar view, see William J. Perry, "Crisis on the Korean Peninsula: Implications for U.S. Policy in Northeast Asia," Brookings Leadership Forum, Brookings Institution, Washington, D.C., January 24, 2003.

p. 99: *"Inspectors in Iraq after Desert Storm. . . ."* Khidhir Hamza with Jeff Stein, *Saddam's Bombmaker* (New York: Touchstone Books; 2000: 333–337).

REFERENCES

p. 99: *"Indeed, the discovery of the nuclear program...."* David Kay, "It Was Never About a Smoking Gun," *Washington Post*, January 19, 2003, B3; David Albright, "The CIA's Aluminum Tubes' Assessment: Is the Nuclear Case Going Down the Tubes?" Institute for Science and International Security, March 10, 2003, available at www.isis-online.org/publications; Mohammed El Baradei, "Let Us Inspect," *Wall Street Journal*, March 7, 2003.

p. 99: *"When provided with good knowledge...."* David E. Sanger and James Dao, "U.S. Says Pakistan Gave Technology to North Korea," *New York Times*, October 18, 2002, 1; Joby Warrick, "Quest for Metal Was Tip-Off," *Washington Post*, October 18, 2002, 1; David Albright, Holly Higgins, and Kevin O'Neill, *Solving the North Korean Nuclear Puzzle*, available at www.isis-online.org/publications/dprk/book/epilogue.html; Central Intelligence Agency, "Unclassified Report to Congress on the Acquisition of Technology Relating to Weapons of Mass Destruction and Advanced Conventional Munitions, January 1 through June 30, 2001," January 2002, 5 of 13, available at www.cia.gov/cia/publications/bian/bian_jan_2002.htm.

p. 100: *"The inspections could be described...."* For a similar argument about applying the U.S.-Russia cooperative threat reduction experience to another part of the world, in this case the Indo-Pakistani nuclear rivalry, see Rose Gottemoeller with Rebecca Longsworth, "Enhancing Nuclear Security in the Counterterrorism Struggle," Carnegie Working Paper no. 29 (Washington, D.C.: Carnegie Endowment; 2002).

p. 100: *"Since the two Koreas and the United States...."* Leon V. Sigal, *Disarming Strangers: Nuclear Diplomacy with North Korea* (Princeton, N.J.: Princeton University Press; 1998: 32, 36, 39).

p. 101: *"It tested the Taepodong 1 three-stage rocket...."* Kongdan Oh and Ralph C. Hassig, *North Korea Through the Looking Glass* (Washington, D.C.: Brookings; 2000: 113); Robert S. Norris, Hans M. Kristensen, and Joshua Handler, "NRDC Nuclear Notebook: North Korea's Nuclear Program, 2003," *Bulletin of the Atomic Scientists* (March/April 2003), 74–77; Ministry of National Defense, Republic of Korea, *Defense White Paper 2000* (Seoul, 2000: 58–59).

p. 101: *"They may be capable...."* Central Intelligence Agency, "Unclassified Report to Congress on the Acquisition of Technology" January 2002, 5 of 13.

p. 101: *"That said, it is not trivial...."* See Janne E. Nolan, *Trappings of Power: Ballistic Missiles in the Third World* (Washington, D.C.: Brookings Institution Press; 1991: 63–73).

p. 102: *"It relaxed some sanctions...."* James M. Lindsay and Michael E. O'Hanlon, *Defending America: The Case for a Limited National*

REFERENCES

Missile Defense (Washington, D.C.: Brookings Institution Press; 2001: 59–65).

p. 102: *"In any case, there has been no movement. . . ."* Michael R. Gordon, "How Politics Sank Accord on Missiles with North Korea," *New York Times*, March 6, 2001, A1.

p. 103: *"Moreover, it was an approach. . . ."* Sigal, *Disarming Strangers*, 66–67.

p. 104: *"It is conventional force reductions. . . ."* For a similar argument, see Seo-Hang Lee, "Arms Control on the Korean Peninsula: Background and Issues," in IFANS, *The Korean Peninsula and Korea-U.S. Relations* (Seoul: Institute of Foreign Affairs and National Security; 1997: 3–13).

p. 106: *"At the same time. . . ."* See CSIS Working Group, *Conventional Arms Control on the Korean Peninsula* (Washington, D.C.: Center for Strategic and International Studies; 2002: 13–17); Lee, "Arms Control on the Korean Peninsula," 11.

p. 107: *"If North Korea wished. . . ."* For an analysis of some of the main elements of the CFE Treaty and prior negotiations, see Frances M. Lussier, "Budgetary and Military Effects of a Treaty Limiting Conventional Forces in Europe," CBO Paper (Washington, D.C.: Congressional Budget Office: 1990: 25–39).

p. 108: *"Using the CFE experience. . . ."* *Treaty on Conventional Armed Forces in Europe*, Paris, November 19, 1990, Protocol on Inspections; *U.S. Costs of Verification and Compliance Under Pending Arms Treaties* (Washington, D.C.: Congressional Budget Office; 1990: 31–34).

p. 109: *"It is also the main, conventional forces. . . ."* North Korea's conventional military forces comprise one million individuals and are backed up by large reserve forces and a large arms industry; what is known of North Korean nuclear, missile, biological, and chemical programs suggests corresponding efforts involving perhaps tens of thousands of individuals. Similarly, while North Korea has several factories to produce chemical weapons, for example, it has several hundred producing conventional military hardware. This suggests that the lion's share of North Korea's defense budget, which represents 20 to 30 percent of its GDP, is gobbled up by conventional forces, so they should be a main focus of any reform proposal. See Marcus Noland, *Avoiding the Apocalypse* (Washington, D.C.: Institute for International Economics; 2000: 71–73); Defense Intelligence Agency, *North Korea: The Foundations for Military Strength—Update 1995* (1996: 12, 24).

p. 111: *"Seoul's interests are similar. . . ."* On the convergence of U.S. and ROK interests, see Oknim Chung, "The U.S.-ROK Alliance: Time to Reinforce, Not to Reconsider," *U.S.-Korea Tomorrow* 6 (April 2003), 10–11.

CHAPTER 4

p. 114: *"The following analysis. . . ."* Much of this chapter is based on Pedro Almeida and Michael O'Hanlon, "Impasse in Korea: A Conventional Arms-Accord Solution?" *Survival* 41 (Spring 1999), 58–72.

p. 114: *"In addition, zonal limitations. . . ."* Defense Intelligence Agency, *North Korea: The Foundations for Military Strength—Update 1995* (Washington, D.C.: Defense Intelligence Agency; 1996: 13).

p. 115: *"Nor would its scope extend. . . ."* This proposal does not include elimination of land mines on the Korean peninsula—but neither is it prejudicial to such a possible future option. The arms control accord we propose should on balance improve the allied conventional military posture relative to the North Korean threat, so it should at least marginally strengthen the case for a land mine ban. But that argument is complex, and we do not take it on here. For a detailed assessment by one advocate of a ban, see Caleb Rossiter, "Winning in Korea Without Landmines," *VVAF Monograph Series* vol. 1, no. 3 (Summer 2000).

p. 116: *"However, North Korea's forces. . . ."* For a longer treatment, see Michael O'Hanlon, "Stopping a North Korean Invasion: Why Defending South Korea Is Easier than the Pentagon Thinks," *International Security* 22 (Spring 1998), 135–170.

p. 121: *"The Korean theater today. . . ."* For information on force densities in Europe during the Cold War, see Frances Lussier, *U.S. Ground Forces and the Conventional Balance in Europe* (Washington, D.C.: Congressional Budget Office; 1988: 7–28, 91–99).

p. 121: *"Even if allied forces..."* See Stephen D. Biddle, David Gray, Stuart Kaufman, Dennis DeRiggi, and D. Sean Barnett, *Defense at Low Force Levels: The Effect of Force to Space Ratios on Conventional Combat Dynamics*, IDA Paper P-2380 (Alexandria, Va.: Institute for Defense Analyses; 1991: 7–41); Joshua M. Epstein, *Conventional Force Reductions: A Dynamic Assessment* (Washington, D.C.: Brookings Institution; 1990: 58).

p. 122: *"As for heavy weapons. . . ."* See O'Hanlon, "Stopping a North Korean Invasion," 155–159.

CHAPTER 5

p. 128: *"Looked at another way. . . ."* Susan Shirk, "A New North Korea?" *Washington Post*, October 22, 2002, A27.

p. 130: *"These trends probably contributed. . . ."* Kongdan Oh and Ralph C. Hassig, *North Korea Through the Looking Glass* (Washington, D.C.: Brookings; 2000: 47–50).

REFERENCES

p. 130: *"But oil price shocks. . . ."* Marcus Noland, *Avoiding the Apocalypse: The Future of the Two Koreas* (Washington, D.C.: Institute for International Economics; 2000: 61–73); Don Oberdorfer, *The Two Koreas: A Contemporary History* (Reading, Mass.: Addison-Wesley; 1997: 97–99).

p. 131: *"But this economic strategy. . . ."* Nicholas Eberstadt, *The End of North Korea* (Washington, D.C.: American Enterprise Institute; 1999: 95–114).

p. 131: *"But even so. . . ."* Noland, *Avoiding the Apocalypse*, 144–145.

p. 131: *"The resulting famine. . . ."* Andrew Natsios, *The Politics of Famine in North Korea* (Washington, D.C.: U.S. Institute for Peace; 1999), available at www.usip.org; Noland, *Avoiding the Apocalypse*, 80, 177; Oh and Hassig, *North Korea*, 42.

p. 131: *"As things have gotten worse. . . ."* The last includes about 10,000 workers in Russia, who send home perhaps $50 million a year in wages. See James Brooke, "North Korea Gives Russia Cheap Labor," *New York Times*, May 18, 2003, 8.

p. 131: *"About 50 percent. . . ."* CIA, *The World Factbook 2002* (2002), available at www.cia.gov/cia/publications/factbook/geos/kn.html; Noland, *Avoiding the Apocalypse*, 89–91, 116–133.

p. 132: *"This is provided mostly. . . ."* Peter S. Goodman, "U.S. Faces Obstacles in Strategy on North Korea," *Washington Post*, December 31, 2002, A1.

p. 132: *"Given its spotty track record. . . ."* For a highly skeptical view, see Eberstadt, *The End of North Korea*, 82–5.

p. 132: *"DPRK leaders undoubtedly fear. . . ."* See Defense Intelligence Agency, *North Korea: The Foundations for Military Strength—Update 1995* (Washington, D.C.: U.S. Defense Intelligence Agency; 1996: 9).

p. 132: *"Functionaries in the Korean Workers Party. . . ."* David Shambaugh, "China and the Korean Peninsula: Playing for the Long Term," *Washington Quarterly* 26 (Spring 2003), 48.

p. 133: *"First, special economic zones. . . ."* Sam-Sik Kim, "Outlook on North Korea's Foreign Economic Relations in 2003," Korea Trade-Investment Promotion Agency, Seoul, Republic of Korea, 2003, available at crm.kotra.or.kr/main/common_bbs.

p. 133: *"Though generally unsuccessful to date. . . ."* Mitsuru Mizuno, "North Korea and International Financial Institutions: Problems that Have to Be Addressed for the Utilization of IFIs," in Sasakawa Peace Foundation, *The Future of the Korean Peninsula and International Cooperation* (Tokyo: Sasakawa Peace Foundation; 2002: 244–260).

p. 134: *"The region's greatest potential. . . ."* Yong-Kyun Cho, "Strategies for Economic Reform in North Korea," in IFANS, *The Korean Peninsula and*

REFERENCES

Korea-U.S. Relations (Seoul, South Korea: Institute of Foreign Affairs and National Security; 1997: 34–35); Noland, *Avoiding the Apocalypse*, 133–139.

p. 134: *"But whatever its prospects...."* James Brooke, "Trial Runs of a Free Market in North Korea," *New York Times*, March 11, 2003, C1.

p. 135: *"We return to this issue below."* Noland, *Avoiding the Apocalypse*, 139–140.

p. 135: *"Indeed, severe inflation...."* John Pomfret, "Reforms Turn Disastrous for North Koreans: Nuclear Crisis May Have Roots in Economic Failure," *Washington Post*, January 27, 2003, A1.

p. 136: *"North Korea already has...."* Scott Kennedy, "Conflicting Logics of Korean Reform," in IFANS, *The Korean Peninsula and Korea-U.S. Relations* (Seoul, South Korea: Institute of Foreign Affairs and National Security; 1997: 46–48); Nicholas R. Lardy, *Integrating China into the Global Economy* (Washington, D.C.: Brookings; 2002: 13); Noland, *Avoiding the Apocalypse*, 281.

p. 136: *"It still faces major economic problems...."* Lardy, *Integrating China into the Global Economy*, 4–16.

p. 136: *"On the latter point...."* See Noland, *Avoiding the Apocalypse*, 273–281, 348 (quote from p. 348).

p. 137: *"The combination of reforms...."* Sumio Kuribayashi, "Economic Interdependence between North Korea and Northeast Asian Countries: Potential for Future Economic Cooperation—An Analysis of International Input-Output Tables," in Sasakawa Peace Foundation, *The Future of the Korean Peninsula and International Cooperation* (Tokyo: Sasakawa Peace Foundation; 2002: 196–216).

p. 137: *"Certainly many scholars and officials...."* For another argument along these lines, see Li Gang-Zhe, "External Economic Policy of North Korea Trying for Market Economy—From Viewpoint of Economic Cooperation in Northeast Asia," in Sasakawa Peace Foundation, *The Future of the Korean Peninsula and International Cooperation* (Tokyo: Sasakawa Peace Foundation; 2002: 77–93).

p. 139: *"A combination of China-style economic reforms...."* On the record of development aid, see Michael O'Hanlon and Carol Graham, *A Half Penny on the Federal Dollar: The Future of Development Aid* (Washington, D.C.: Brookings Institution; 1997).

p. 140: *"It could then gradually spread out...."* See O'Hanlon and Graham, *A Half Penny on the Federal Dollar*, 59–65.

p. 140: *"It does not seem a particularly appropriate model...."* Ullrich Heilemann and Wolfgang H. Reinecke, *Welcome to Hard Times* (Washington, D.C.: Brookings Institution; 1995: 26); Marcus Noland,

Avoiding the Apocalypse: The Future of the Two Koreas (Washington, D.C.: Institute for International Economics; 2000: 285–295).

p. 141: *"Japan provided a total of $500 million...."* See, for example, Michael J. Green, *Japan's Reluctant Realism* (New York: Palgrave; 2001: 114).

p. 141: *"But it would be roughly comparable...."* See "Country/Account Summaries ('Spigots'), FY 2004," Department of State, February 2003, available at www.state.gov.

p. 142: *"China's role would be critical...."* Peter S. Goodman, "U.S. Faces Obstacles in Strategy on North Korea," *Washington Post*, December 31, 2002, A1; James Brooke, "Trial Runs of a Free Market in North Korea," *New York Times*, March 11, 2003, C1.

CHAPTER 6

p. 149: *"Perhaps even more important...."* See Richard K. Betts, "Wealth, Power, and Instability: East Asia and the United States after the Cold War," *International Security* 18 (Winter 1993/94), 46.

p. 150: *"What would be the overarching purposes...."* For a similar argument about the future of the U.S.-Japan alliance after the Korean confrontation is defused, see Mike Mochizuki and Michael O'Hanlon, "A Liberal Vision for the U.S.-Japanese Alliance," *Survival* 40 (Summer 1998), 127–134.

p. 150: *"In addition, what specific types...."* Some of the ideas discussed below appear in Michael O'Hanlon, "Keep U.S. Forces in Korea after Reunification," *The Korean Journal of Defense Analysis* 10 (Summer 1998), 5–19.

p. 151: *"In other words, to the extent...."* See Robert Ross, "Assessing the China Challenge," Henry Stimson Center, Washington, D.C., May 14, 1997.

p. 151: *"This conclusion is reinforced...."* See David Shambaugh, "China's Security and Military Policy and the Potential for CBMs in the Region," Henry Stimson Center, Washington, DC, December 17, 1996.

p. 152: *"Knowing in advance...."* See Barry R. Posen and Andrew L. Ross, "Competing Visions for U.S. Grand Strategy," *International Security* 21 (Winter 1996/97), 15–16; Richard N. Haass, *The Reluctant Sheriff: The United States After the Cold War* (Washington, D.C.: Council on Foreign Relations; 1997: 85).

p. 152: *"With U.S. military facilities...."* See Robert Crumplar, "A Future U.S. Military Presence on a Unified Korean Peninsula," paper presented at Brookings-IFANS Conference, Washington, DC, July 1997, 3; Haass, *The Reluctant Sheriff*, 85.

p. 153: *"The U.S.-Japan and U.S.-Korea security relationships...."* See Kishore Mahbubani, "An Asia-Pacific Consensus," *Foreign Affairs* 76

(September/October 1997), 149–158; for evidence of Japanese views, see Mike M. Mochizuki, "American and Japanese Strategic Debates: The Need for a New Synthesis," and Takuma Takahashi, "Economic Interdependence and Security in the East Asia–Pacific Region," in Mike M. Mochizuki, ed., *Toward a True Alliance: Restructuring U.S.-Japan Security Relations* (Washington, D.C.: Brookings; 1997: 56–72 and 114, respectively).

p. 153: *"If they are increasingly integrated. . . ."* For more on the vision of closer security ties between Japan and South Korea and the associated benefits, see Victor Cha, "Values After Victory: The Future of U.S.-Japan-Korea Relations," paper presented at the Pacific Forum CSIS April 2002 Conference on Future Relations among the U.S., Korea, and Japan, available at www.csis.org/pacfor/annual/2002_full.pdf.

p. 153: *"They are also better than paper treaties. . . ."* See Kenneth N. Waltz, *Theory of International Politics* (Reading, Mass.: Addison-Wesley; 1979: 129–193); Aaron L. Friedberg, "Ripe for Rivalry: Prospects for Peace in a Multipolar Asia," *International Security* 18 (Winter 1993/94), 5–10; Donald Kagan, "Locarno's Lessons for NATO," *Wall Street Journal*, October 28, 1997, 22.

p. 154: *"But many Korean scholars and officials. . . ."* See for example, Byung-joon Ahn, "The Future of Korea in Northeast Asian Regional Security," in IFANS, *The Korean Peninsula and Korea-U.S. Relations* (Seoul, South Korea: Institute of Foreign Affairs and National Security; 1997: 79–80); Keun-Sik Kim, "Inter-Korean Relations and the Future of the Sunshine Policy," *Journal of East Asian Affairs* 16, (Spring/Summer 2002), 115–117; Ministry of National Defense, *Defense White Paper 2000* (Seoul, 2000), 115.

p. 154: *"Therefore, the stabilizing benefit. . . ."* For a thoughtful Chinese view admitting the potential for specific tension and conflict but underscoring the region's general commitment to peaceful relations, see Tian Xinjian and Feng Haixia, "Asian Security and CBMs Over the Next Decade," in Michael Krepon, ed., *Chinese Perspectives on Confidence-building Measures*, Report No. 23 (Washington, D.C.: Henry Stimson Center; 1997: 39–50).

p. 154: *"Some have argued against a long-term U.S.-Korea alliance. . . ."* Selig Harrison, *Korean Endgame* (Princeton, N.J.: Princeton University Press; 2002: 285–356).

p. 154: *"Such a positive result. . . ."* David Shambaugh, "China and the Korean Peninsula: Playing for the Long Term," *Washington Quarterly* 26 (Spring 2003), 51–52).

p. 154: *"Keeping the bilateral alliances intact. . . ."* See Richard L. Kugler, *Changes Ahead: Future Directions for the U.S. Overseas Military Presence* (Santa Monica, Calif.: RAND; 1998: 84).

p. 154: *"Leaders in Seoul, Tokyo, and Washington. . . ."* For one possible approach, see Ashton B. Carter, William J. Perry, and John D. Steinbruner,

A New Concept of Cooperative Security (Washington, D.C.: Brookings Institution; 1992: 64–65); for a related and more recent view, see Zbigniew Brzezinski, "A Geostrategy for Eurasia," *Foreign Affairs* 76 (September/October 1997), 63–64.

p. 155: *"These types of efforts. . . ."* On this point, see Ashton B. Carter and William J. Perry, *Preventive Defense: A New Security Strategy for America* (Washington, D.C.: Brookings Institution; 1999: 106–111).

p. 155: *"The United States has conducted peacekeeping exercises. . . ."* See Dennis C. Blair and John T. Hanley, Jr., "From Wheels to Webs: Reconstructing Asia-Pacific Security Arrangements," *Washington Quarterly* (Winter 2001), 13.

p. 155: *"Such measures and dialogues. . . ."* Marie-France Desjardins, "Rethinking Confidence-Building Measures," *Adelphi Paper 307* (Oxford: Oxford University Press; 1996: 60–63).

p. 156: *"Because the U.S.-Japan and U.S.-Korea alliances. . . ."* Andrew Mack and Pauline Kerr, "The Evolving Security Discourse in the Asia-Pacific," *Washington Quarterly* 18 (Winter 1995), 129.

p. 156: *"Alliances between various Asian powers. . . ."* See Kishore Mahbubani, "An Asia-Pacific Consensus"; Michael H. Armacost, *Friends or Rivals?* (New York: Columbia University Press; 1996: 212); Satoshi Morimoto, "The Security Environment in East Asia," in Mike M. Mochizuki, ed., *Toward a True Alliance* (Washington, D.C.: Brookings Institution; 1997: 84–85).

p. 156: *"Even with its new emphasis. . . ."* Michael E. O'Hanlon, Susan E. Rice, and James B. Steinberg, "The New National Security Strategy and Preemption," *Brookings Policy Brief No. 113* (Washington, D.C.: Brookings Institution; 2002).

p. 158: *"Additional supplies for U.S. forces. . . ."* See Assistant Chief of Staff, Resource Management, U.S. Forces Korea, "U.S. Forces Korea in the Republic of Korea 1997," Department of Defense, 1997; International Institute for Strategic Studies, *The Military Balance 1996/1997* (Oxford, England: Oxford University Press; 1996: 29).

p. 159: *"It could have four to five divisions there. . . ."* See Michael O'Hanlon, *Defense Planning for the Late 1990s: Beyond the Desert Storm Framework* (Washington, D.C.: Brookings Institution; 1995: 50–65); Rachel Schmidt, *Moving U.S. Forces: Options for Strategic Mobility* (Washington, D.C.: Congressional Budget Office; 1997: 7).

p. 161: *"Taking this step could help prove to China. . . ."* See Russ Swinnerton, "Piracy Remains a Concern for Southeast Asian Nations," *Defense News*, August 25–31, 1997, 8.

REFERENCES

p. 162: *"However, enough potential danger zones. . . ."* For example, the Senkaku Islands are about 650 miles from southern South Korea, the Taiwan Straits roughly 750 miles distant, and the Paracel Islands in the South China Sea about 1,500 miles away. At a distance of roughly 1,000 miles from its base and with one in-flight refueling, an AWACS surveillance aircraft can maintain station for about 15 hours, and an F-16 can conduct a combat mission (but with only modest loiter time). The Navy's P-3 land-based maritime surveillance aircraft could loiter about 5 hours at that distance. See Colonel Timothy M. Laur and Steven L. Llanso, *Encyclopedia of Modern U.S. Military Weapons* (New York: Berkley Books; 1995: 59, 78, 91).

p. 162: *"Moreover, the Army has gained considerable experience. . . ."* William E. Odom, "Transforming the Military," *Foreign Affairs* 76 (July/August 1997), 60. Odom makes the point in specific regard to Japan, but it is valid more generally.

p. 163: *"Secretary of Defense Donald H. Rumsfeld. . . ."* Sonni Efron and Mark Magnier, "Rumsfeld May Reduce Forces in S. Korea," *Los Angeles Times*, February 14, 2003.

p. 164: *"Cost arguments should simply. . . ."* See Michael O'Hanlon, "Restructuring U.S. Forces and Bases in Japan," in Mike M. Mochizuki, ed., *Toward a True Alliance: Restructuring U.S.-Japan Security Relations* (Washington, D.C.: Brookings Institution; 1997: 159–161).

APPENDIX 1

p. 167: *"Structured quantitative and. . . ."* This appendix, like Chapter 2, is also derived in part from Michael O'Hanlon, "Stopping a North Korean Invasion: Why Defending South Korea Is Easier than the Pentagon Thinks," *International Security*, vol. 22, no. 4 (Spring 1998), pp. 135-170.

p. 167: *"This conclusion is. . . ."* Zalmay M. Khalilzad and David A. Ochmanek, "Rethinking U.S. Defence Planning," *Survival*, Vol. 39, No. 1 (Spring 1997), pp. 43-64; National Defense Panel, "Assessment of the May 1997 Quadrennial Defense Review" (Arlington, Va.: National Defense Panel, May 15, 1997), p. 8; General John Shalikashvili, "Comments by the Chairman of the Joint Chiefs of Staff," in Cohen, *Report of the Quadrennial Defense Review*, p. 66; Eliot A. Cohen, "Toward Better Net Assessment: Rethinking the European Conventional Balance," *International Security*, Vol. 13, No. 1 (Summer 1988), pp. 50-89.

In 1990-1991, analysts such as Joshua Epstein, Barry Posen, and Trevor Dupuy predicted that total U.S. casualties would number no more than 10,000 to 15,000—and thus that 2,000 to 3,000 might be killed (assuming one death for every four to five casualties). Press reports suggest that the Pentagon's estimates were two to three times higher; actual U.S. killed totaled about 400, including those killed in training and deployment during Operation Desert Shield. See Congressional Budget Office, "Costs of Operation Desert Shield" (Washington, D.C.: U.S. Congressional Budget Office, January 1991), p. 15.

p. 168: *"A thorough analysis. . . ."* See Beldecos and Heginbotham, "The Conventional Military Balance in Korea," *Breakthroughs*, p. 6.

p. 168: *"Once the buildup. . . ."* Some might argue that U.S. and Korean forces would ignore a buildup even once they detected it, given the tendency of countries to find themselves surprised in battle despite observing a number of warning signs in the period leading up to hostilities. But that argument does not seem convincing in the Korean context, given the absence of a peace accord, the most militarized terrain in the world, and a number of serious war scares in recent years. For the general tendency of states to be surprised, see Richard K. Betts, *Surprise Attack* (Washington, D.C.: Brookings Institution, 1982), pp. 3-24.

p. 168: *"In the Gulf War,. . . ."* Thomas A. Keaney and Eliot A. Cohen, *Gulf War Air Power Survey Summary Report* (Washington, D.C.: Government Printing Office, 1993), pp. 127-128.

p. 169: *"Mechanized ROK units. . . ."* Approximately 40 percent of South Korea's infantry forces are in the first line of defenses; in addition, three armor-heavy mechanized infantry divisions would be available to counterconcentrate against the North Korean attack, though their equipment is not figured into these frontline numbers. See Beldecos and Heginbotham, "The Conventional Military Balance in Korea," *Breakthroughs*, p. 4.

p. 170: *"Modern TOW missiles. . . ."* See Jeffrey Record, "Armored Advance Rates: A Historical Inquiry,"*Military Review*, Vol. 53, No. 9 (September 1973), pp. 63-66; Epstein, *Conventional Force Reductions*, p. 69; Robert H. Scales, Jr., *Certain Victory: The U.S. Army in the Gulf War* (McLean, Va.: Brassey's, 1994), p. 81; Colonel Timothy M. Laur and Steven L. Llanso, *Encyclopedia of Modern U.S. Military Weapons* (New York: Berkley Publishing Group, 1995), pp. 227, 232-235, 270-271; and Department of Defense, *Conduct of the Persian Gulf War: Final Report to Congress* (1992), pp. T-126 through T-129.

p. 172: *"But North Korean. . . ."* U.S. Army, *Ranger Handbook* (Fort Benning, Ga.: U.S. Army Infantry School, 1992), pp. 6-15 through 6-24, 15-3; W.J. Schultis et. al., *Comparison of Military Potential: NATO and Warsaw Pact* (Alexandria, Va.: Weapon System Evaluation Group, June 1974); and Dunnigan, *How to Make War*, p. 64.

p. 172: *"Also, if the weather. . . ."* Allied artillery might typically have inaccuracies of a few meters, whereas North Korean rounds might typically be off by several tens of meters, at least initially. For data on modern artillery-tracking radars, see, for example, Jane's Information Group, *Jane's Weapon Systems 1988-1989* (Alexandria, Va.: Jane's Information Group, 1988), pp. 291-292.

p. 173: *"North Korean biological...."* Steve Fetter, *Toward a Comprehensive Test Ban* (Cambridge, Mass.: Ballinger Publishing, 1988), pp. 169-174; and Congressional Budget Office, *Implementing START II* (Washington, D.C.: U.S. Congressional Budget Office, March 1993), p. 48; Defense Intelligence Agency, *North Korea: The Foundations for Military Strength* (Washington, D.C.: 1991), pp. 60-62.

p. 174: *"They would make...."* Victor A. Utgoff, *The Challenge of Chemical Weapons: An American Perspective* (New York: St. Martin's Press, 1991), pp. 172-181; U.S. Forces Korea, "U.S. Forces Korea in the Republic of Korea, 1997," p. 18; U.S.-Japan Security Consultative Committee, "The Guidelines for U.S.-Japan Defense Cooperation," September 23, 1997, Section V.2.(2).a; and Schmidt, *Moving U.S. Forces*, p. 25.

p. 175: *"And even if...."* Office of Technology Assessment, *Proliferation of Weapons of Mass Destruction: Assessing the Risks*, OTA-ISC-559 (Washington, D.C.: U.S. Congress Office of Technology Assessment, August 1993), pp. 52-57; Lisbeth Gronlund, George Lewis, Theodore Postol, and David Wright, "The Weakest Line of Defense: Intercepting Ballistic Missiles," in Joseph Cirincione and Frank von Hippel, *The Last 15 Minutes* (Washington, D.C.: Coalition to Reduce Nuclear Dangers, 1996), pp. 51-60. The lethal radius of a one-ton chemical warhead might be about half a kilometer on a cloudy day with low wind. See Janne E. Nolan, *Trappings of Power* (Washington, D.C.: Brookings Institution, 1991), pp. 33, 70-72; and Office of Technology Assessment, *Proliferation of Weapons of Mass Destruction*, p. 54.

p. 176: *"Given that allied...."* Cordesman and Wagner, *The Lessons of Modern War, Volume 2*, p. 518; Trevor N. Dupuy, *Attrition: Forecasting Battle Casualties and Equipment Losses in Modern War* (Fairfax, Va.: HERO Books, 1990), p. 58; Utgoff, *The Challenge of Chemical Weapons*, pp. 6-7.

INDEX

Adaptive dynamic model, 168
Adoption of grand bargain, 20
Afghanistan, U.S. aid to, 141
Agreed Framework between the
    United States of America and
    the Democratic People's
    Republic of Korea, 4, 177–181
  and DPRK extortion, 84
  and DPRK reforms, 31
  inception of, 12
  plutonium release conditions in, 6
  value of, to DPRK, 96
  violations of, 15, 39, 96, 98
Aid, 19, 89
  conditions for, 7, 89–90
  duration of, 111, 138
  economic, 19, 48–49, 89–90
  and economic reform, 138–142
  forms of, 3
  probable amounts needed,
    139–140
Air Force troops in Korea, 158,
    160–162
Aircraft:
  under CFK accord, 106
  50 percent cuts in, 117–121
  fire from, 77–78
Albright, Madeleine, K., 13, 29
Alliances, 156 (*See also* Long-term
    U.S.—ROK alliance)
Allies (*see* Regional partners)
Analytical Science Corporation, 67,
    118
Appeasement, charges of, 3
Armored attack, modeling DPRK
    breakthrough with, 169–171
Armored personnel carriers:
  under CFK accord, 106
  50 percent cuts in, 117–120
Arms cuts (*see* Conventional arms
    reduction)
Arms sales, DPRK, 30

Army troops in Korea, 157–160, 162,
    163
Artillery:
  under CFK accord, 106
  50 percent cuts in, 117–120
  modeling DPRK breakthrough
    using infantry and, 171–173
  vulnerabilities to, 76
Asia-Pacific region:
  current U.S. troops in, 148
  desire for stability in, 154
  long-term security structures in,
    153–156
Attrition-FEBA expansion model, 168
Australia, grand bargain negotiations
    and, 8
Avoiding the Apocalypse (Marcus
    Noland), 136–137
"Axis of evil," 14, 27, 37, 41, 95

Ballistic missiles, 8
  grand bargain requirements for, 91
  production of, 100
  testing of, 100, 102
Beldecos, Nick, 168
Benchmarks, 5, 7
Bilateral talks, multilateral talks vs.,
    7–8, 17, 37
Biological weapons:
  acceptance of conventions against,
    8
  grand bargain requirements for, 8,
    50, 86, 91
Blackmail, charges of, 3, 12
Bush administration policy, 2, 4, 5,
    14–16
  and buy-out of DPRK missile
    program, 44
  during current nuclear crisis,
    35–38
  and diplomatic relations, 95
  DPRK fears about intentions of, 17

INDEX

Bush administration policy *(Cont.)*:
   new approach needed in, 11
   for preemptive use of force, 60, 156–157
Bush, George W.:
   changes to Clinton policies by, 11
   during current nuclear crisis, 36–38
   and current ROK—U.S. relations, 41–42
   and direct, bilateral talks, 45
   and DPRK blackmail, 143
   and DPRK in "axis of evil," 14, 27, 37
   and DPRK nuclear exports, 34
   hard line policy of, 4, 14
   and Kim Jong Il, 15, 36
   and limited engagement school, 85
   and national security strategy, 183–193
   and sunshine policy, 41

Camp Red Cloud U.S. Army Base, 157
Canada, grand bargain negotiations and, 8
Cash transfers (to DPRK), 134–135
Center for Strategic and International Studies (CSIS) report, 50–51
CFE Treaty (*see* Conventional Forces in Europe Treaty)
CFK accord (*see* "Conventional Forces in Korea" accord)
Challenge inspections, 6, 97, 108
Chemical weapons:
   acceptance of conventions against, 8
   grand bargain requirements for, 8, 50, 86, 91
   modeling DPRK breakthrough using, 173–176
China:
   aid from, 7, 89, 110, 132, 142
   in April 2003 talks, 16
   development assistance from, 139
   and DPRK nuclear weapons development, 33
   DPRK trade with, 132
   energy resources from, 131

China *(Cont.)*:
   engagement policy endorsed by, 84
   as example of economic reform, 49–50, 135–136
   hypothetical attacks from, 146, 148, 151–152
   Kim Jong Il's visits to, 132
   and need for hard line policy, 2
   in negotiations for grand bargain, 8
   and options for U.S. forces in reunified Korea, 158–163
   perception of long-term U.S.—ROK alliance in, 149
   and post-crisis security tasks, 155
   technical assistance from, 19, 49, 89
   "third way" of, 131
   and unification of regional partners, 53–54, 111–112
   and U.S.—ROK long-term alliance, 154–157
Chorwon corridor, 63
Clinton administration policy, 11–14, 94–95
   on DPRK missile capabilities, 102–103
   and DPRK sanctions, 39
   and ROK vs. U.S. difference in views, 42
   tactical approach in, 43–44
"Coercion" approach, 2, 4, 37–38, 83–84
Colombia, U.S. aid to, 141
Combat aircraft:
   under CFK accord, 106
   50 percent cuts in, 117–119
Commando forces, 79
Communications systems, 117
Confidence-building measures, 155
Conventional arms reduction, 6–7, 113–126
   aid tied to, 52–53
   for aircraft, 120–121
   apportioning of allies' resources in, 115
   for armored personnel carriers, 117–119
   for artillery, 120

Conventional arms reduction *(Cont.)*:
  capabilities of allied firepower after, 121–124
  for combat aircraft, 117–119
  economic aid tied to, 48–49
  economic benefits of, 114
  50 percent cut proposal for, 104–106, 114–117
  grand bargain requirements for, 6–7, 48–49, 85–86, 91–92, 104–109
  for large-bore artillery, 117–119
  for light tanks/armored personnel carriers, 119–120
  precedents for, 54
  for tanks, 117–119
  zonal limitations in, 114–115
Conventional Forces in Europe (CFE) Treaty, 85, 105–108
"Conventional Forces in Korea" (CFK) accord, 6, 85–86, 104–109, 124 (*See also* 50 percent cut proposal)
Conventional military balance, 57–81
  DPRK military capabilities, 65–68
  as greatest threat to ROK, 17–18
  military analysis of attempted DPRK invasion, 73–80
  and military geography of peninsula, 63–64
  and preemptive ROK—U.S. attack, 60–62
  ROK military capabilities, 68–70
  and surprise DPRK attack, 58–60, 64–65
  United States' forces in potential war, 70–73
Council on Foreign Relations, 54
Counterfeiting, 8, 50, 86
CSIS report (*see* Center for Strategic and International Studies report)
Cult of personality, 24–25

Defense Intelligence Agency, 59
Demilitarized zone (DMZ):
  conventional arms cuts near, 6, 7, 105, 107, 108

Demilitarized zone (DMZ) *(Cont.)*:
  DPRK forces in, 26
  forces deployed near, 65
  under grand bargain, 48
  impediments to movement in, 75–76
  proposed drawdowns along, 54
Democratic People's Republic of Korea (DPRK):
  cult of personality in, 24–25
  and current nuclear crisis, 31–39
  dangers of nuclear arsenal in, 40
  economic conditions in, 26–27
  economic history of, 129–131
  grand bargain demands on, 18–19
  history of, 23–31
  human rights abuses in, 24
  juche system in, 27, 130
  military capabilities of, 65–68
  military options of, 10
  military spending in, 18, 26, 58, 66, 130
  modeling of attempted breakthrough by, 167–176
  and nuclear non-proliferation accord with ROK, 15, 31, 34–35
  nuclear weapons capabilities of, 8–11, 15–16, 31
  past negotiation patterns of, 17, 52
  probable response to preemptive attacks by, 10–11
  quality of military in, 10, 62, 79–80
  recent reforms in, 28–31
  reverence for political leadership in, 24–25
  starvation in, 24
  threat of ROK invasion by, 73–80, 115–116
  threat posed by, 26–28
  U.S. sanctions on, 87–89
  vital statistics for, 64
Denuclearization, 92–100
  and aid for economic reform, 138
  factors complicating, 93–94
  grand bargain requirements for, 5–6, 46, 48, 85, 96–98

223

Denuclearization *(Cont.)*:
  inspections related to, 98–100
  and recent diplomatic history,
    94–96
  as top priority, 5–6
Détente policy (DPRK—ROK), 29, 45
Development aid, 3, 19, 110, 139–141
Diplomatic relations, 19
  during Bush administration, 95
  during Clinton administration,
    94–95
  between DPRK and ROK, 29
  following 1994 accord, 12–13
  between U.S. and DPRK, 8, 50, 86,
    90–92
DMZ *(see* Demilitarized zone)
DPRK *(see* Democratic People's
  Republic of Korea)
Drug trafficking, 8, 50, 86
Dupuy, Trevor, 70

East Germany, 140
Economic aid, 19
  conventional arms reduction
    required for, 48–49
  under grand bargain, 89–90, 92,
    109–111
Economic conditions (in DPRK):
  current, 24, 26–27
  under grand bargain, 49
  history of, 127–131
Economic reform, 6, 7, 127–143
  aid conditional upon, 7, 49
  current prospects for, 135–137
  DPRK attempts at, 20, 131–135
  grand bargain requirements for, 6,
    7, 92, 109
  and history of DPRK economy,
    127–131
  and political power, 132
  role of external aid in, 138–142
Economic zones, 133–135, 139, 140
Education (in DPRK), 130, 135, 139,
  141
Egypt, U.S. aid to, 141
Energy sources:
  development of, 19
  under grand bargain, 89, 97

Engagement, traditional policy of,
  84–85
Epstein "adaptive dynamic model,"
  168
European Union, aid from, 132
Exports, 132
  arms, 131
  missile, 8, 13, 26
Extortionist behavior (of DPRK), 4,
  29, 84, 109

Failure of grand bargain, 1–2, 20–21,
  129
50 percent cut proposal, 104–106, 125
Fighting vehicles (under CFK accord),
  106
Foreign investment (in DPRK), 134
France, U.S. military operations and,
  150
Fuel oil shipments:
  restoration of, 6, 91
  suspension of, 15

Gaeseong Industrial Zone, 133
Geography, military, 63–64
Germany, 140
Geumgang Mountain Special Tourism
  Zone, 133
Grand bargain, 1, 3–4, 83–112
  aid provisions in, 7, 19, 89–90
  broad goal of, 3
  and charges of
    appeasement/blackmail, 3
  and chemical/biological weapons,
    8, 50, 86
  as choice for DPRK, 5, 11, 20
  conventional arms reductions in,
    6–7, 48–49, 85–86, 104–109
  counterfeiting issues in, 8, 50, 86
  countries involved in, 7–8
  demands coupled with incentives
    in, 43
  demands on DPRK in, 18–19
  denuclearization issues in, 5–6, 46,
    48, 85, 92–100
  diplomatic ties with ROK in, 86
  diplomatic ties with U.S. in, 4,
    90–91

INDEX

Grand bargain *(Cont.)*:
  drug trafficking issue in, 8, 50, 86
  economic aid issues in, 48, 49, 89–90, 109–111
  economic reform issues in, 6, 7, 109
  and failure of prevailing schools of thought, 83–85
  goals of, 46
  human rights issues in, 8, 50, 86
  implementation of, 53, 91–92
  Japanese kidnapping victims provisions in, 8, 50, 86
  missiles issues in, 8, 85, 100–104
  negotiation of, 42–43
  precedent for, 54–55
  reasons for, 51–54
  regime change in, 3, 49–50
  results from potential failure of, 1–2, 20–21
  terrorism support issues in, 8, 86
  uniting regional parties behind, 111–112
  U.S. pledges in, 8, 50, 86–87, 90
  and U.S. preemptive military strikes, 46–47
  as vision and roadmap, 43
  vision of, 5
Gulf War, 168, 170, 171

Haass, Richard, 43
Hard-line policies, 2, 4, 5
Health improvements (in DPRK), 139, 141
Heginbotham, Eric, 168
Helicopters (under CFK accord), 106
"Hermit kingdom," 23
Howard, John, 34
Human rights issues, 8, 24, 50, 86
Humanitarian aid, 141, 155
Hussein, Saddam, 62

IAEA inspectors *(see* International Atomic Energy Agency inspectors)
Implementation of grand bargain, 53, 91–92
Imports, DPRK, 131, 132
Incentives to reform, 4
  as catalysts to reform, 16
  demands coupled with, 43, 51–52

Infantry, modeling DPRK breakthrough using artillery and, 171–173
Infrastructure development, 139–141
Inspections, 97–100
  under CFK accord, 108
  challenge, 6, 97, 108
  of conventional arms, 91
  as deterrent to surprise attack, 117
  in Iraq, 99
  for nuclear programs, 6, 98–99
  possible objection to, 99–100
  to verify end of uranium enrichment program, 97
International Atomic Energy Agency (IAEA) inspectors, 32, 98
International financial institutions, 138–139
Iraq war, 33, 34, 42, 61, 62
Iraq's nuclear program, 99
Israel, 44, 103, 141

Japan:
  aid from, 7, 89, 132
  compensation for colonization from, 19, 110, 141
  DPRK attempted rapprochement with, 133
  and DPRK nuclear weapons development, 33
  DPRK trade with, 132
  engagement policy endorsed by, 84
  kidnapping victims from, 8, 30, 50, 86, 90–92
  and long–term U.S. forces in Korea, 152–153
  and need for hard line policy, 1–2
  in negotiations for grand bargain, 8
  and post-crisis security, 155, 156
  preemptive strike views of, 93–94
  ROK aid from, 141
  and unification of regional partners, 53–54, 111–112
  U.S. forces in, 71, 147, 148, 162
Jordan, U.S. aid to, 141
Juche system, 27, 130

225

INDEX

KEDO (Korean Energy Development Organization), 32
Kelly, James, 30, 32, 35, 36
Kidnapping victims, Japanese, 8, 30, 50, 86, 90–92
Kim Dae Jung, 12, 14, 45, 54, 95
Kim Il Sung:
  and Korean War, 130
  required homage to, 27
  reverence for, 24–25
Kim Jong Il, 5, 9, 15, 20, 50
  Bush's statements about, 36
  characteristics of, 25–26
  and economic reforms, 128, 132
  and military acceptance of CFK accord, 108, 116
  personal safety fears of, 33
  possibility of grand bargain acceptance by, 47–48
  reform attempts by, 28–29
  required homage to, 27
  reverence for, 24, 25
Kim Young Sam, 42
Koizumi, Junichiro, 94
Korean Energy Development Organization (KEDO), 32
Korean War armistice of 1953, 35
Kugler-Posen "attrition-FEBA expansion model," 168
Kunsan U.S. Air Force Base, 158, 164

Laney, James, 54
Large-bore artillery:
  under CFK accord, 106
  50 percent cuts in, 117–119
Lee Hoi Chang, 41
Libya, U.S. military operations and, 150
Light tanks, 50 percent cuts in, 119–120
Long-term U.S.—ROK alliance, 145–165
  and defense against Chinese attacks, 146, 148
  looser and more inclusive structure vs., 155–157
  and options for U.S. forces in reunified Korea, 157–163
  as peace-keeping mechanism, 153–155

Long-term U.S.—ROK alliance *(Cont.)*:
  political/diplomatic groundwork for, 149
  and purpose of U.S. military presence in Korea, 150–157
  and stability in Asia-Pacific community, 153, 154
  support of South Korean people for, 148–149
  and U.S. forces in Korea, 146

Marines in Korea, 162, 163
Marshall Plan, 140
Mideast war of 1973, U.S. military operations during, 150
Military capabilities:
  of allies after 50 percent cuts, 121–124
  of DPRK, 65–68 (*See also* Nuclear weapons capabilities (DPRK))
  reduction in (*see* Conventional arms reduction)
  of ROK, 68–70
  of U.S. for war in Korea, 70–73
  of U.S. in ROK, 157–158
  and U.S. troops in foreign countries, 146–148
Military geography, 63–64
Military issues and options, 8–11
  cost of DPRK military, 7, 8, 18, 26
  for destroying DPRK nuclear capability, 9–10
  for DPRK response to preemptive attacks, 10–11
  if grand bargain fails, 20
  for U.S. forces in reunified Korea, 146, 157–163
  Yongbyon strike possibility, 46–47
  (*See also* Conventional military balance)
Military spending (DPRK), 18, 26, 58, 66
Missiles, 100–104
  Clinton administration concern with, 102–103
  export of, 8, 13, 26, 100
  grand bargain requirements for, 8, 85, 100–104

Missiles *(Cont.)*:
  nuclear issue vs., 100
  possible deals related to, 103–104
  proposed buy-out of, 13, 44, 102–103
  threats posed by, 101
Modeling of DPRK breakthrough, 167–176
  and build-up of forces, 168–169
  for chemical weapons use, 173–176
  for massive artillery/infantry assaults, 171–173
  for traditional armored attack, 169–171
Monitoring:
  resumption of, 91
  suspension of, 15
Multilateral talks, bilateral talks vs., 7–8, 17, 37
Munsan corridor, 63

National security strategy of the U.S., 183–193
  overview of, 187–189
  presidential preface to, 183–187
  strengthening alliances as part of, 189–193
NATO-Warsaw Pact Conventional Forces in Europe Treaty, 6
Navy forces in Korea, 158, 160–162
Negotiation:
  of Agreed Framework, 20
  of grand bargain, 8, 42–43
  past DPRK patterns of, 17, 52
  U.S.—ROK initial position in, 125–126
No first use of weapons of mass destruction pledge, 8, 50, 90
Noland, Marcus, 128, 136–137
Nonaggression pledge, U.S., 8, 50, 86, 90, 92
North Korea (*see* Democratic People's Republic of Korea)
Northeast Asia:
  balance of power in, 149
  DPRK threat to, 26
  nuclear arms trade in, 10

NPT (see Nuclear Non-Proliferation Treaty)
Nuclear crisis, current, 31–39
  DPRK actions in, 31–35
  U.S. actions in, 35–38
  (*See also* Denuclearization)
Nuclear non-proliferation accord (DPRK—ROK), 15, 31, 34–35
Nuclear Non-Proliferation Treaty (NPT), 14, 15, 31–32
  DPRK official withdrawal from, 34
  and uranium enrichment program, 98
Nuclear reactors, 8, 9
  under Agreed Framework, 12, 39
  DPRK's possible completion of, 35
  under grand bargain, 98
  "research," 32–33
  Yongbyon, 8–9
Nuclear weapons capabilities (DPRK), 8–11, 35
  DPRK flexibility toward, 94
  as of early 2003, 31
  under grand bargain, 46
  lack of conclusive evidence for, 102
  near future of, 38
  possible current expansion of, 15–16
  risks associated with, 40
  (*See also* Denuclearization)
Nuclear/missile engagement school, 84–85

Office of Net Assessment (Pentagon), 67
Okinawa, U.S. Marine Corps in, 162, 165
O'Sullivan, Meghan, 43
Osan U.S. Air Force Base 158, 164

Paek Nam Sun, 33
Pakistan, U.S. aid to, 141
Peace keeping, security structures and, 153, 155
Peace treaty, 8, 19, 50, 92
Perry, William J., 9, 29, 44–45, 72, 92
Personality, cult of, 24–25
Plutonium, 34
  cessation of activities related to, 91–92

Plutonium *(Cont.)*:
  DPRK's release of, 6
  potential DPRK production of, 35
  potential DPRK sales of, 4
  reprocessing facility for, 32–33
  from Yongbyon reactor, 8–9
Political leadership:
  DPRK reverence for, 24–25
  and economic reform, 136, 137
Powell, Colin, 36, 37
Power plants:
  under Agreed Framework, 12
  conventional vs. nuclear, 6
Precedent (for grand bargain proposal), 54–55
Precision-guided munitions, 117
Preemptive attacks:
  and current conventional military balance, 60–62
  by DPRK, 10
  DPRK denuclearization and possibility of, 46–47
  under grand bargain, 19
  possible DPRK response to, 9–10
  regional partners' views on, 93–94
  against uranium enrichment program, 93
  against Yongbyon, 93
Prices (in DPRK), 135
Proliferation resistant reactors, 12
Propaganda, DPRK, 24–25

Rajin-Sonbong special economic zone, 134
Reactors, nuclear (*see* Nuclear reactors)
Reagan, Ronald, 11
Reconnaissance capabilities, 77, 117
Reform, DPRK attempts at, 20, 28–31, 131–135 (*See also* Economic reform)
Regime change, 2
  coercion approach to, 2, 4, 37–38, 83–84
  grand bargain demands for, 3
  soft form of, 50

Regional partners:
  military capabilities of, after 50 percent cuts, 121–124
  in potential peninsula war, 116–117
  preemptive attack view of, 93–94
  unification of, 53–54, 111–112
  (*See also specific countries*)
Republic of Korea (ROK), 26
  aid from, 7, 89, 110, 132, 142
  allied prospects for defense of, 59
  current U.S. relations with, 40–42
  defense spending in, 69
  DPRK détente policy with, 29, 45
  DPRK invasion threat to, 73–80, 115–116
  and DPRK nuclear weapons development, 33
  DPRK submarine landing in, 39
  DPRK tourists from, 133–134
  DPRK trade with, 132
  engagement policy endorsed by, 84
  long-term U.S. alliance with, 145–165
  military capabilities of, 68–70
  military spending by, 130
  and need for hard line policy, 1–2
  in negotiations for grand bargain, 8
  nuclear non-proliferation accord with, 15, 31, 34–35
  past Japanese aid to, 141
  and people's support of U.S.–ROK alliance, 148–149
  preemptive strike views of, 93
  realignment of U.S. forces in, 49, 59
  and unification of regional partners, 53–54, 111–112
  U.S. forces in, 157–158
  and U.S. hard line policy, 2
  vital statistics for, 64
Road map (*see* Grand bargain)
Roh Moo Hyun, 36–37, 41–42, 45, 84, 94, 95
ROK (*see* Republic of Korea)
Rumsfeld, Donald H., 37, 48–49, 59, 163

Index

Russia:
  arms reduction guidance from, 107
  and DPRK nuclear weapons development, 33
  engagement policy endorsed by, 84
  in negotiations for grand bargain, 8
  and post-crisis security tasks, 155

Sale of fissile materials, 4, 10, 34, 92
Sanctions on DPRK, 87–89
  during Clinton administration, 39
  DPRK reaction to tightening of, 84
  lifting of, 8, 50, 86, 92
  lobbying for end of, 133
Saudi Arabia, U.S. military operations and, 150–151
Search-and-rescue exercises, 155
Security dialogues, 155
Security structure, post-crisis, 153–156
Seoul, potential damage to, 9–10
Sinuiju Special Administrative Region, 133
Solarz, Stephen, 85
South Korea (*see* Republic of Korea)
Soviet Union, 130–131
Special economic zones, 133, 134, 139, 140
Spent fuel rods, 8, 9
  under Agreed Framework, 12
  plutonium from, 32
Starvation, 24, 131
Strangulation policy, 4
Summits, 12–13
Sunshine policy, 14, 29, 37, 41, 54

Tanks:
  under CFK accord, 106
  50 percent cuts in, 117–120
Team Spirit exercise, 73
Technical assistance, 19, 49, 89
Tenet, George, 94
Terrain, 61

Terrorism support:
  DPRK decline in, 30
  and DPRK in "axis of evil," 14, 27
  as grand bargain issue, 8, 86
  and lack of DPRK links to terrorists, 15
  removing DPRK from list of countries providing, 50, 86, 133
Tourism, 133–135
Tumen River delta, 134
Turkey, U.S. military operations and, 150–151
Two-war framework, 58

Ulchi Focus Lens exercise, 73
United Nations Commission on Human Rights, 24
United States:
  aid from, 7, 89, 110, 132, 141
  current ROK relations with, 2, 40–42
  grand bargain requirements for, 8, 19, 50, 86–87, 90
  long-term ROK alliance with, 145–165
  military capabilities of, for war in Korea, 70–73, 106
  military options of, 9–10
  national security strategy of, 183–193
  and purpose of forces in Korea after reunification, 150–157
  sanctions on DPRK by, 87–89
  troops of, in foreign countries, 146–148
  troops of, in ROK, 157–158
  two-war framework of, 58
  and unification of regional partners, 53–54, 111–112
  vital statistics for, 64
United States policy, 3–5
  during Bush administration, 14–16
  during Clinton administration, 11–14
  during current nuclear crisis, 35–38

United States policy *(Cont.)*:
  if grand bargain fails, 1–2, 20–21
  narrow/tactical approach of, 3–4, 43–45
  national security strategy, 183–193
  need for new approach in, 11
  proposed new approach for, 16–21
Uranium enrichment program, 91, 98
  and Bush administration policy, 15
  as definitive end of Agreed Framework, 39
  discovery of, 99
  eventual inspection of, 6, 97, 98
  identification of sites involved in, 98
  initiation of, 13, 95
  perceived need for, 14
  preemptive strike against, 93
  recent nuclear crisis and discovery of, 31, 32
  unknown location of, 10
  verifying end of, 97
  as violation of Agreed Framework, 98

U.S.—Japan Defense Cooperation Guidelines, 174
U.S.—ROK alliance:
  hard line policy and strains on, 2
  long-term, 148–165

Vietnam, economic reform in, 134, 135
Vision, grand bargain as, 43

Wages (in DPRK), 135
Wang Yi, 33
War:
  models of, 167–168
  potential damage from, 9–10

Yongbyon, 6, 8, 46–47
  grand bargain requirements for, 96, 97
  potential preemptive attack against, 93, 96
  return of monitors to, 91, 96

Zonal limitations (in 50 percent cut proposal), 114–115
Zones, economic, 133–135, 139, 140

www.ingramcontent.com/pod-product-compliance
Lightning Source LLC
Chambersburg PA
CBHW071900160426
43198CB00011B/1183